JESUS AND THE EVANGELISTS

JESUS AND THE EVANGELISTS
The Ministry of Jesus and Its Portrayal in the Synoptic Gospels

Philip A. Cunningham

UNIVERSITY
PRESS OF
AMERICA

Lanham • New York • London

ISBN 0–8191–9216–3

The paper used in this publication meets the minimum requirements of
American National Standard for Information Sciences—Permanence
of Paper for Printed Library Materials, ANSI Z39.48–1984.

CONTENTS

Contents

Chapter Eight
GOD'S REIGN AND THE MISSION OF JESUS

Chapter Nine
THE DEATH OF JESUS

Chapter Ten
THE RESURRECTION AND THE MESSIANIC AGE

Epilogue
CONSEQUENCES OF A CRITICAL AWARENESS OF
THE SYNOPTIC GOSPELS

ACKNOWLEDGEMENTS

I must express my deep gratitude to the following friends who undertook the labor of critiquing the manuscript of this book. Their assistance in keeping technical jargon to a minimum and in developing the Questions for Reflection and Discussion was invaluable. I thank them especially for their enthusiasm and support, which is both treasure and blessing to me:

Leon E. Abbott, Jr.
Teresa V. Baker
Ruth Bamford
John Bell
Edward J. Breitkopf
Gail Capriole
Edith S. Daley
Ros Ebacher
Beverly Fisher
Lucretia Ganley
Phyllis M. Heble, N.D.
Stuart M. Hernandez
Gordon Pew
Joan Pew
Joyce Rollins
Julia Anne Walsh

To the faithful of the
Salem Deanery
in the Roman Catholic
Diocese of Manchester, New Hampshire,
whose dedication to growing in Christ
is inspiring and energizing.

THE THREE STAGES
OF GOSPEL TRADITION

Stage I:

The Ministry of Jesus

Stage II:

The Preaching of the Apostles
After the Resurrection

Stage III:

The Work of the Evangelists

INTRODUCTION

*S*ince the conclusion of Vatican Council II in 1965, the Roman Catholic tradition has witnessed the awakening of a tremendous interest in the Bible. Dozens of ecclesial documents have motivated Catholics in large numbers to explore a Bible which had previously been unfamiliar to them.

Besides encouraging the widespread use of Scripture, the Catholic tradition has also been promoting what might be called a *critical awareness* of the sacred writings. Such an awareness recognizes that the biblical writers, frequently motivated by the historical events of their times, expressed their inspired insights according to the norms of their culture. In order for modern readers, living thousands of years later in a completely different society, to accurately discern these insights they must seek to bridge the temporal and cultural gap which separates them from the sacred authors. In other words, when reading the Bible one must "carefully investigate what meaning the sacred writers really intended" (*Dei Verbum*, 12) by hearing their words in the context of the writers' historical setting.

The Catholic tradition, and others as well, makes a distinction between revelation and inspiration. Everything in the Bible is inspired because the sacred authors were moved by God to reflect, pray, and write about his involvement in their lives. However, only certain of the writers' insights are revealed truths about God and humanity. For instance, the author of Genesis 1 was inspired to compose a description of the creation of the world. Since his society understood the earth to be flat, the writer portrayed God fashioning a flat earth. This pre-scientific geographical knowledge is not part of the Bible's divine message, but the *religious* insight that God is the sole Creator of the universe is certainly a revealed and timeless truth! It is by discerning the historically and culturally conditioned features of the inspired writings that the revelation of God in the Bible becomes apparent.

This principle is most important when reading the Gospels. The Pontifical Biblical Commission has in recent years issued a series of statements which call for a critical awareness of the Gospels by all believers. They insist that to fully appreciate the profound Gospel messages the concerns and historical setting of every evangelist must be considered.

Because each Gospel was addressed to particular concerns in each evangelist's church community, and because different writers had varying sources of information available to them, every Gospel offers a unique perspective on the meaning of Jesus' life and death. Different Gospels will present the same incident in startlingly contrasting manners because of the authors' divergent theological interests. For example, the Gospel of Mark portrays Jesus in Gethsemane in great distress and anguish, wishing somehow to escape his impending ordeal (Mk 14:33–36), while in the Gospel of John a Jesus in complete command of the situation purposefully strides forth to meet his arresters and causes them to collapse to the ground by majestically stating "I am" the one being sought (Jn 18:1–6).

This diversity among the Gospels must be considered in coming to an understanding of the ministry of Jesus. For people whose exposure to the Gospels is restricted to hearing selected passages proclaimed at Sunday liturgies, the special, distinctive emphases of each evangelist are not readily apparent. Rather, the listener unconsciously "homogenizes" the Gospels into a harmonious blend in which any unique characteristics are lost. Such a listener would come to believe that all the Gospels say pretty much the same thing, and is usually shocked to discover that this is not the case.

Furthermore, it seems that people who possess only this "homogenized" view of the Gospels find it very difficult to imagine Jesus as a truly human person—they tend to conceive of him exclusively in divine terms. By contrasting and critically evaluating the Gospels, however, it becomes apparent that the early Church came to perceive Jesus as divine only gradually and only in the light of experiencing his resurrection. All of the Gospels were written long after the raising of Jesus by people who had reflected for decades on the religious meaning of what had occurred. Equipped with this realization, the modern reader can come to know Jesus as he was seen and heard by his Jewish followers *before* the resurrection—as a kinsman through whom the Almighty was working for the restoration of Israel. By noting the gradual development of the Church's theological insight, it becomes possible to reconstruct some of the historical events in Jesus' life, and to perceive the goals and aims of his ministry in the very human terms of first-century Palestinian Jewish expectations.

The Pontifical Biblical Commission issued an Instruction in 1964 which stated that the Gospels had to be understood in terms of three stages of developing tradition. Using this perspective as a guide, this book will introduce the reader to recent scholarly consensus on the three "synoptic" Gospels of Mark, Matthew, and Luke. These critical studies have provided an enormous wealth of insight into the ministry of Jesus; insights which are of benefit to all Christians. As was stated in 1984, "the Pontifical Biblical Commission judges that, if one prescinds from details of minor importance, such studies have made sufficient progress that *any believer can find in their results a solid basis for his/her study about Jesus Christ*" (*Bible & Christology*, 1.3.3; italics in the original).

Accordingly, after exploring the origins of these three Gospels, and some ground-rules for reading them, each of them will be examined in turn in order to discover the situation in each author's church community and each evangelist's unique concerns and insights. Once the authors' contributions have been determined, we will turn our attention to traditions about Jesus which date back to his ministry and use those traditions to describe that ministry historically. Finally, some reflections on the significance of our findings for the faith-life of modern Christians will be offered.

To facilitate ease of reading, the text will not be cluttered with footnotes and excessive cross-references. However, the reader should realize that this book is based upon the labors and efforts of the scholars whose works are listed in the bibliography. In particular, the translations of the Pontifical Biblical Commission's decrees undertaken by Joseph A. Fitzmyer, S.J. must be acknowledged. For further information on scholarly research the reader is urged to consult the bibliography. I am greatly indebted to all of the authors listed therein for the insights I have tried to convey in these pages.

It would be well to state at the outset that this exploration will ultimately result in the portrayal of a Jewish Jesus not very familiar to most Catholics, and indeed to most twentieth-century Christians. Whereas we have all been the heirs of two thousand years of thought on the Jesus-event *as seen through the faith-filled eyes of the resurrection experience*, our considerations will reveal to some extent the Jesus *before* the resurrection, who was seen by his contemporaries as either a prophet announcing the arrival of God's kingdom, an uneducated northerner leading the people astray, or a potentially dangerous revolutionary. In any case, Jesus will be encountered according to the terms of his first-century Galilean Jewish roots, not in terms of subsequent theological realizations. Such a portrayal, although disorienting at first, makes the humanity of Jesus much more accessible to his followers today. He becomes a real, live, flesh-and-blood person whose faithfulness to his mission and to his Father one can seek to imitate in the modern world.

NOTES FOR THIS 1993 REPRINT

The reprinting of this work has provided the opportunity to make a number of minor revisions to the text. However, some significant changes have been incorporated into chapter 3, which discusses the Matthean Jesus. Among them is a shift of the chapter's subtitle from "Wisdom of God Incarnate" to "Living Wisdom of God." This more accurately conveys Matthew's christology and avoids confusion with the more properly incarnational outlook of the Gospel of John. In addition, the treatment of Matthew's attitude toward his Jewish contemporaries has been refocused in light of recent scholarship which heightens the intramural character of the evangelist's rivalry with Pharisaic Judaism. The following studies greatly clarify the Matthean social context and are recommended to anyone who would like to explore this subject further: Daniel J. Harrington, *The Gospel of Matthew* [Sacra Pagina Commentary] (Collegeville: The Liturgical Press/Michael Glazier, 1991); J. Andrew Overman, *Matthew's Gospel and Formative Judaism: The Social World of the Matthean Community* (Minneapolis: Fortress Press, 1990); and Anthony J. Saldarini, "Delegitimation of Leaders in Matthew 23," *Catholic Biblical Quarterly* 54/4 (October, 1992): 659-680.

Finally, I would like to reiterate and expand the original volume's dedication to the Catholic faithful of New Hampshire. Their commitment to growing in faith continues to inspire and energize. Thank you.

Notre Dame College
Manchester, New Hampshire
1993

Part I

THE EVANGELISTS

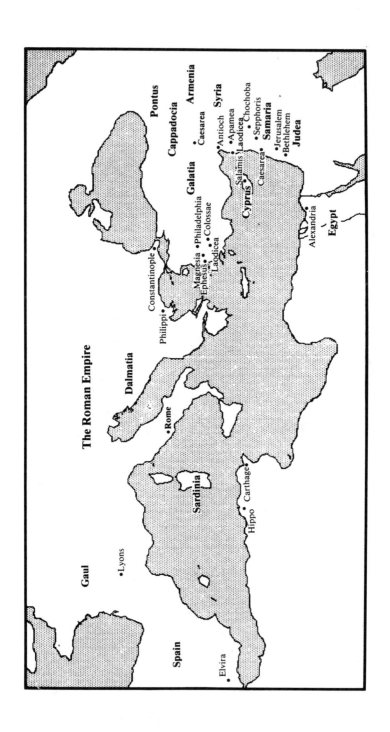

The Roman Empire

Gaul

Spain

Lyons

Elvira

Sardinia

Rome

Dalmatia

Hippo

Carthage

Constantinople

Philippi

Magnesia

Ephesus

Laodicea

Colossae

Philadelphia

Galatia

Pontus

Cappadocia

Armenia

Caesarea

Antioch

Apamea

Laodicea

Syria

Chochoba

Sepphoris

Samaria

Jerusalem

Bethlehem

Judea

Caesarea

Salamis

Cyprus

Alexandria

Egypt

Chapter One

THE ORIGINS OF THE GOSPELS

The Pre-Gospel Period

*O*ver the past several decades, Scripture scholars have arrived at a practically unanimous consensus regarding when the Gospels were authored and how they relate to each other. The Gospel of Mark seems to have been written first, having been composed close to the year 70. Since the ministry of Jesus apparently occurred during the early 30s, with his crucifixion taking place in the year 33 at the latest, almost four decades had elapsed before this first of the Gospels was completed. Such a delay on the part of the evangelists might seem surprising to twentieth-century believers who are used to our culture's instantaneous communicating and documenting of historic events. Clearly, the early Christians lived with different expectations, interests, and circumstances than we do today.

It would be inconceivable to most first-century believers that people might be discussing their writings two thousand years in the future. Many were positive that the Lord Jesus would be returning in glory very soon, certainly within their own lifetimes. For example, the apostle Paul, whose letters are the oldest parts of the New Testament, had apparently preached about Christ's impending return with such vigor that the church in Thessalonica was thrown into turmoil when some of their number died. They feared whether their loved ones might be lost forever since they had not survived until the close of the age. Paul consoles them with the message that those "who are still alive, who are left until the coming of the Lord, shall not precede those who have fallen asleep. For . . . the dead in Christ will rise first" (1 Thess 4:15–16).

It may be that the earliest Christians did not feel it was necessary to write long accounts about Jesus' life for the benefit of future generations. They did not expect that there would *be* many future generations! Their attention was not fixed on recording the past; it was centered on preparing for the rapidly inbreaking future. (The reasons for the expectation of the Lord Jesus' imminent return will be explored in chapter 10.)

Although in the first four decades of the Church some Christians might have been uninterested in composing records for posterity, it does seem certain that various types of "collections" of Jesus' words and deeds circulated, probably for missionary purposes.

Compilations of Jesus' sayings and parables appear to have been prepared by people who revered him as a great teacher of wisdom. Some composed short descriptions of his passion and death in order to emphasize that he who died had been raised. Others collected accounts of his miraculous deeds because they esteemed Jesus as a wonder-worker. Some of these sorts of writings, together with various strands of oral traditions, were available to the evangelists when they began to prepare their Gospels.

As the years passed, the generation of apostles and eyewitnesses began to pass away. The deaths of those who had had direct contact with Jesus no doubt contributed to a desire to preserve early reports and traditions. Note that the Gospel of Luke begins with the observation that "many have undertaken to compile a narrative of the things which have been accomplished among us, just as they were delivered to us by those who from the beginning were eyewitnesses and ministers of the word" (Lk 1:1–2).

It may not be coincidental that the composition of the first Gospel, the Gospel of Mark, occurs within a few years of the deaths of three of the most important "first-generation" Christians. James, known as the brother of the Lord, was killed in Jerusalem around the year 60, while Paul and Peter were executed in Rome in the mid-60s.

The Gospel Years

The author of Mark appears to have had a collection of miracle stories about Jesus which he incorporated and modified in his Gospel. Furthermore, his church community was evidently suffering persecution and distress. An ancient tradition, supported by a slight majority of recent Scripture scholarship, declares that this Gospel was written in Rome. If so, then the Gospel could have been composed shortly after the persecution of Christians by the Emperor Nero (64–66) and in the midst of the Jewish-Roman War (66–70). Living during such tumultuous and painful events would certainly influence the way Jesus was portrayed and would color the evangelist's expectations of the future.

During the decade of the 80s, the Gospel of Matthew and the Gospel of Luke were composed, independently of each other. But while these writers were unaware of each other's work, it seems plain that both possessed some form of the Gospel of Mark. This gives modern researchers the ability to perceive the individual preferences and styles of these two writers with greater ease than with the author of Mark because the finished products can be compared with one of their sources.

For example, Mk 6:5–6 in recounting the scene often referred to as "the rejection of Jesus at Nazareth" comments that "he *could* do no mighty work there . . . he marveled because of their unbelief." Mt 13:58, however, observes that "he *did* not do many mighty works there, because of their unbelief." Apparently, the writer of Matthew is uncomfortable with the Marcan Jesus who "could not" do something, and he alters the Marcan text accordingly. Similarly, when Jesus breathes his last in Mk 15:39, the centurion exclaims, "Truly this man was Son of God!" But in Lk 23:47 he cries, "Certainly this man was righteous!" Clearly, the two writers want to emphasize different ideas about the death of Jesus, as will be explored later. At this point, it is enough to observe that the ability to contrast Matthew and Luke with their source Mark gives us the opportunity to really see the hand of the evangelist at work.

Such comparisons have revealed even more about Matthew and Luke. After filtering out the Marcan material in both Luke and Matthew, there still remains a considerable amount of writing that both have in common. These remaining commonalities are practically all sayings of Jesus. Consequently, the vast majority of Scripture scholarship holds that both Matthew and Luke had, in addition to Mark, a collection of Jesus' sayings which they utilized. This "sayings source," known as "Q" from the German word for "source," is an example of one of the pre-Gospel writings mentioned above.

Both the Gospel of Matthew and that of Luke also contain materials unique to each which can shed still further light on their respective authors. The Gospel of Matthew seems to have been composed by a Christian of Jewish heritage who considers Jesus to be the ultimate revelation of God's Wisdom, completely fulfilling the Hebrew Scriptures. If the reference in 13:52 is autobiographical ("every scribe who has been trained for the kingdom of heaven is like a householder who brings out of his treasure what is new and what is old"), the evangelist might see his role as teaching how Jesus has perfected and fulfilled the best in Judaism.

The Gospel of Luke emphasizes the peace and healing that accompany Jesus wherever he goes. The Church's mission to the Gentiles is very prominently featured, possibly because the author imagined that his work might have a widely scattered readership. Since Acts of Apostles was written by the same author, one can see how the themes of the Gospel are continued into the second volume. Christianity in both works is pictured as friendly to Rome and originating among pious and deeply religious Jews according to God's divine plan. The climax of this writer's presentation is the scene in which the apostle Paul, the hero of the Gentile churches, is freely preaching the good news in the capital city of a global empire.

Because of the Matthean and Lucan dependency on Mark, all three Gospels are highly interrelated. For this reason they are referred to as the "synoptic" Gospels, "seeing the whole together." Their similarities make it possible to compile Gospel "parallels," in which all three Gospels are listed side by side in three columns, permitting a rapid assessment of where their narratives agree and where they differ.

Such ease of comparison cannot be found when considering the Gospel of John. This last of the Gospels to be written (in the mid-90s) diverges from the synoptic Gospels in many important ways. For instance, Jesus almost never speaks in parables, but in long discourses; he preaches not about the kingdom of God as in the synoptics but about himself; and he overturns tables in the temple at the very beginning of his ministry, not at its conclusion. In addition, the Johannine writer employs a unique vocabulary including such terms as "from above," "Paraclete," "lifted up," and "light/darkness." Most scholars understand such differences to have occurred for several reasons: (1) the writer does not possess the synoptic accounts, although he obviously has access to presynoptic traditions about Jesus (including possibly a collection of Jesus' miracles); (2) the author's community has a distinctive history which has shaped its views; (3) the evangelist's church is in the midst of certain controversies which have affected it deeply.

In any case, this quick presentation of current scholarly consensus about the origins and relationships of the Gospels could profitably be displayed in graphic form. The chart on page 14 illustrates the approximate year in which each Gospel was written, the sources used by the various evangelists, and important contemporary events.

Reading the Gospels

Before continuing, the reader might wish to consult the accounts of the baptism of Jesus which will be alluded to in this section. See Mk 1:9-11; Mt 3:13-17; Lk 3:21-22; Jn 1:29-34.

The critical tools which have enabled scholars to investigate how the Gospels came into being do not merely provide interesting historical information. They also have produced new awarenesses of how the gospels are to be read and appreciated today. Such realizations have been vigorously advanced by official agencies in the Roman Catholic tradition (including the most authoritative Catholic body—an ecumenical council), although the effect of these proclamations is only just beginning to be perceived by the vast majority of the Catholic faithful.

In 1964, the Pontifical Biblical Commission issued *An Instruction Concerning the Historical Truth of the Gospels*. The Commission's work was repeated and defined as dogma by Vatican Council II's *Dogmatic Constitution on Divine Revelation*. The perspective which

THE RELATIONSHIP OF THE GOSPELS

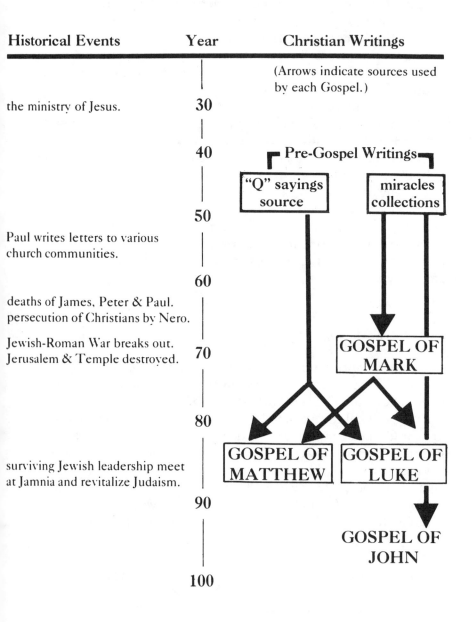

Historical Events	Year	Christian Writings

(Arrows indicate sources used by each Gospel.)

the ministry of Jesus. — 30

40 — **Pre-Gospel Writings**

"Q" sayings source — miracles collections

50

Paul writes letters to various church communities.

60

deaths of James, Peter & Paul. persecution of Christians by Nero.

Jewish-Roman War breaks out. Jerusalem & Temple destroyed. — 70

GOSPEL OF MARK

80

surviving Jewish leadership meet at Jamnia and revitalize Judaism.

GOSPEL OF MATTHEW **GOSPEL OF LUKE**

90

GOSPEL OF JOHN

100

both of these documents offer is tremendously important. As we shall see, they both assert that the Gospels cannot be considered simply as "biographies" of Jesus in a twentieth-century sense. Instead, they are writings designed to reflect and to promote the saving faith of the early Church.

Basically, the *Instruction* (denoted by Roman numerals in these paragraphs) stated that modern readers of the Gospel must be aware that the text they are reading contains materials which date from "three stages of tradition" in the early Church's developing theological awareness (VI.2). The Gospels do not represent a one-dimensional statement of faith. Rather, they bear witness to the fact the early Church's faith-awareness experienced a process of development as the decades of the first century unfolded. The resurrection of Jesus was an especially crucial milestone in this developmental process.

The Three Stages of Tradition in the Gospels

Stage One: THE MINISTRY OF JESUS
the historical preaching and activity of Jesus   (early 30s)

Stage Two: THE PREACHING OF THE APOSTLES
the proclamation about the Christ after the resurrection   (34–65)

Stage Three: THE WORK OF THE EVANGELISTS
the personal contributions and concerns of the writers   (70–95)

First, there are certainly materials and traditions which originated in the ministry of Jesus in the early 30s, passed on by eyewitnesses of that ministry. For example, all four of the Gospels, in various ways, refer to the historic fact of Jesus' baptism by John the Baptist. While their presentations of this incident may vary (as will be seen below), they are clearly all aware that the incident did occur. In describing this first stage of tradition, the *Instruction* notes that Jesus taught and spoke according to "the modes of reasoning and of exposition which were in vogue at the time" (VII). It would seem, then, that for twentieth-century Christians to clearly understand Jesus' words they must have some acquaintance with the world of first-century Palestinian Judaism.

Second, the Gospels contain insights which occurred during the preaching of the apostles, *after the raising of Jesus from death.* "After Jesus rose from the dead and his divinity was clearly perceived . . . the apostles passed on to their listeners what was really said and done by the Lord with that fuller understanding which they enjoyed" (VIII). In other words, after the resurrection, the followers of Jesus came to realize that God himself had been present to them in the person of their Nazarean companion, and they began to preach about Jesus using such titles as "Lord" and "Son of God." These honorifics could have been bestowed upon Jesus only in the light of the resurrection experience. The early Christian missionaries' preaching about Jesus was permeated with their post-resurrectional awareness of his divinity. Returning to our previous example of the baptism of Jesus, it can be seen how this second stage of tradition manifests itself in the Gospels. In Mk 1:11, after Jesus is baptized a voice from heaven tells him, "You are my beloved Son; with you I am well pleased." The statement is clearly intended for the readers' benefit because this rather startling announcement provokes no reactions from the bystanders in the Jordan. (This is true even in Mt 3:17 where the evangelist has altered the heavenly proclamation to "*This* is my beloved with whom I am well pleased," apparently directed not just at Jesus but at anyone within earshot. Still, there is no response from those on hand.) The early Church's post-resurrectional insight into Jesus is being announced to the *reader* right at the commencement of Jesus' ministry.

Third, the Gospels have definitely been influenced by the evangelists' concerns, interests, and circumstances. Each Gospel was written according to "a method suited to the particular purpose which each [author] set for himself. From the many things handed down they selected some things, reduced others to a synthesis, others they explicated as they kept in mind the situation of the churches" (IX). Once again the baptism accounts provide an example. There appear to have been adherents of John the Baptist who believed that he was, in reality, the Messiah, and who were rivals of the emerging Christian movement. The historic fact that Jesus had been baptized by John proved to be an embarrassment to some Christians in their debates with these "Baptists" because it could be argued that the baptism showed that Jesus considered himself subordinate to John. This embarrassment seems to have motivated the writer of Matthew to add this exchange to his version of Mark's baptism scene:

> John would have prevented [Jesus from being baptized], saying, "I need to be baptized by you, and do you come to me?" But Jesus answered him, "Let it be so now; for thus it is fitting for us to fulfill all righteousness." Then he consented (Mt 3:14–16).

The insertion of this passage, which is unique to Matthew, is the writer's way of informing his readers that even John realized who should really be baptizing whom. Similarly, the Gospel of John deals with the same uneasiness about Jesus' being baptized by John. The writer repeatedly emphasizes the Baptist's status: "There was a man sent from God whose name was John. He was *not* the light, but came to bear witness to the light" (Jn 1:6,8); "He who comes after me ranks *before* me" (1:15,30); "[John] confessed, he did not deny, but confessed, 'I am *not* the Christ' " (1:20). After this series of disclaimers, the evangelist avoids the embarrassing baptism scene by not presenting it! Instead, he has the Baptist refer to the incident obliquely (Jn 1:30–34). Again, the point of drawing attention to these varying baptism accounts is to illustrate how the concerns of the Gospel writers in the 70s, 80s, or 90s influenced their depiction of the ministry of Jesus.

In discussing the third stage of tradition, the time of the evangelist, the *Instruction* makes the extremely important observation that in reading the Gospels one must "seek out the meaning intended by the Evangelist in narrating a saying or a deed in a certain way or in placing it in a certain context" (IX). This statement indicates that we should try to perceive Jesus the way the sacred author does. The Gospels must be appreciated on their own terms, and not treated as if they had been composed by twentieth-century believers.

The Nature of the Gospels

Superficially, the Gospels look like modern biographies. They narrate the story of Jesus' life, two of them beginning with his birth and concluding with the events shortly after his death. This outward appearance has given the Gospels an historical veneer which encourages today's readers to regard them, at least initially, as if they were reading an historian's biography of a famous person like Abraham Lincoln. A closer inspection quickly reveals that the evangelists are not interested in our notions of history. They want to communicate only their faith-filled, inspired insights into the *religious* meaning of Jesus of Nazareth.

An excellent example of this theological purpose can be seen by comparing the two Gospels which have infancy narratives, Matthew and Luke. Because of the beauty and pageantry of our Christmas observances, we all know about the events surrounding Jesus' birth. A careful reading of the Gospel accounts, however, shows that most people are only aware of (again) a "homogenized" blending of the two narratives. Their contradictions on an historical level are usually not discerned. Even more regrettably, the writers' profound notions about Jesus are also unperceived. It would be useful to first read Mt 1:1–2:23 and Lk 1:1–2:52, 3:23–38, and then peruse this summary chart which shows the *historical* discrepancies:

A Comparison of the Infancy Narratives

MATTHEW	LUKE
Genealogy of Jesus from Abraham to Joseph, including five women (1:1–17).	Zechariah and Elizabeth are told they will have a son (despite their advanced age), whose name will be John (1:5–25).
Joseph considers divorcing his betrothed, Mary, because she is pregnant before their marriage (1:18–19).	Mary of Nazareth is told by an angel that she will conceive a son by the Holy Spirit. She consents (1:26–38).
Joseph is told in a dream that Mary has conceived by the Holy Spirit. He obeys the command to marry her (1:20–24).	Mary visits her cousin Elizabeth (1:39–56). Elizabeth's son John is born (1:57–80).
	Caesar orders a census which causes Mary and Joseph to travel to Bethlehem (2:1–5).

Joseph does not have relations with Mary until she has borne a son whom he names Jesus (1:25).

While in Bethlehem, Mary gives birth to a son, wraps him in swaddling cloths and lays him in a manger, because there had been no room for them in the inn (2:6–7).

When Jesus is born in Bethlehem, magi from the east arrive in Jerusalem seeking the "King of the Jews." They are instructed to look in Bethlehem and to report back (2:1–10).

An angel tells shepherds in the fields that Christ, the Lord, the Savior, has been born, and directs them to go to Bethlehem (2:8–14).

Arriving in Bethlehem, the magi go into *the house*, see the child with Mary, worship him and present gifts of gold, myrrh, and frankincense. Being warned in a dream not to report to Herod they take another route home (2:11–12).

Going quickly, the shepherds find Mary and Joseph, and the child in the manger. They recount the angel's words and Mary ponders them in her heart. The shepherds depart, praising God (2:15–20).

Joseph is warned in a dream to flee to Egypt to escape the imminent murderous designs of Herod. He obeys (2:13–15).

At the end of eight days, at his circumcision, the child is named Jesus (2:21).

Herod, enraged at the failure of the magi to report, orders the killing of all male babies younger than two years old in Bethlehem and its environs (2:16–18).

They bring Jesus to Jerusalem for a purification ritual. In the temple, Simeon rejoices at seeing the child. Anna, an elderly prophetess, speaks about the child to all awaiting the salvation of Jerusalem (2:22–38).

After Herod's death, Joseph is told in a dream to return to Israel. But hearing that Herod's son is in power, Joseph, guided in a dream, withdraws to Galilee and settles in Nazareth (2:19–23).

When they had fulfilled the law, they return to Nazareth (2:39–40).
*
Jesus at twelve years of age (2:41–52).
*
Genealogy of Jesus from Joseph back to Adam (3:23–38).

On a mere historical level, the two accounts pose interesting problems. Luke's version makes it clear that Mary and Joseph are natives of Nazareth who must journey to Bethlehem for a census and then return home. Matthew, however, has Joseph and Mary in Bethlehem right from the start (2:1 is the first mention of locale), the magi visit them in their *house* (2:11), and subsequently Joseph decides to put down roots in Galilee out of fear of Herod's son. Luke shows no awareness of magi from the east or a massive slaughter of infants and Herod's murderous frenzy. Instead, Joseph and Mary peacefully worship right in the heart of Herod's Jerusalem capital, while the prophetess Anna and Simeon, heedless of any danger to the child, publicly proclaim Jesus as the Christ. Matthew, on the other hand, is not aware of any census, of any family relationship between Jesus and John the Baptist, of mangers or of shepherds. Historical records from the first century contain no reference to Matthew's Herodian infanticide (although many other negative things about Herod are mentioned) or to a census of the type Luke describes as emanating from Rome.

All these questions are not to imply that the infancy narratives are devoid of any historical information, but only that history is not the evangelists' principal concern. Both writers have traditions that Jesus' parents were Joseph and Mary (but Luke highlights Mary's role, while Matthew's spotlight is on Joseph), that Jesus was born in Bethlehem and grew up in Nazareth (although Matthew starts with Joseph and Mary in Bethlehem and must get them eventually to Nazareth, while Luke begins with them in Nazareth and must bring them to Bethlehem for the birth), and that Jesus was conceived by the Holy Spirit. This last item is the most significant of the traditions because of its theological meaning for the sacred authors. And so, let us turn our attention to what is really important—the evangelists' religious points.

It has been suggested that both infancy narratives introduce and encapsulate all the various insights which the evangelists will further develop as their Gospels unfold. As was mentioned earlier, the writer of Matthew's Gospel conceives of Jesus as the ultimate manifestation of divine revelation, bringing to perfection all the qualities of Israel's heroes in the Old Testament. Like Moses, the infant Jesus' life is sought by a wicked king who orders the deaths of all male babies (Ex 1:22), but he escapes because he is destined to save his people. Joseph, who like his namesake receives messages in dreams (Gen 37:5–11; 40:5–19; 41:14–36), learns that "those who were seeking the child's life are dead," just as Moses was told by the Lord that "all those who were seeking your life are dead" (Ex 4:19). Jesus being called out of Egypt (Mt 2:15) echoes yet another Old Testament theme.

The evangelist's awareness of the importance of Jesus' death also appears in the infancy narrative. The magi from the east come seeking "the king of the Jews," a title which will not again appear in Matthew until the trial of Jesus and his crucifixion. As we will see in a later chapter, the author of Matthew's Gospel also believes that those Jews who have not come to faith in Jesus have been replaced in God's favor by the believing Gentiles. Notice that the pagan magi learn something of God's plan through a manifestation of nature, but they must discover its details by consulting with the Jews who have the sacred Scriptures (Mt 2:2), but who, according to Matthew, do not accept its contents. It is also interesting that the corrupt ruler Herod summons the chief priests and scribes (Mt 2:4), two groups who with another corrupt ruler, Pilate, appear again at the trial of Jesus. The magi's gifts of gold, frankincense, and myrrh all have funereal overtones, again foreshadowing Jesus' saving death. Furthermore, just as the significance of Jesus' birth was unexpectedly perceived by pagan magi through a startling event of nature, so, too, the significance of his death will first be realized by pagan Romans following a remarkable natural phenomenon (Mt 27:54—"When the centurion and those who were with him . . . saw the earthquake and what had taken place, they were filled with awe, and said, 'Truly this was the Son of God!' ").

Luke's infancy narrative also contains important theological perspectives. Notice that Mary and Joseph are portrayed as pious, completely law-abiding Jews. They (especially Mary) hear God's word and follow it, they circumcise the child according to Mosaic practice, they participate in a presentation and a purification ceremony, and they worship in the temple every Passover. (They are also depicted as obedient to Roman law as the census requirement shows—evidence of a concern of the evangelist in the 80s.) This religious piety is continued in the Gospel's later presentation of Jesus as a man who often prays. The Lucan Jesus, as will be discussed in detail later, also has a special concern for the poor and lowly. Unlike the Matthean Jesus who receives dignitaries from afar, the Lucan infant is placed in a manger where he is visited by shepherds from the fields who are seeking the Savior. At his presentation in the temple, two elderly, deeply religious, prophetic figures, Simeon and Anna, appear, praising Jesus as the salvation of God for all peoples, and the rise and fall of many in Israel. Luke's interest in portraying Mary as the prime example of a disciple is also evident in the infancy narrative. Besides following God's word, she keeps and ponders it in her heart (Lk 2:19,51), although her soul will be pierced through by it (2:35).

This quick skimming of the religious orientations of the authors of the infancy narratives only scratches the surface of those texts. Hopefully, it has served to demonstrate that the Gospels are essentially statements of *faith* and not primarily historical biographies. Settings, characters, and the words of the characters in any particular Gospel scene are all aimed at promoting the authors' theological interests. Just as the Gospels themselves should not be approached as if they were written according to twentieth-century literary norms, the statements made by particular persons in the Gospel should not be assumed to be direct quotations recorded on the spot. As a quick example, all the Gospels have some form of the incident we have come to call Peter's confession. The following chart presents the words of Jesus and Peter in each account:

	Mk 8:27–29	Mt 16:13–20	Lk 9:18–21	Jn 6:67–70
Jesus:	"But who do you say that I am?"	"But who do you say that I am?"	"But who do you say that I am?"	"Do you also wish to go away?"
Peter:	"You are the Christ."	"You are the Christ, the Son of the Living God."	"The Christ of God."	"Lord, to whom shall we go? You have the words of eternal life; and we have believed and have come to know that

		you are the Holy One of God."
Jesus:	"Blessed are you Simon Bar-Jona! For flesh and blood have not revealed this to you, but my Fa- ther who is in heaven. I tell you, you are Peter, and on this rock I will build my church. . . ."	"Did I not choose you, the twelve, and one of you is a devil?"

While these passages will be examined further in later chapters, it is clear that the different authors are using a common memory of a certain incident to reveal varying insights about Jesus and Peter, and that the words of both are presented accordingly. Notice, also, how the second stage of Gospel tradition, the time after the resurrection, permeates the vocabulary used in these verses. While calling Jesus "the Christ" or the "Anointed One" reflects a high esteem for him as the Agent of God, "Son of the living God" carries divine resonances which developed only after the resurrection.

This reference to the Pontifical Biblical Commission's *Instruction* brings us to one final point. It might have been noticed that the Commission distinguished between the apostles and the evangelists. The first preaching of the apostles was defined as stage two, while the writing of the evangelists occurred later in stage three. This reflects the conclusion of modern Scripture scholarship that none of the Gospels were written by actual eyewitnesses to Jesus' ministry, but by second or third generation Christians. There are several reasons for this opinion, but an obvious one is the fact that all the Gospels were composed many decades after the events of which they speak. Furthermore, the Gospels originally circulated anonymously. The writers apparently did not feel that their identities were as important as their messages. The names now associated with the Gospels—Mark, Matthew, Luke, and John—were not attributed to them until far into the second century. For the sake of convenience, these names will be used when referring to a certain evangelist or to his Gospel, without making any assertions about the writers' actual identities.

This is not to say that the Gospels do not have apostolic traditions underlying them, but only that the actual authors were not the apostles themselves. This is important because it is sometimes asserted that the Gospels of Matthew, and especially John, are somehow superior to those of Mark and Luke because their writers were members of the Twelve and actually witnessed many of the events described. Since we do not know the evangelists' identities, each Gospel must be appreciated for the unique and valuable inspired composition that it is. One writer's presentation of a particular incident—the confession of Peter, for example—must not be considered better than another's because it adds to or enhances upon certain passages. Rather, each Gospel must be respected and read because of its one-of-a-kind insights into the meaning of Jesus. After all, the significance of the life of Jesus can never be exhausted, but can be conceived of in an infinite variety of ways.

Having explored what is currently known about the origins and natures of the Gospels in a general way, our attention will now be directed to exploring the three synoptic Gospels a little more closely. While multi-volume commentaries could be written about each of them, our purpose will simply be to become reasonably familiar with the overall themes, concerns, and perceptions of each of the three synoptic writers.

QUESTIONS FOR REFLECTION AND DISCUSSION

1. If the Gospels should not be understood as modern, historical biographies, what would be better ways to describe them?

2. Since the Gospels present four unique perspectives on the significance of Jesus, what might be done at liturgies to reduce the tendency of worshipers to overlook their distinctiveness by unconsciously blending them together?

3. What are some of the dangers in reading the Gospels without an awareness of the three stages of tradition contained in them?

4. Why is it important for modern readers to be familiar with the insights of *all* of the Gospels, rather than concentrating on only one?

5. Why is an awareness of Judaism important for understanding Jesus of Nazareth?

6. What are some consequences of the realization that the Gospels were all written by anonymous authors many decades after the events of Jesus' ministry?

Chapter Two

THE MARCAN JESUS:
SUFFERING SON OF MAN

Preliminary Reading of the Gospel

*B*efore beginning this chapter, it would be beneficial to read through the entire Gospel of Mark from start to finish, in one sitting if possible. This would avoid dealing with this evangelist in a piece-meal fashion, and would make his personal style more apparent. It might be helpful to keep handy the outline of the Gospel given below and to pay special attention to the following points:

1. the pace of the narrative
2. what Jesus is doing most of the time
3. the content of Jesus' preaching
4. the sequence in which the various incidents occur
5. the portrayal of the disciples
6. the titles which are given to Jesus and by whom they are given

---

Rough Outline of the Gospel of Mark

I. JESUS' ACTIVITIES PRODUCE AWE, BUT NO ONE PERCEIVES THEIR REAL SIGNIFICANCE
    A. The Beginnings of Jesus' Ministry [1:1–15]
        Transitional Summary [1:14–15]:
        after John's arrest Jesus begins preaching the Gospel

B. Jesus Speaks and Acts with Authority [1:16–3:12]
Transitional Summary [3:6–12]:
enemies conspire to destroy Jesus; great crowds surround
him; demons are continually silenced

C. Jesus Encounters Widespread Disapproval [3:13–6:6]
Transitional Episode [6:1–6]:
Jesus is rejected at Nazareth; he travels around other vil-
lages teaching

D. The Disciples Also Misunderstand Him [6:7–8:26]
Transitional Episode [8:22–26]:
healing in stages of blind man

II. JESUS' SUFFERING REVEALS THE TRUE MEANING
OF HIS MESSIAHSHIP AND MODELS AUTHENTIC
DISCIPLESHIP

A. Jesus Discusses His Death and Being His Follower [8:27–
10:52]
Transitional Episode [10:46–52]:
healing of blind Bartimaeus

B. Conflict in Jerusalem [11:1–12:44]
Transitional Episode [12:41–44]:
the widow who gives all that she has

C. The End Times [13:1–14:11]
Transitional Episode [14:1–11]:
the authorities seek Jesus' life;
a woman anoints Jesus;
the authorities conspire with Judas

D. The Passion Narrative [14:12–16:8]
Concluding Episode [16:1–8]
the women discover the empty tomb, but out of fear tell
no one.

An Amazing Story

One way to gain insights into the evangelist's purposes is to
consider the manner in which he has incorporated various traditions
about Jesus into his narrative. An obvious structural feature of the

Gospel is that it is divided in half, the mid-point being 8:27–30ff, the scene known as Peter's confession. Before that passage, there is a great emphasis on Jesus as miracle-worker. About fifteen individual miracles occur (and many others are alluded to in a general way) in the first half of the Gospel, while only four or five take place in the second half. The events in the first eight chapters of the Gospel apparently race by at breakneck speed due to the frequent use of the Greek word for "immediately" or "at once." The term appears fifteen times before 8:27, but only twice afterward.

Although Jesus performs many wondrous feats in the Gospel's opening chapters, his deeds and words produce only bafflement and wonder, not faith:

1:22	And they were astonished at his teaching, for he taught them as one who had authority . . .
1:27	"What is this? A new teaching! With authority he commands even the unclean spirits and they obey him."
2:12	They were all amazed and glorified God saying, "We never saw anything like this!"
4:41	And they were filled with awe, and said to one another, "Who then is this, that even wind and sea obey him?"
5:20	. . .and all men marveled.
5:42	. . .and they were immediately overcome with amazement.
6:2	"Where did this man get all this? What is the wisdom given to him? What mighty works are wrought by his hands!"
6:51	And they were utterly astounded, for they did not understand about the loaves, but their hearts were hardened.
7:18	"Then are you also without understanding?"
7:37	And they were astonished beyond measure, saying, "He has done all things well; he even makes the deaf hear and the dumb speak."
8:4	"How can one feed these men with bread here in the desert?" [after aiding in the feeding of the five thousand in 6:41]
8:21	"Do you not yet understand?"
10:32	And they were on the road, going up to Jerusalem . . . and they were amazed, and those who followed were afraid.

11:18   . . .all the multitude was astonished at his teaching.
12:17   And they were amazed at him.

This series of bewildered reactions is notably concentrated in the first half of the Gospel, just as the miracles are. Only three of the above incidents take place after the pivotal 8:27 scene.

The focus on the awesome and remarkable is intensified by several occasions when demons are forbidden to cry out statements about Jesus' identity. Although these demons seem to possess a supernatural awareness about Jesus, the only ones who benefit from their knowledge are the readers. Like the chorus in a Greek play, the demons' utterances have no effect whatsoever on the action which is taking place. But their constant exclamations hammer home to Mark's readers the true nature of Jesus which has escaped everyone else in the Gospel narrative. Once more, notice that all of these incidents occur before the central 8:27 passage:

1:23–25   And immediately there was in their synagogue a man with an unclean spirit; and he cried out, "What have you to do with us, Jesus of Nazareth? I know who you are, the Holy One of God." But Jesus rebuked him saying, "Be silent, and come out of him!"

1:34   And he healed many who were sick with various diseases, and cast out many demons; and he would not permit the demons to speak, because they knew him.

3:11–12   And whenever the unclean Spirits beheld him, they fell down and cried out, "You are the Son of God." And he strictly ordered them not to make him known.

5:7   And crying out with a loud voice he said, "What have you to do with me, Jesus, Son of the Most High God? I adjure you by God, do not torment me."

Not only have the demons' outcries progressively heightened in their grandeur (from "Holy One of God" to "Son of God" to "Son of the Most High God"), but the reader has already encountered two additional statements about Jesus' identity. The Gospel opened with the words "The beginning of the Gospel of Jesus Christ, the

Son of God" (1:1); and at his baptism a heavenly voice said to Jesus, "You are my beloved Son; with you I am well pleased" (1:11).

Significantly, none of Jesus' contemporaries in the narrative have any inkling of these things—only the reader benefits from the writer's *post-resurrectional* knowledge of his identity. Those who have not yet experienced his death and raising seem to be incapable of such insights. Almost everyone in the Gospel is apparently drawn to Jesus only because he is so amazing, but their amazement leads no further. Some have faith that Jesus can heal, but they do not perceive who he really is.

The Failure To Perceive

The evangelist carefully includes almost every group imaginable among those who reject or disapprove or simply do not understand Jesus. As early as 3:6, the Pharisees and Herodians plot to destroy him. His family comes to take charge of Jesus because people are saying that he is out of his mind (3:20–22, 31–34). The scribes accuse him of being involved in a satanic alliance (3:23–30). The Gentile Gerasenes ask him to leave their neighborhood (5:17) and his fellow-Nazareans take offense at him (6:3).

Even his own disciples do not comprehend, in fact, the evangelist portrays them more negatively than any of the other Gospel writers. Their failings are aggravated because they are repeatedly the recipients of private instruction by Jesus.

4:10–11   And when he was alone, those who were about him with the twelve asked him concerning the parables. And he said to them, "To you has been given the secret of the kingdom of God, but for those outside everything is in parables."

4:33–34   With many such parables he spoke the word to them, as they were able to hear it; he did not speak to them without a parable, but privately to his own disciples he explained everything.

7:17–18   And when he had entered the house, and left the

people his disciples asked him about the parable. And he said to them, "Are you also without understanding?"

9:28   And when he had entered the house, his disciples asked him privately, "Why could we not cast it out?"

10:10   And in the house the disciples asked him again about this matter.

Despite this personal tutoring, the disciples understand Jesus no better than anyone else. The best (or worst) example of their blindness occurs in relation to the two miraculous feedings of the multitude. Even though they had distributed the multiplied loaves and fish to five thousand individuals (6:41), they cannot imagine how four thousand are going to be fed only two chapters later (8:4). Worse yet, shortly after this second feeding they become upset when they realize that they have taken only one loaf of bread into the boat with them (8:14–16)! It appears to be an exasperated Jesus who inquires, "Why do you discuss the fact that you have no bread? Do you not yet perceive or understand? Are your hearts hardened? Having eyes do you not see, and having ears do you not hear? And do you not remember?" (8:17–18).

To sum up what has been noted thus far, Mark seems to have deliberately divided his Gospel in half. Most of Jesus' miracles occur in quick succession in the first half, and although it is observed that he teaches often, more words are devoted to describing his wondrous feats than to recounting his preaching. While the reader is aware from several sources, most notably the perceptive demons, that Jesus is the Son of God, this post-resurrectional awareness never dawns on the witnesses to Jesus' ministry. The enthusiastic crowds, which on occasion make it impossible for Jesus to eat a decent meal (3:20), are apparently only interested in his healings and exorcisms. They marvel at his teachings, but never seek them. The Pharisees, scribes, Herodians, his family, friends, townsfolk, and the Gentile Gerasenes all are opposed to Jesus in one way or another. The disciples are particularly obtuse even though they have had the benefit of private explanations from Jesus.

All this brings us to the crucial passage 8:27–30ff, the scene in which Jesus asks the disciples point blank the question that has-

been confounding everyone up to that point (except the reader)—
the question of his identity.

The Son of Man Must Suffer

Immediately before presenting Peter's confession, Mark describes a unique healing of a blind man in 8:22–26. The cure is
unusual because it occurs gradually, not immediately. After an initial
laying of Jesus' hands on him, the blind man can only see indistinctly
(8:24). Following a second laying on of hands, his vision is completely restored. It is surely no accident that Mark presents this
episode about the gradual and imperfect arrival of perception right
before Peter makes the insightful, though incomplete, observation,
"You are the Christ" (8:29). This is the first time in the Gospel that
any human character has said anything of this sort, but like the
demons who had made even more profound utterances, Jesus does
not allow such ideas to be widely proclaimed (8:30). Instead, he
overlooks the title Peter has given him by immediately speaking
about the "Son of Man," the only title which Jesus uses of himself in
the Gospel.

Mk 8:31 introduces a completely new thought into the Gospel
narrative, the idea that the Son of Man will suffer, be rejected, and
be killed. Up to this point, the focus has been on Jesus as wonder-
worker who remains a mystery to all. But now, in this pivotal verse,
the concept that will dominate the remainder of the Gospel
appears—the Son of Man will suffer and die.

In the section of the Gospel which follows, Jesus will make a
total of three such "passion predictions," and they will become
progressively detailed:

8:31   And he began to teach them that the Son of Man
            must suffer many things, and be rejected by the
            elders and the chief priests and the scribes, and be
            killed, and after three days rise again.

9:31   "The Son of Man will be delivered into the hands of
            men, and they will kill him; and when he is killed,
            after three days he will rise."

10:33–34   "Behold, we are going up to Jerusalem; and the Son of Man will be delivered up to the chief priests and scribes, and they will condemn him to death, and deliver him to the Gentiles; and they will mock him, and scourge him, and kill him; and after three days he will rise."

Keeping in mind the three stages of Gospel tradition, one might strongly suspect that these predictions (especially the last one) have been written from hindsight through the post-resurrectional perspective of the early Church. Such a suspicion is confirmed by the non-synoptic tradition in the Gospel of John, which also depicts Jesus making three passion predictions, but in a much more general way:

3:14 "And as Moses lifted up the serpent in the wilderness, so must the Son of Man be lifted up, that whoever believes in him might have eternal life."

8:28 "When you have lifted up the Son of Man, then you will know that I am he, and that I do nothing on my own authority but speak thus as the Father taught me."

12:32 "And I, when I am lifted up from the earth, will draw all men to myself."

It would seem that Jesus, in his historical ministry, knew that death was likely to be his fate, and communicated this knowledge to his followers together with the belief that God would ultimately vindicate him. After experiencing his death and resurrection, these followers remembered Jesus' forebodings and preached how Jesus remained faithful to his mission even in the face of death (see Phil 2:8, for example). Jesus' realistic assessment of his fate (during his ministry in the early 30s) is later expressed by the evangelists (writing in the 70s, 80s, or 90s) in the terms of the Church's post-resurrectional insights. The Gospel writers use the predictions to reveal the significance of Jesus' death (such as John 12:32, "when I am lifted up from the earth, I will draw all men to myself"). This point about the place of the predictions in the historical ministry of Jesus will be discussed further in chapter eight, but let us return to the present topic—namely, how the writer of the Gospel of Mark uses the prediction traditions he has received.

Each time Jesus discusses his imminent passion and death, Mark depicts some misunderstanding or negative behavior occurring, which prompts Jesus to explain further to his disciples what being a follower of his is all about:

8:31–32a First passion prediction

8:32b–33 Peter takes Jesus aside and remonstrates with him.

8:34–9:1 "If any man would come after me, let him deny himself and take up his cross and follow me" (vs. 34).

9:30–32 Second passion prediction

9:33–34 Disciples argue about who among them is the greatest.

9:35–37 Whoever would be greatest must be servant of all and even concerned for children.

10:32–34 Third passion prediction

10:35–41 Zebedee brothers ask to be Jesus' lieutenants in the Kingdom; other disciples are indignant.

10:42–45 You must not be domineering like pagan lords, you must be slaves of all because "the Son of Man also came not to be served, but to serve, and to give his life as a ransom for many" (vs. 45).

This brilliant arrangement is intended by the evangelist to demonstrate that just as Jesus was servant and slave of all by his suffering, so, too, his followers must be slaves and servants of all and be willing to suffer. Such a message would be especially relevant to Mark's church community if it was indeed in the throes of persecution and pain as most scholars believe.

Notice, also, how the theme of the disciples' misunderstanding persists. Right from the initial title switch from Peter's "Christ" to Jesus' "Son of Man," the teaching about suffering messiahship is not accepted. Peter apparently tries to talk Jesus out of suffering (8:32b); shortly after hearing about being servants of all, the disciples vie for the title of "greatest" (9:33–34); and James and John are ambitious (and seemingly, by their indignation, so are all the rest) for power and glory (10:37,41).

In between the passion prediction scenes, the evangelist has inserted other incidents which accentuate the disciples' inability to absorb Jesus' teaching. This entire section of the Gospel expresses in a variety of ways the evangelist's fundamental conviction: Jesus' true significance, the nature of his messiahship, and the meaning of discipleship can only be perceived by experiencing Jesus' suffering, death, and raising. Note how cleverly the writer has arranged his materials in this section:

8:22–26	healing in stages of blind man of Bethsaida
8:27–9:1	first passion prediction cycle
9:2–29	Jesus is transfigured; disciples fail to exorcise a dumb spirit
9:30–37	second passion prediction cycle
9:38–10:31	disciples complain about a strange exorcist; a divorce discussion; disciples reject children; discussion about riches
10:32–45	third passion prediction cycle
10:46–52	healing of blind Bartimaeus

After hearing about taking up one's cross and following Jesus, Peter, James, and John are taken up on a mountain where they behold Jesus in glory (9:2–3). Despite what they have seen and been taught both publicly and in private, the disciples are "exceedingly afraid" (9:6). As if to emphasize that they must start to pay attention to what Jesus has been saying about suffering, a heavenly voice identifies who Jesus is and what Peter, James, and John should be doing: "This is my beloved Son; *listen to him!*" (9:7 italics added). The episode concludes with Jesus telling the three not to speak of what has occurred to anyone until the Son of Man has risen from the dead. They are puzzled as to what this might mean (9:9–10), although Jesus had already explained it previously (in 8:31). Neither Jesus' glory, nor his identity, nor his mission can be understood until his suffering, death, and resurrection have been experienced.

Following the second passion prediction cycle, with its teaching on being servants and accepting of little children, the disciples are jealous of a successful exorcist not of their number (9:38–41; recall that they had been unable to exorcise a spirit of dumbness in 9:17). Then they try to keep children from coming to Jesus (10:13)—not only do they not understand, they do the exact opposite of what Jesus has taught! Indignantly, Jesus rebukes them, saying, "Whoever does not receive the kingdom of God like a child shall not enter it" (10:15, echoing the child saying of 9:36–37).

The third passion prediction cycle is followed by the healing of a blind man named Bartimaeus (10:46–52). Just as this whole section opened with the giving of sight to a blind person, so now it ends in a similar fashion. The opening miracle was unique because it occurred gradually. Here, the Gospel's only other curing of blindness is notable because of Bartimaeus' persistent calling out to Jesus, despite being rebuked by bystanders. He addresses Jesus as "Son of David," the title which is closest to the evangelist's preferred "Son of Man," and is the only healed person to actually follow Jesus (vs. 52). His unflagging faith in Jesus and his decision to follow him is a fitting conclusion to this discipleship section. Perhaps the evangelist is reminding his church community that continuing faith in Jesus to show the way, even in the face of ridicule and opposition, is the hallmark of genuine discipleship.

The Gospel proceeds immediately to the onset of Jesus' suffering by depicting his humble entrance, riding upon a colt, into Jerusalem (11:1–11). The two chapters which follow show Jesus in increasing conflict with the temple leadership. Jesus overturns tables in the temple (11:15–19, a scene bracketed by the cursing and subsequent death of a fruitless fig tree, 11:12–14,20–25). The authority of Jesus is questioned and he responds with riddling words and a pointed parable about the wicked tenants of a vineyard, a familiar image for Israel (11:27–12:12). The leadership try to trick Jesus with a loaded question about paying taxes to Caesar (12:13–17), and continue their efforts with other inquiries about marriage in the afterlife and the greatest commandment, though this latter conversation is noticeably amiable (12:18–34). After issuing a warning about the scribes (12:38–40), this Jerusalem section concludes with a widow donating her entire savings to the poor (12:41–44). Jesus is also about to give everything he has, including life itself.

The Passion and Death of the Son of Man

Temporarily postponing our consideration of chapter 13, let us follow the narrative as it sweeps along to its inevitable conclusion. While a woman prophetically anoints Jesus beforehand for his burial (14:3–9), the authorities seek to kill Jesus (14:1–2) by conspiring with Judas, one of the Twelve (14:10–11). Ever since the scene of Peter's confession, Jesus has been expressing the major theme of this Gospel—the necessity of the suffering of the Son of Man. The companions of Jesus have been consistently unable to accept such a notion, or its implications for their discipleship. When Jesus shows no signs of resisting or avoiding his imminent death, they will leave him to endure his fate totally alone.

During the passover meal with his disciples, Jesus once again speaks of his ministry in terms of suffering. He will be betrayed by one of the Twelve, by one of those now sharing table-fellowship with him (14:18–20). The Son of Man goes to his Scripture-appointed destiny (14:21), a destiny which requires the breaking of his body and the pouring forth of his blood before the kingdom of God can fully arrive (14:22–25). When the disciples are warned that they will all abandon him, Peter asserts his own loyalty, prompting Jesus to predict Peter's denials (14:27–30). Peter and the rest are vehement in their denials of any such faithlessness, even expressing willingness to die alongside Jesus (14:31).

Although Jesus has been depicted throughout the second half of the Gospel as resigned to his fate, the evangelist does not want his readers to conclude that he felt no misgivings about it. Taking the special three companions along with him once more, Jesus tells Peter, James, and John that he is desperately sorrowful and asks them to keep watch (14:33–34). Then, "falling to the ground" he prays to the Father that somehow his ordeal might be avoided (14:35–36). When he discovers Peter, James, and John sound asleep rather than watchful, his words seem to apply as much to his own distressed mood as to them, "Watch and pray that you may not enter into temptation; the spirit is indeed willing, but the flesh is weak" (14:38). Three different times he returns to his three friends from his prayer only to find them asleep and unable to be of any support (14:37–42). The arresters arrive. Judas, one of those who had been closest to Jesus, who had received private instruction from him, betrays him with a gesture of intimate affection (14:44–45). Jesus does not resist capture. The evangelist is poignantly blunt about his companions' reaction: "They all forsook him, and fled" (14:50). One of them in panic upon being seized abandons his very clothing and escapes naked (14:51). Just as the first disciples had left everything to follow Jesus (1:16–20; 2:14), so now this one leaves everything in order to get away from him.

Facing the chief priests and council, Jesus is asked if he is "the Christ, the Son of the Blessed" (14:61). This is the very first time in the Gospel that a human being has called Jesus Son of God, although in this context it is obviously not meant to be a statement of faith. Jesus responds affirmatively by referring to the coming of the Son of Man on the clouds of heaven with divine power (14:62). This event, remember, is exactly what Mark's church community would be waiting for—the return of Christ in glory to vindicate his followers. Such longing would be intensified if, as most scholars suspect, the Marcan church is experiencing persecution or violence. Despite reading of their Lord being insulted, spat upon, and struck (14:65), the readers are urged by the evangelist to trust that Jesus' words will be proven correct. For even as he is being taunted to prophesy, another of Jesus' predictions is coming to pass.

True to Jesus' words, "all the sheep have been scattered" (14:27), but Peter is just outside in the courtyard, accused of being Jesus' accomplice. His responses to these charges are noteworthy. First, he declares, "I neither know nor understand what you mean" (14:68). The evangelist would have been hard put to find better words to describe the Peter he has presented throughout his entire Gospel! Second, Peter denies "being one of them" (14:69). It is difficult not to associate this passage with later disciples, perhaps members of the Marcan church, being persecuted for "being one of them." Third, Peter curses and swears his non-friendship with Jesus (14:71). The situation of persecuted Christians later in the first century again comes to mind. One way of proving their disavowal of the Christian movement was for the accused to curse Christ. Although the Greek text here is ambiguous as to whether Peter actually curses Jesus, the parallel is suggestive nonetheless.

In the first half of the Gospel we noted how the writer had carefully showed a wide variety of groups not comprehending Jesus. Similarly, during his passion he is rejected by everyone. The disciples have betrayed, denied, and abandoned him; the chief priests and council have condemned and abused him; the crowd prefers Barabbas to him and urges Jesus' crucifixion (15:6–14); the Roman soldiers scourge and torment him as a pitiable "King of the Jews" (15:15–20), and while suspended in agony from the cross he is jeered and derided by passers-by (15:29), by the chief priests (15:31–32a), and by those crucified with him (15:32b). Unlike the other Gospels, there is not a single friendly voice to speak on Jesus' behalf. He is utterly alone.

The sense of total abandonment is powerful. "My God! My God! Why have you forsaken me?" (15:34), Jesus cries, and, after a second scream, he dies.

At once the temple curtain is torn (15:38). This probably has a twofold significance for the evangelist. First, it seems to indicate divine wrath against the temple which is destined for destruction (13:2, "There will not be left here one stone upon another that will not be thrown down"). Recall that the episode of Jesus' "cleansing of the temple" was bracketed by the scene of a fruitless fig tree being cursed by Jesus and later being found withered (11:12–14,20–25). Second, the tearing of the curtain could be seen as the opening up of access to God for the Gentile pagans. In this regard it is noteworthy that Mark's Gospel is the only one in which Jesus proclaims during the temple cleansing that the Lord's house would be a house of prayer *"for all the nations"* (11:17).

Finally, the curtain's destruction could also relate to the parable Jesus had told in the temple about the wicked vineyard tenants, who, after killing the owner's beloved son, will feel his wrath. "He will come and destroy the tenants, and give the vineyard to others" (12:9). These "others" clearly must mean the Gentiles, indicating that the Marcan church is a largely Gentile one. This impression is confirmed by the evangelist's earlier presentation of Jesus' dispute with the Pharisees about purity (7:1–23). The writer parenthetically explains Jewish purification customs in a distant and not completely accurate manner—a sign that the Marcan community, and possibly the evangelist himself, is not Jewish. In a second editorial statement, the author declares that "thus [Jesus] declared all foods clean" (7:19), a comment which insures that Gentile Christians need not worry about observing the Jewish law. It might also reveal a belief that the law has become obsolete for Jews as well, an opinion which would not endear the Marcan church to Jewish contemporaries. The temple curtain being torn at Jesus' death might, therefore, be an attack by the evangelist on the continuing validity of Judaism.

Jesus' death also inspires the most important exclamation of any character in the Gospel. The Gentile centurion, after observing Jesus' death, is able to perceive that "Truly this man was the Son of God" (15:39). These were the words with which the evangelist had opened his Gospel. They were the words spoken by the heavenly voice, by various demons, and mockingly asked of Jesus by the high priest. *But no human being has been able to say these words with true conviction and insight until witnessing the death of the Son of Man.* The centurion's statement is really the climax of Mark's Gospel. Although witness to authoritative words and deeds, even though privately instructed, no one can truly understand Jesus without experiencing his passion.

The Marcan Community

This message would be of especial interest to the Marcan church community if it is the victim of some sort of persecution or distress as many scholars believe. It has already been noted how Jesus' teaching on the suffering service of the Son of Man was related to being his follower. The central discipleship section (8:27–10:52) contains several references to the need for disciples of Jesus to be willing to serve and endure suffering:

8:34–9:1   And he called to him the multitude with his disciples, and said to them, "If any man would come after me, let him deny himself and take up his cross and follow me. For whoever would save his life will lose it; and whoever loses his life for my sake and the gospel's will save it. For what does it profit a man, to gain the whole world and forfeit his life? For whoever is ashamed of me and my words in this adulterous, sinful generation, of him will the Son of Man also be ashamed, when he comes in the glory of his Father with the holy angels." And he said to them, "Truly, I say to you, there are some standing here who will not taste death before they see that the kingdom of God has come with power."

9:35   And he sat down and called the twelve and said to them, "If any one would be first, he must be the last of all and servant of all."

9:43-47   "And if your hand causes you to sin, cut it off; it is better for you to enter life maimed than with two hands to go to hell, to the unquenchable fire. And if your foot causes you to sin, cut it off; it is better for you to enter life lame than with two feet to be thrown into hell. And if your eye causes you to sin, pluck it out; it is better for you to enter the kingdom of God with one eye than with two eyes to be thrown into hell."

10:29-31   Jesus said, "Truly, I say to you, there is no one who has left house or brothers or sisters or mother or father or children or lands, for my sake and for the gospel, who will not receive a hundredfold now in this time, houses and brothers and sisters and mothers and children and lands, with persecutions, and in the age to come eternal life. But many that are first will be last, and the last first."

10:38-39   But Jesus said to them, "You do not know what you are asking. Are you able to drink the cup that I drink, or to be baptized with the baptism with which I am baptized?" And they said to him, "We are able." And Jesus said to them, "The cup that I drink you will drink; and with the baptism with which I am baptized you will be baptized."

10:42-45   And Jesus called to them and said to them, "You know that those who are supposed to rule over the Gentiles lord it over them, and their great men exercise authority over them. But it shall not be so among you; but whoever would be great among you must be your servant, and whoever would be first among you must be slave of all. For the Son of Man also came not to be served but to serve, and to give his life as a ransom for many."

All of these passages can be readily seen to relate to the predicament of a persecuted Marcan church sometime in the 60s. Living through a period of torment, these believers anxiously anticipate the return of Jesus in glory to rescue and vindicate them. By being willing to "take up their cross" in imitation of their Lord, they can be sure to receive his blessings upon his return. If they prove faithless in the face of suffering, then the Son of Man will be

ashamed of them. The Marcan church is exhorted to remain steadfast because Christ will appear in their lifetimes (13:30).

The references to the amputation of limbs and organs which
encourage sinfulness (9:43ff) could also have been understood in a
very concrete way by Mark's community. If they are being tortured
by persecutors by having arms and feet cut off, or by being blinded,
these verses would be a tremendous consolation. Better to suffer
such losses than to betray the Lord. Those who have endured the
loss of family, friends, homes or property are comforted too. Although in the midst of persecution in the present age, they will
enjoy the eternal life of the age to come.

Finally, the disciples are plainly told that they will share in the
baptism and drink the cup of Jesus. These are common references
to Jesus' passion throughout the New Testament writings. Such a
fate is only to be expected if followers imitate the master who will
"give his life as a ransom for many" (10:45).

Clearly, chapter 13 is intended specifically for the evangelist's
contemporaries. After indicating that there would be "wars, and
rumors of wars, earthquakes, and famines" (13:7–8; all of which
occurred in the 50s–60s), Jesus goes on to describe what must
actually be taking place in the Marcan church:

> "But take heed to yourselves; for they will deliver you up to
> councils; and you will be beaten in synagogues; and you will
> stand before governors and kings for my sake, to bear testimony
> before them. And the gospel must first be preached to all the
> nations. And when they bring you to trial and deliver you up, do
> not be anxious beforehand what you are to say; but say what-
> ever is given you in that hour, for it is not you who speak, but
> the Holy Spirit. And brother will deliver brother up to death,
> and the father his child, and children will rise against parents
> and have them put to death; and you will be hated by all for my
> name's sake. But he who endures to the end will be saved"
> (13:9–13).

If these verses indeed relate the recent or current history of Mark's
community, then the Gospel's central concern about Jesus' suffering and death becomes very understandable. Notice the similarities
with Jesus—he, too, was "delivered up" (15:1,15), he was beaten

and stood before the governor, and he was rejected and abandoned by family, friends, and kinfolk. The evangelist has two particular messages for his church in this passage. The temporary delay in Jesus' return must happen so that the good news can be preached to all the pagans (although he will come back soon—13:30). Most importantly, those who remain faithful and do not succumb to the pain with which they are afflicted will be rescued.

And so, it is evident that the sacred author has been at least partially motivated to write his Gospel because of the traumatic ordeal his community is undergoing. His entire Gospel has been colored by his intention to bolster his church's resolve, endurance, and faith in the crucified Lord who will save them.

It is also possible that the evangelist has had the additional aim of correcting views about Jesus that he finds dangerously erroneous. There may be people in his community, or perhaps visitors from elsewhere, who are perpetuating the idea that it is the miraculous power of Jesus which is of prime importance. Such people would dwell on Jesus' miracles and mighty works, would consider the performance of similar feats to be the tests of true discipleship, might assert that they have been the recipients of secret, private revelations from Jesus, and would encourage Christians to avoid persecution. From what can be discerned from various sources, these revelers in Jesus' glory, or "glory-hounds," tended to write and speak only about Jesus' power, and compiled accounts of his miracles. The influence of their perspective can be seen not only in the Gospel of Mark, but also in 2 Corinthians (where Paul forcefully asserts that the mark of true discipleship is not power, but suffering; see 2 Cor 11:1–31, for example), the Gospel of Luke (which is comfortable with the outlook), and the Gospel of John (which, like Mark, finds sign-faith superficial).

The fact that the first half of the Gospel presents a mostly "miracle-man" image of Jesus is certainly no accident. The writer possibly uses his opponents' own miracles-collection against them. While not denying that Jesus healed people, he consistently shows that these actions do not produce faith in Jesus as Son of God. The portrayal of the disciples as privately tutored, yet still ignorant (and unable to exorcise), serves to undercut any claims to private revelation that the "glory-hounds" might assert.

Moreover, in his discourse about the end of time and the necessary preliminary suffering in chapter 13, the Marcan Jesus warns his followers to be particularly alert:

> "Take heed that no one leads you astray. Many will come in my name, saying, 'I am he!' and they will lead many astray. . . And then if anyone says to you, 'Look, here is the Christ!' or 'Look, there he is!' do not believe it. False Christs and false prophets will arise and show signs and wonders, to lead astray, if possible, the elect" (13:6,21–22).

It appears that in the desperate times of suffering which the Marcan church is experiencing, and as the believers eagerly and desperately long for the coming of their Savior, some of the "gloryhounds" are claiming that the power of the resurrection has returned in their own miraculous abilities.

The writer of Mark's Gospel counters such ideas by his presentation of Jesus' ministry and the role of the disciples in it. Peter and the rest of the disciples did not come to true faith in Jesus either by witnessing or by sharing in his power. They did not understand him through private lessons from him. They were faithless, and they abandoned, denied, and maybe even cursed him once danger arose.

Nor did true faith develop because of witnessing miraculous resurrection appearances. The Gospel originally ended with this scene:

> And entering the tomb, they saw a young man sitting on the right side; and they were amazed. And he said to them, "Do not be amazed; you seek Jesus of Nazareth, who was crucified. He is risen, he is not here; see the place where they laid him. But go, tell his disciples and Peter that he is going before you to Galilee; there you will see him as he told you." And they went out and fled from the tomb; for trembling and astonishment had come upon them; and they said nothing to anyone, for they were afraid (Mk 16:5–8).

Once more, a spectacular event does not promote faith in Jesus as Son of God. The evangelist has deliberately ended his account, not with a glorious manifestation of the Risen Christ, but simply with an empty tomb. The empty tomb confronts Mark's readers with a challenge. Will their faith be shallow and superficial, dependent on wondrous signs, the kind of faith fostered by the "glory-hounds"? Or will their faith be like that of the disciples of Jesus, who ultimately became witnesses to the Lord, founding communities such as Mark's, only because they had lived through the despair and guilt of his passion to a realization of Jesus' true glory?

The evangelist has provided powerful role-models for his readers. Even if in the midst of persecution they succumb to threats or violence and deny their faith, like the apostles before them they can yet become sharers in the glory of the Son who was crucified.

QUESTIONS FOR REFLECTION AND DISCUSSION

1. What lesson should modern Christians learn from Jesus' willingness to endure suffering?

2. What is this evangelist's opinion of faith in Jesus based on miracles and wondrous signs? How does he convey this viewpoint in his Gospel?

3. How do we understand the role of Jesus' miracles? Does our understanding enhance or hinder our ability to imitate him?

4. Define discipleship according to Mark. Do you know of anyone living today who fits this description? Do you?

5. Mark's church could readily identify with the sufferings of Jesus, but Christians who are relatively free from persecution might find it difficult to do so. What other, more subtle forms of "persecution" might we be subjected to in our lives today?

6. Over the centuries, many Christians have tried to forget Jesus' passion by thinking only of his power, glory, and authority. What do you think the writer of Mark's Gospel would say to such people?

Chapter Three

THE MATTHEAN JESUS:
THE LIVING WISDOM OF GOD

Preliminary Reading of the Gospel

As we begin consideration of this evangelist, a sense of his particular style and emphases would be obtained by reading the entire Gospel. The reader may find the following outline useful, and might also take special note of these features:

1. any differences from Mark's Gospel
2. the frequency of "this was to fulfill" passages
3. what Jesus is doing most of the time
4. the portrayal of the disciples
5. the author's attitude toward Judaism
6. the importance of doing God's will

Rough Outline of the Gospel of Matthew

I. JESUS' BEGINNINGS [1:1-4:16]
   A. Jesus Comes in fulfillment of God's Promises of Old
   1. Jesus, son of David, son of Abraham, comes according to God's plan [1:1-17].
   2. Jesus' coming means that "God is with us" [1:18-25].
   3. At Jesus' coming, foreign magi worship him and a Jewish king seeks to kill him [12:1-23].

46

B. Jesus' Ministry Is Introduced
1. The Baptist preaches the imminence of God's reign [3:1–12].
2. Obedient to God, Jesus is baptized by John [3:13–17].
3. Jesus remains faithful despite satanic temptations [4:1–11].
4. Jesus settles in Capernaum [4:12–16].
II. THE PUBLIC MINISTRY OF JESUS [4:17–16:20]
   * Transitional Verse [4:17]:
   From that time Jesus began to preach, saying "Repent, for the kingdom of heaven is at hand."
   A. Jesus Ministers to "the House of Israel"
   1. Jesus calls disciples [4:17–22].
   2. The Sermon on the Mount [4:23–7:29].
   3. Jesus performs ten mighty deeds [8:1–9:34].
   4. Jesus commissions and instructs the Twelve [9:35–11:1]
   B. Jesus Is Rejected by his Own People
   1. Opposition mounts:
      a. the Baptist questions Jesus' identity [11:2–15].
      b. Jesus upbraids the cities he has visited [11:16–24].
      c. He is criticized for various reasons [11:25–12:37].
      d. A sign is demanded [12:38–45].
      e. Jesus is visited by his family [12:46–50].
   2. Jesus tells parables and instructs his disciples [13:1–52].
   3. Despite his words and deeds, Jesus is not accepted:
      a. the rejection at Nazareth [13:53–58].
      b. the execution of the Baptist [14:1–12].
      c. Jesus heals and feeds, but is repeatedly attacked and demanded for a sign [14:13–16:12].
   4. Peter acknowledges Jesus' divine Sonship [16:13–20].
III. THE DISCIPLES AND THE EVENTS IN JERUSALEM [16:21–28:20]
   *Transitional Verse [16:21]:
   From that time Jesus began to show his disciples that he must go to Jerusalem and suffer many things from the elders and chief priests and scribes, and be killed, and on the third day be raised.

A. The Way to Jerusalem
   1. Jesus discusses his death and his Church with the disciples [16:22–18:35].
   2. After entering Judea, Jesus is tested by Pharisees, and teaches the disciples [19:1–20:34].
   3. In fulfillment of the Scriptures, Jesus enters the city of Jerusalem [21:1–11].
B. In the Temple, the Hostility with the Scribes and the Pharisees Escalates [21:12–23:39]
C. Jesus Discusses the End of This Age and the Arrival of the Age to Come [24:1–25:46]
D. The Passion Narrative [26:1–27:66]
E. Jesus Risen from the Dead [28:1–20]
*Concluding Verse [28:20b]:
   . . .*and lo, I am with you always to the close of the age.*

The Opening of Matthew's Gospel

As mentioned previously, one of the advantages that scholars have in studying Matthew's Gospel is the ability to contrast it against one of its sources, the Gospel of Mark. Even at first glance there are several obvious differences between the two.

Unlike Mark's Gospel which began its presentation of Jesus with the events surrounding his baptism, Matthew's commences with a genealogy of Jesus and the circumstances of his birth. Mark frequently mentioned that Jesus taught, although there was not a great deal of space devoted to recounting that teaching. Matthew, which has the "Q" sayings collection as one of its sources, provides many examples of Jesus' teachings.

While the writer of the Gospel of Matthew would certainly agree with the Marcan stress on the importance of Jesus' suffering, his Gospel has other concerns and insights as well. These unique Matthean contributions naturally result from the evangelist's different background, church community, and situation, and are evident in the very first pages of the Gospel.

One of the writer's favorite themes is introduced right from the start—his interest in identifying Jesus with the expectations of the Jewish people and with the divine plan of God himself:

1:22–23   All this took place to fulfill what the Lord had spoken by the prophet: "Behold a virgin shall conceive and bear a son, and his name shall be called Emmanuel" (which means, God with us).

2:5–6   They told him [where the Christ was to be born], "In Bethlehem of Judea; for so it is written by the prophet: 'And you, O Bethlehem, in the land of Judah, are by no means least among the rulers of Judah; for from you shall come a ruler who will govern my people Israel.' "

2:14–15   And he rose and took the child and his mother by night, and departed to Egypt, and remained there until the death of Herod. This was to fulfill what had been spoken by the prophet, "Out of Egypt have I called my son."

2:17–18   [After Herod orders the slaying of male children:] Then was fulfilled what was spoken by the prophet Jeremiah: "A voice is heard in Ramah, wailing and loud lamentation, Rachel weeping for her children; she refused to be consoled, because they were no more."

2:23   And he went and dwelt in a city called Nazareth, that what was spoken by the prophets might be fulfilled, "He shall be called a Nazarene."

There are two points that should be made concerning these "fulfillment" passages. First, one should not assume that the Old Testament verses to which the evangelist refers were all predictions concerning a future Messiah and his characteristics. For example, in Mt 2:15 the evangelist has cited Hosea 11:1, "When Israel was a child, I loved him, and out of Egypt I called my son," which depicts God reflecting on his past deeds during the exodus events on behalf of his son, Israel. It is not referring to the future at all! The evangelist's use of the Old Testament texts must be understood in the proper direction. From the perspective of their post-resurrectional awareness of Jesus as Lord, the early Christians gazed *backward* to the Hebrew Scriptures searching for incidents and themes which resonated with their current experiences. Here the evangelist sees a parallel between Jesus' and Israel's situations in being guided by God out of Egypt. But no one would have taken Hosea 11:1 in such a manner unless that person already had come to know the Christ. One would not look *forward* from Hosea 11:1 and anticipate that an eventual Messiah would come up out of Egypt.

Second, it is important to recognize the effect that this compilation of fulfillment passages would have upon a contemporary of the writer. It indicates that Jesus' coming is unfolding according to God's designs and in harmony with Jewish expectations. It also indicates that in the person of his Son, God himself is about to dwell with his people. Jesus is conceived "of the Holy Spirit" (1:20), will be called "God with us" (1:23), and is God's Son who is watched over by his Father (2:13–15).

These ideas about fulfillment and divine presence were actually presented even earlier in the Gospel, right in its opening genealogy. As son of David and son of Abraham, Jesus embodies the kingly qualities of his legendary ancestors and their role in the covenant between God and his people (1:1). The genealogy's most notable feature, however, is the unconventional inclusion of five women: "Tamar" (1:3), "Rahab," (1:5), "Ruth" (1:5), "the wife of Uriah" (1:6; in other words, Bathsheba), and "Mary, of whom Jesus was born" (1:16). Since it is unusual in the writer's time for women to be listed in a genealogy, and since only these five were mentioned instead of the female ancestor for each generation, the evangelist must have had some special motive for including them.

The most obvious commonality among the five is that even though they were all involved in some sort of unseemly or out-of-the-ordinary sexual behavior, they were still instruments of God's divine plans:

—TAMAR—

[After the death of her husband, Judah's eldest son] Judah said to Tamar his daughter-in-law, "Remain a widow in your father's house, till Shelah my son grows up.". . . So Tamar went and dwelt in her father's house. In the course of time the wife of Judah died. . . . And when Tamar was told, "Your father-in-law is going up to Timnah to shear his sheep," she put off her widow's garments, and put on a veil, wrapping herself up, and sat at the entrance to Ennaim; for she saw that Shelah was grown up, and she had not been given to him in marriage. When Judah saw her, he thought her to be a harlot, for she had covered her face. He went over to her at the roadside, and said, "Come, let me come in to you," for he did not know that she was his daughter-in-law. . . . And she conceived by him. . . .

About three months later Judah was told, "Tamar your daughter-in-law has played the harlot; and moreover she is with child by harlotry. . . . Then Judah acknowledged [what had happened] and said, "She is more righteous than I, inasmuch as I did not give her to my son Shelah" (Gen 38:11–16,18,24,26).

—Rahab—

And Joshua the son of Nun sent two men secretly from Shittim as spies, saying, "Go, view the land, especially Jericho." And they went, and came into the house of a harlot whose name was Rahab, and lodged there. Then the king of Jericho sent to Rahab, saying, "Bring forth the men that have come to you, who entered your house; for they have come to search out all the land." But the woman had taken the two men and hidden them. . . . She brought them up to the roof, and hid them with stalks of flax which she had laid in order on the roof. She came up on the roof and said to them, "I know that the Lord has given you the land, and that the fear of you has fallen upon us, and that all the inhabitants of the land melt away before you. Now then, swear to me by the Lord your God that as I have dealt kindly with you, you will also deal kindly with my father's house, and give me a sure sign, and save alive my father and mother, my brothers and sisters, and all who belong to them, and deliver our lives from death. And the men said to her, "Our life for yours! If you do not tell this business of ours, then we will deal kindly and faithfully with you when the Lord gives us the land" (Jos 2:1,3,4,6,8–9,12–14).

—Ruth—

Then Naomi her mother-in-law said to her [Ruth, the Moabite], "My daughter, should I not seek a home for you, that it may be well with you? Now is not Boaz our kinsman, with whose maidens you were? See, he is winnowing barley tonight at the threshing floor. Wash therefore and anoint yourself, and put on your best clothes and go down to the threshing floor; but do not make yourself known to the man until he has finished eating and drinking. But when he lies down, observe the place where he lies; then, go uncover his feet and lie down; and he will tell you what to do." And she replied, "All that you say I will do."

So she went down to the threshing floor and did just as her mother-in-law had told her. And when Boaz had eaten and drunk, and his heart was merry, he went to lie down at the end of the heap of grain. Then she came softly, and uncovered his feet, and lay down. At midnight the man was startled, and turned over, and behold, a woman lay at his feet! He said, "Who are you?" And she answered, "I am Ruth, your maidservant; spread your skirt over your maidservant, for you are next of kin." And he said, "May you be blessed by the Lord, my daughter . . . you have not gone after young men whether poor or rich. And now, my daughter, do not fear, I will do for you all that you ask." . . . So Boaz took Ruth and she became his wife; and he went in to her, and the Lord gave her conception, and she bore a son. They named him Obed; he was the father of Jesse, the father of David (Ru 3:1–11; 4:13,17).

—BATHSHEBA—

And it happened, late one afternoon, when David arose from his couch and was walking on the roof of the king's house, that he saw from the roof a woman bathing; and the woman was very beautiful. And David sent and inquired about the woman. And one said, "Is this not Bathsheba, the daughter of Eliam, the wife of Uriah the Hittite?" So David sent messengers, and took her; and she came to him, and he lay with her. . . . Then she returned to her house. And the woman conceived; and she sent and told David, "I am with child" (2 Sm 11:2–5).

—MARY—

Now the birth of Jesus took place in this way. When his mother Mary had been betrothed to Joseph, before they came together she was found to be with child of the Holy Spirit; and her husband Joseph, being a just man and unwilling to put her to shame, resolved to divorce her quietly. But as he considered this, behold, an angel of the Lord appeared to him in a dream, saying, "Joseph, son of David, do not fear to take Mary your wife, for that which is conceived in her is of the Holy Spirit; she will bear a son, and you shall call his name Jesus, for he will save his people from their sins." . . . When Joseph woke from sleep, he did as the angel of the Lord had commanded him; he took his wife, but he knew her not until she had borne a son; and he called his name Jesus (Mt 1:18–22,24–25).

In each of these cases, God's plan is furthered even though there is something distasteful about the circumstances. One woman poses as a prostitute to trick her father-in-law, another actually is a prostitute who cleverly aids enemy spies. A third woman is a pagan who in effect seduces her future husband, while a fourth commits adultery with the king. Lastly, the mother of Jesus is found to be pregnant before her wedding to Joseph has occurred. Yet despite these untoward events, all of the women are not only heroically portrayed, but they are all instruments in the implementation of God's designs.

The "gang of four" women from the Old Testament might also be playing a secondary purpose in the evangelist's mind. It is possible that all of the four are Gentile foreigners. Tamar and Rahab appear to be native Canaanites, Ruth is a Moabite, and Bathsheba, as wife of Uriah the Hittite, may be a Hittite as well. The inclusion of such pagans would certainly add a universal dimension to the divine plans which are coming to fruition in Jesus, and as such would be of great interest to the Matthean church in the 80s in which Gentiles are coming to assume the dominant position.

This concern for Gentile involvement in God's purposes would seem to be underscored by the appearance, in the same sentence as Jesus' birth, of the presumably pagan magi from the east (Mt 2:1). They recognize that the king of the Jews has come, and since when they find him they fall down in worship (2:11), they apparently also perceive that God is present.

Such insight is in marked contrast to the Jewish king Herod and his priestly advisors. Although they have access to the sacred writings which the magi lack, they not only fail to perceive the hand of God in the unfolding events, but they actively seek to thwart his plans (2:3–8,16). This negative portrayal of the Jewish leadership continues in the first scene after the infancy narrative in which the Baptist angrily denounces the Pharisees and Sadducees (3:7–10).

The conclusion of the Gospel's opening episodes incorporates all of the themes which have been noted thus far. As the perfectly obedient Son, Jesus is baptized to "fulfill all righteousness" (3:15), and is thereupon praised by a heavenly voice as "my beloved Son in whom I am well pleased" (3:17).

That Jesus deserves such approval is made clear in the following scene in which he is tempted by the devil. Unlike Mark, Matthew and Luke present three detailed temptations, although they disagree about their sequence. As was noted earlier, Matthew again sees an important connection between Jesus and the experience of Israel in the Old Testament.

And you shall remember all the way which the Lord your God has led you these forty years in the wilderness, that he might humble you, testing you to know what was in your heart, whether you would keep his commandments, or would not (Dt 8:2).

Then Jesus was led up by the Spirit into the wilderness to be tempted by the devil. And he fasted forty days and forty nights, and afterward he was hungry (Mt 4:1–2).

They set out from Elim, and all the congregation of the people of Israel came to the wilderness of Sin, which is between Elim and Sinai, on the fifteenth day of the second month after they had departed from the land of Egypt. And the whole congregation of the people of Israel murmured against Moses and Aaron in the wilderness, and said to them, "Would that we had died by the hand of the Lord in the land of Egypt, when we sat by the fleshpots and ate bread to the full; for you have brought us out into this wilderness to kill this whole assembly with hunger" (Ex 16:1–3).

And the tempter came and said to him, "If you are the Son of God, command these stones to become loaves of bread." But he answered, "It is written, 'Man shall not live by bread alone, but by every word that proceeds from the mouth of God' " (Mt 4:3–4).

All the congregation of the people of Israel moved on from the wilderness of Sin by stages, according to the commandment of the Lord, and camped at Rephidim; but there was no water for the people to drink. Therefore the people found fault with Moses and said, "Give us water to drink." And Moses said to them, "Why do you find fault with me? Why do you put the Lord to the proof?" And he called the name of the place Massah and Meribah, because of the faultfinding of the children of Israel, and because they put the Lord to the proof by saying, "Is the Lord among us or not?" (Ex 17:1–2,7).

Then the devil took him to the holy city, and set him on the pinnacle of the temple, and said to him, "If you are the Son of God, throw yourself down, for it is written, 'He will give his angels charge of you,' and 'On their hands they will bear you up, lest you strike your foot against a stone.' " Jesus said to him, "Again it is written, 'You shall not test the Lord your God' " (Mt 4:5–7).

When the people saw that Moses delayed to come down from the mountain, the people gathered themselves together to Aaron and said to him, "Up, make us gods, who shall go before us; as for this Moses, he who brought us up out of the land of Egypt, we know not what has become of him." And Aaron said to them, "Take off the rings of gold which are in the ears of your wives, your sons, and your daughters, and bring them to me." So all the people took off the rings of gold which were in their ears, and brought them to Aaron. And he received the gold at their hand and fashioned it with a graving tool and made a molten calf; and they said, "These are your gods, O Israel, who brought you up out of the land of Egypt" (Ex 32:1–4).

Again, the devil took him to a very high mountain, and showed him all the kingdoms of the world and the glory of them; and he said to him, "All these I will give you, if you will fall down and worship me." Then Jesus said to him, "Begone, Satan! for it is written, 'You shall worship the Lord your God and him only shall you serve' " (Mt 4:8–10).

When listed in parallel columns like this, the evangelist's ideas about Jesus' experience and the story of the ancient Israelites become obvious. Although God declares that "Israel is my first-born son" (Ex 4:22), the people persist in disregarding God's wishes. However, Jesus, the Son of God, successfully resists all of the temptations to which Israel of old succumbed. Indeed, Jesus' rejects the tempter's overtures by repeatedly quoting the Torah against him, citing Dt 8:3, Dt 6:16, and Dt 6:13, respectively. It could be said, then, that Jesus in this episode shows himself to be the perfect Jew, the ultimate expression of what it means to be God's Son. He completely conforms himself to God's will, using the sacred expression of that will, the Torah, to ward off inducements to faithlessness.

The evangelist notes that after these temptations, Jesus settled in the town of Capernaum, and he sees in this still another "fulfillment." By referring to the region as "Galilee of the Gentiles," and its inhabitants as the "people who sat in darkness have seen a great light," Matthew again weaves the Gentile theme into his tapestry (4:13–15). While in its original setting the Isaiah passage (Is 9:1–2) commented on the then pagan population of that region north of Judah, the Gospel writer perceives another application in his situation. Although Jesus, who is perfectly obedient to God's will, is the fulfillment of all of Israel's hopes and goals, his coming also affects the lives of the pagan Gentiles.

It might be beneficial at this point to summarize the various topics and emphases which are present in these opening chapters of Matthew:

(1) Jesus is the Son of God, and with his coming God is directly revealed to his people. He is virginally conceived of the Holy Spirit, and will be known as "God with us."

(2) Jesus is the culmination of a centuries-old divine plan of salvation. His ancestry, the references to various Old Testament "fulfillment passages," and the providential events surrounding his birth all indicate that God's designs are being carried out.

(3) Jesus embodies all of Israel's previous experience. His birth is portrayed so as to evoke memories of such legendary heroes as Abraham, Joseph, Moses, and David. He is kingly and ever-faithful. Jesus, Son of God, is Torah-obedient and does not yield to the temptations which corrupted the son of God, Israel.

(4) Beginning even in these early portions of the Gospel, the Jewish authorities are depicted unfavorably. Herod, the chief priests, the scribes, the Pharisees, and the Sadducees all appear in negative roles.

(5) Jesus' coming is of great importance for the pagan Gentiles. The Gentile ancestral strain represented by the four unconventional women, the uniquely perceptive pagan magi, and Jesus' ministry in "Galilee of the Gentiles" are manifestations of this concern "for the nations."

As shall be seen below, these Matthean features continue to be developed as the Gospel unfolds. They are all intrinsically related to the evangelist's conception of Jesus.

The Living Torah

Shortly after he has begun his ministry, Jesus goes up on a mountain and teaches his disciples (5:1—7:29). This long discourse has come to be known as the Sermon on the Mount. It is worth noting that the Gospel of Luke's version of this event takes place on a level plain before a vast crowd (Lk 6:17—7:1). Because of the law-oriented sayings which occur in the Matthean discourse, and because of the mountain setting, one is reminded again of a Mosaic pattern, here that of law-giving from a mountain.

Jesus makes a number of interesting remarks about the Mosaic law, or the Torah. The fulfillment motif recurs, as well as more polemic against the Jewish leadership. There is also evidence of a deep concern on the evangelist's part for the keeping of God's law:

> Think not that I have come to abolish the law and the prophets; I have not come to abolish them but to fulfill them. For truly I say to you, till heaven and earth pass away, not an iota, not a dot, will pass from the law until all is accomplished. Whoever then relaxes one of the least of these commandments and teaches others to do so shall be called least in the kingdom of heaven; but he who does them and teaches them shall be called great in the kingdom of heaven. For I tell you, unless your righteousness exceeds that of the scribes and Pharisees, you will never enter the kingdom of heaven (5:17–20).

As will be indicated later in this chapter, these words have particular significance for the situation in the Matthean church community. But it is plain that the Jesus portrayed by Matthew is one who does not seek to overturn Jewish customs, but rather to "fulfill" them. How such fulfillment occurs is apparently shown by the series of six "antitheses" which follows next. Note that each statement contains the formula "You have heard that it was said . . . but I say to you that. . . ."

5:21–22   You have heard that it was said to the men of old, "You shall not kill; and whoever kills is liable to judgment." But I say to you that every one who is angry with his brother shall be liable to judgment; whoever insults his brother shall be liable to the council, and whoever says, "You fool!" shall be liable to the hell of fire.

5:27–28   You have heard that it was said, "You shall not commit adultery." But I say to you that everyone who looks at a woman lustfully has already committed adultery with her in his heart.

5:31–32   It was also said, "Whoever divorces his wife, let him give her a certificate of divorce." But I say to you that everyone who divorces his wife, except on the ground of unchastity, makes her an adulteress; and whoever marries a divorced woman commits adultery.

5:33–37   Again you have heard that it was said to the men of old, "You shall not swear falsely, but shall perform to the Lord what you have sworn." But I say to you, do not swear at all, either by heaven, for it is the throne of God, or by the earth, for it is his footstool, or by Jerusalem, for it is the city of the great King. And do not swear by your head, for you cannot make one hair white or black. Let what you say be simply "Yes" or "No"; anything more than this comes from evil.

5:38–41   You have heard that it was said, "An eye for an eye and a tooth for a tooth." But I say to you, do not resist one who is evil. But if anyone strikes you on the right cheek, turn to him the other also; and if anyone would sue you and take your coat, let him have your

5:43–45   cloak as well; and if anyone forces you to go one mile, go with him two miles.
You have heard that it was said, "You shall love your neighbor and hate your enemy." But I say to you, love your enemies and pray for those who persecute you, so that you may be sons of your Father who is in heaven; for he makes his sun rise on the evil and on the good, and sends rain on the just and on the unjust.

Except for the last antithesis, Jesus has first quoted the Torah, and then expounded upon it (Mt 5:21 = Dt 5:17; Mt 5:27 = Dt 5:18 and Ex 20:14; Mt 5:31 = Dt 24:1–4; Mt 5:33 = Lev 19:12; Mt 5:38 = Dt 19:21, Ex 21:23–25, and Lev 24:19–20). The last saying may refer to Lev 19:17–18 which calls for love of neighbor, but not for the hating of enemies.

In each case Jesus does not contravene the law, but he intensifies its ideas, extending them further in the same direction. Not only is murder evil, but even a purely attitudinal hostility between people is wrong. Lusting after a woman has already reduced her to the status of a thing, whereas promiscuity simply puts that dehumanization into action. The Mosaic restriction that divorces had to be legally authenticated is intensified to the point of virtually outlawing divorce. Swearing is needed only when the possibility of falsehood exists, so the command against swearing falsely was devised in order to promote the truth. Jesus has simply extended that aim by requiring truthfulness constantly, thereby rendering oath-taking unnecessary. The law which sought to limit retribution, Jesus magnifies to the ultimate by prohibiting retribution at all, and even beyond that by mandating generosity to an oppressor. The commandment to love one's neighbor is intensified to loving even enemies. Jesus, then, is not presenting a radically new law; he "fulfills" the law by enhancing its principles to the ultimate.

However, the Matthean Jesus does this by means of the "but I say to you. . ." formula, which denotes an astonishing level of authority—greater than Moses or any contemporary students of the Mosaic law (7:28–29). How does the evangelist understand this supreme authority of Jesus to teach God's will? Certainly it is rooted in Jesus' identity as Son of God, but for Matthew there is still more to it than even that.

After performing ten miracles, which might be reminiscent of the ten mighty deeds that resulted in Israel's release from Egyptian slavery (8:1—9:34), Jesus makes two remarks which bear on his own identity, and, as one might suspect, they must be understood in the light of the Hebrew Scriptures:

> 11:16–19 But to what shall I compare this generation? It is like children sitting in the marketplaces and calling to their playmates, "We piped to you, and you did not dance; we wailed, and you did not mourn." For John came neither eating nor drinking, and they say, "He has a demon"; but the Son of Man came eating and drinking, and they say, "Behold, a glutton and a drunkard, a friend of tax collectors and sinners!" *Yet wisdom is justified by her deeds.*
>
> 11:28–30 *Come to me,* all who labor and are heavy-laden, and I will give you *rest.* Take my *yoke* upon you, and *learn from me;* for I am gentle and lowly in heart, and you will find rest for your souls. For my yoke is easy, and my burden is light.

Both of these passages refer to the Wisdom of God, a feminine manifestation of God's divine order who appears in several books of the Old Testament. Note in particular these references to her:

> My son, from your youth up choose instruction, and until you are old you will keep finding wisdom. *Come* to her like one who plows and sows, and wait for her good harvest. For in her service you will toil a little while, and soon you will eat of her produce. . . . Listen, my son, and accept my judgment; do not reject my counsel. Put your feet into her fetters, and your neck into her collar. Put your shoulder under her and carry her, and do not fret under her bonds. *Come* to her with all your soul, and keep her ways with all your might. Search out and seek, and she will become known to you; and when you get hold of her, do not let her go. For at last you will find the *rest* she gives, and she will be changed to joy for you. Then her fetters will become for you a strong protection, and her collar a glorious robe. Her *yoke* is a golden ornament, and her bonds a cord of blue. You will

wear her like a glorious robe, and put her on like a crown of gladness.... Reflect on the statutes of the Lord and meditate at all times on his commandments. It is he who will give insight to your mind, and your desire for wisdom will be granted (Sirach 6:18-19, 23-31, 37).

[Wisdom says,] "Come to me, you who desire me, and eat your fill of my produce. For the remembrance of me is sweeter than honey, and my inheritance sweeter than the honeycomb. Those who eat me will hunger for more, and those who drink me will thirst for more. Whoever obeys me will not be put to shame, and those who work with my help will not sin." All this is the book of the covenant of the Most High God, the law which Moses commanded us as an inheritance for the congregation of Jacob (Sirach 24:19-24).

Draw near to me, you who are untaught, and lodge in my school. Why do you say you are lacking in these things, and why are your souls very thirsty? I opened my mouth and said, Get these things for yourselves without money. Put your neck under the *yoke*, and let your souls receive instruction; it is to be found close by. See with your eyes that I have labored little and found for myself much *rest* (Sirach 51:23-27).

These passages indicate the primary Matthean understanding of Jesus. He is the Living Wisdom of God. He brings with him the perfected expression of God's will, God's Torah. Those who "come to him" and take "his yoke upon them" will experience the rest and joy that come from living in accord with the designs of God.

Jesus as God's Wisdom has further implications for Matthew. In the Old Testament the Torah was often referred to as the "yoke" to which a member of God's covenant with Abraham joyfully submits. Note how in the second Sirach citation above how the Wisdom of God is identified with "the book of the covenant of the Most High God, the law...." Jesus by referring to his "yoke" and by being presented as God's Wisdom is also being conceived of as God's Torah come to life.

Moreover, Sirach 24:1-12 describes how Wisdom has traversed all of creation searching for a place in which to dwell. Under God's command she "pitches her tent" in Jacob; "in the holy tabernacle I ministered before him, and so I was established in Zion" (Sir 24:10). The Matthean Jesus, then, is also God's temple, the point at which God dwells with his people (recall Mt 1:23: "God with us").

All of these various images interrelate. In the original temple, the ark of the covenant, containing the tablets of the law, was placed in the holy sanctuary. Jesus as the Wisdom of God is the law/ Torah of God and the temple in which God dwells. This is why Matthew so often speaks of Jesus "fulfilling" the law and the prophets—he is the ultimate expression of that law. It is also the reason why Jesus can proclaim, "You have heard that it was said . . . but I say to you that. . . ." Jesus is the living embodiment of the law who intensifies it to perfection.

The evangelist reinforces this perspective with several passages in the very next chapter which use the formula "something greater than . . . is here." In response to opponents who criticize his disciples for plucking grain on the sabbath, Jesus states, "I tell you, something greater than the temple is here" (12:6). The Matthean Jesus is the supreme temple in which God is perfectly revealed. For this reason he is "Lord of the sabbath" (12:8). As the living expression of God's will, Jesus then proceeds to authoritatively teach that "it is lawful to do good on the sabbath" (12:12).

It might be observed that throughout this section of his Gospel the writer constantly shows the Jewish leadership in active opposition to Jesus, taking counsel to destroy him (12:14). Typically, Matthew sees this hostility fulfilling the Scriptures. His related theme of Jesus' importance for the Gentiles appears again in a reference to Isaiah through which Matthew indicates that Jesus "shall proclaim justice to the Gentiles . . . and in his name will the Gentiles hope" (12:18,21). (Once more, it is important to realize that the evangelist has looked *backward* from his experience of Jesus in order to detect compatible ideas in Isaiah. No one looking *forward* from Isaiah's comments about the humanity-saving destiny of God's chosen people would anticipate their connection with a single individual in the future. It is through his post-resurrectional perspective that Matthew has perceived that Isaiah is applicable to Jesus.)

Matthew continues to unfold his understanding of Jesus' nature by recounting an incident in which adversaries demand a sign. Jesus responds:

> An evil and adulterous generation seeks for a sign; but no sign shall be given it except the sign of the prophet Jonah.
>
> For as Jonah was three days and three nights in the belly of the whale, so will the Son of Man be three days and three nights in the heart of the earth.
>
> The men of Nineveh will arise at the judgment with this generation and condemn it; for they repented at the preaching of Jonah, and behold *something greater than Jonah is here.*
>
> The queen of the South will arise at the judgment with this generation and condemn it; for she came from the ends of the earth to hear the wisdom of Solomon, and behold, *something greater than Solomon is here* (Mt 12:39–42).

In effect, Jesus has presented two "signs of Jonah." One of them is clearly rooted in the writer's post-resurrection experience. The other is much more likely to come from the actual ministry of Jesus, especially since it is so similar to the "sign of the queen of the South." Both of these latter remarks demonstrate the Matthean conception of Jesus. As the embodiment of God's law Jesus can speak on behalf of God far more accurately than any prophet. Although the wisdom of Solomon was fabled throughout many lands, it is far exceeded by the Wisdom of God enfleshed.

Such a wisdom-oriented Christology, or approach to Jesus, is a perfectly natural one for this particular evangelist to have developed. He is certainly Jewish as his reluctance to refer to the kingdom of "God" demonstrates. Not caring to repeatedly mention the divine name, he prefers to use the expression kingdom of "heaven." He is obviously very familiar with the Torah and the Hebrew Scriptures, displaying a knowledge which one might expect of a scholar. Indeed, he could well be referring to himself in 13:52 as a "scribe who has been trained for the kingdom of heaven . . . who brings out of his treasure what is new and what is old." It is not surprising that such a person, who reveres and honors the Torah of God, would apply this perspective to his experience of Christ. Jesus is seen as the ultimate expression of the law, whose perfect teachings must be followed.

This viewpoint also colors the author's understanding of the Church and of the Jewish people.

The Church Built Upon Rock

The Gospel of Matthew has always been held in high esteem because of its concern for the community life of the Church. Of all the Gospels, it is only Matthew which employs the Greek term "ekklesia," meaning "assembly" or "Church." Just as the Matthean Christology is formed according to the evangelist's Jewish heritage, so too is his ecclesiology, his view of Church.

Since Jesus has been presented as the Wisdom/Torah of God enfleshed, it is to be expected that the assembly of Jesus must live according to his teachings. The law of Christ must be done. In addition, that law is to be authoritatively interpreted and preached by community leaders according to the norms established by the Matthean Jesus:

> Now when Jesus came to the district of Caesarea Philippi, he asked his disciples, "Who do men say that the Son of Man is?" And they said, "Some say John the Baptist, others says Elijah, and others Jeremiah or one of the prophets." He said to them, "But who do you say that I am?" Simon Peter replied, "You are the Christ, the Son of the living God." And Jesus answered him, "Blessed are you Simon Bar-Jona! For flesh and blood has not revealed this to you, but my Father who is in heaven. And I tell you, you are Peter, and on this rock I will build my church [ekklesia], and the powers of death shall not prevail against it. I will give you the keys of the kingdom of heaven, and whatever you bind on earth shall be bound in heaven, and whatever you loose on earth shall be loosed in heaven." Then he strictly charged the disciples to tell no one that he was the Christ (Mt 16:13–20).

> [Jesus said to the disciples:] "Truly, I say to you, whatever you bind on earth shall be bound in heaven, and whatever you loose on earth shall be loosed in heaven" (Mt 18:18).

The Matthean account of the "confession of Peter" is different from Mark's version in several important ways. Whereas in Mark

Peter simply exclaimed that Jesus was "the Christ" (Mk 8:29), here Jesus is also identified as "the Son of the living God," a far more exalted title. Jesus' subsequent response to Peter is found only in the Gospel of Matthew. In addition to claiming that Peter's knowledge has been a divine gift, Jesus goes on to rename Simon as Peter, "the Rock." Upon whom the Church is to be built. Furthermore, Peter is to receive the "keys of the kingdom," giving him the authority to "bind and loose." Finally, there is no title switching from "Christ" to "Son of Man" as occurred in Mark. Instead the Matthean Jesus is comfortable being called Christ.

The uniqueness of Matthew's presentation, as well as the use of the post-resurrectional term "ekklesia," indicates that this passage has been fashioned to convey the evangelist's beliefs about how the Church should function. It should come as no surprise that the writer's understanding of the Church is rooted in his Jewish heritage and modified by his conception of Christ as the Wisdom/Torah of God come to life.

The authority to "bind and loose" is a rabbinic power which can have two different, though related, applications. First, the rabbi can declare authoritatively those teachings and beliefs to which the people are "bound." He can declare that the community must affirm certain statements or that other ideas are optional. For example, in the time of Jesus all Jews were "bound" to believe that God is One, but they could decide for themselves whether or not to accept the idea of a general resurrection of the dead.

This first meaning of the power to "bind and loose" seems to be operative in Jesus' words to Peter in Mt 16:19. Peter has, in fact, been appointed the chief rabbi in Jesus' ekklesia. He must authoritatively interpret the perfected law proclaimed by the Living Wisdom of God.

The second rabbinic application of "binding and loosing" refers to the ability of rabbis to hold or to release people from membership in the community. Persons who refused to conduct themselves according to the law of God could ultimately be "loosed" or expelled from the assembly. Subsequently, they could be readmitted or "bound" to the community once more. This appears to be the sense of Jesus' statement in 18:18. The disciples as a group have the authority to regulate membership status in the Church. (Notice how much more favorably Matthew depicts the disciples than Mark did. He softens or eliminates the most negative Marcan material. This is because of his different purposes and interests.)

It is important to consider the verses immediately preceding 18:18. In them the evangelist indicates the power to "loose" is only to be used as a last resort:

> If your brother sins against you, go and tell him his fault, be-
> tween you and him alone. If he listens to you, you have gained
> your brother. But if he does not listen, take one or two others
> along with you, that every word may be confirmed by the evi-
> dence of two or three witnesses. If he refuses to listen to them,
> tell it to the "ekklesia"; and if he refuses to listen even to the
> "ekklesia," let him be to you as a Gentile and a tax collector.
> Truly, I say to you, whatever you bind on earth shall be bound
> in heaven, and whatever you loose on earth shall be loosed in
> heaven (Mt 18:15–18).

Once more the use of the Christian terms "ekklesia" and "brother" indicates that the writer is addressing issues in his own community. He is asserting that the leaders of the Matthean church have the ability to speak definitively about membership status in the community. Perhaps there are some who are causing "little ones" in Matthew's church to sin (18:6). They are saying or doing things which the writer perceives as temptations (18:7ff). This may be the same group referred to as "wolves in sheep's clothing" in 7:15–20. He is warning them that their disturbances may eventually have to be corrected by "loosing" them from the community, although only when all else fails.

[This idea is also operating in the Judaism of the 80s. While the Gospel of Matthew is being composed by a Jewish scribal Christian, the Pharisaic leaders of Judaism are simultaneously meeting at a town called Jamnia. They are attempting the monumental task of restructuring their faith now that the temple has been destroyed forever. Among other things, they too are exercising the rabbinic right to "loose" from the Jewish community those who hold ideas deemed incompatible with the Judaic tradition. Matthew is proba-bly aware of this activity as will be seen below. At this point it is interesting to note that both the Jewish scribal evangelist and the

Pharisees at Jamnia make use of the rabbinic practice of binding and loosing" in divergent ways.]

The evangelist's concern for legal propriety might seem to denote an attitude of cold-hearted legalism. But the writer is very careful to stress the absolute priority of forgiveness within the assembly of Christ. He concludes chapter 18, which has been described as an instruction on Christian community life, by emphasizing reconciliation. After Jesus informs his disciples of their responsibility to "bind and loose," Peter asks how often a "brother" must be forgiven (18:21). Jesus replies that a brother must be forgiven, in effect, a limitless number of times. The evangelist then inserts the parable of the unforgiving servant, climaxing with the idea that God will punish everyone who does "not forgive his brother from his heart" (18:35).

The overriding Matthean concern for forgiveness within the Church community can be seen in an earlier passage from chapter 5 in which the Matthean Jesus was intensifying the Jewish tradition by means of the six antitheses. After indicating that mere anger against a brother, not just murder, was condemnable, Jesus declares:

> So if you are offering your gift at the altar, and there remember that your brother has something against you, leave your gift there before the altar and go; first be reconciled to your brother, and then come and offer your gift (5:23-24).

It is difficult not to see in these verses a statement aimed directly at the evangelist's community. The writer seems to feel that worship (and Matthew's worship was, of course, the Eucharist) should not take place if mutual harmony is not present among all community members. The law of Christ is above all else a law of love.

Matthew is aware of the danger of emphasizing "law." It can become an end unto itself. He, therefore, stresses the love and forgiveness which lie at the heart of the perfected law taught by God's Living Wisdom. He also repeats the warning from the Gospel of Mark that those in authority must use their power as a service, not to domineer:

> But Jesus called them to him and said, "You know that the rulers of the Gentiles lord it over them, and their great men

exercise authority over them. It shall not be so among you; but whoever would be first among you must be your slave; even as the Son of Man came not to be served but to serve, and to give his life as a ransom for many" (20:25-28).

And so, we have seen that the evangelist's conception of Church flows from his Jewish-based understanding of Jesus as the Living Wisdom of God. The Church is that community of persons pledged to live the perfected Torah of Christ, a law of love and forgiveness. They are guided by leaders who have the rabbinically-modeled authority to interpret that law. Such leaders exercise their authority as a service, never to dominate, and only "loose" members from the community as a last resort.

It is plausible that the evangelist's church community is being beset by some sort of internal unrest. There are members who might be disturbing the faith of others, and some are apparently refusing to settle differences with members with whom they are quarreling. The writer is thus facing a situation very different from the persecution afflicting the Marcan community at least a decade earlier. He responds by emphasizing the law of forgiveness revealed by the Living Wisdom of God.

The Synagogue and the Church

Although the evangelist is very concerned about reconciliation within the Church assembly, events occurring at the time he is composing his Gospel cause him to have a somewhat different outlook toward certain Jews who are not members of his community.

As mentioned earlier, the leaders of Judaism gathered in Jamnia in the 80s in order to reconstruct the elements of their faith after the disaster of the Jewish-Roman War (66-70). Of all the various groups and parties within the Judaism of Jesus' day, it was mostly Pharisees who survived the war's destruction. The Zealots, Herodians, Sadducees, and Essenes were all involved in the fighting in one way or another, and declined. The Pharisees then faced the enormous responsibility of preserving and adapting their traditions now that the temple, the focus of their worship, was gone forever.

As they interpreted the law to meet this new situation, the Pharisees at Jamnia felt that they had to clearly delineate what constituted authentic Jewish teaching. They thus came into conflict with certain Jews who had become part of various movements and sects. One such group with whom they had to contend were Christians of Jewish heritage. The writer of Matthew's Gospel is clearly engaged in a dispute with the local synagogue over the correct interpretation of Jewish traditions. He insists that the law has been authoritatively reinterpreted and perfected by the Wisdom of God, and that genuine Jewish leaders should acknowledge that fact. Vying for leadership of the Jewish community in the power-vacuum caused by the destruction of the Temple, Matthew considers his Pharisaic rivals to be hypocritical and illegitimate.

This ongoing debate with his synagogue contemporaries completely colors Matthew's Gospel. Consider these passages from the Sermon the Mount:

5:20   For I tell you, unless your righteousness exceeds that of the scribes and Pharisees, you will never enter the kingdom of heaven.

6:1-6   Beware of practicing your piety before men in order to be seen by them; for then you will have no reward from your Father who is in heaven. Thus, when you give alms, sound no trumpet before you, as the hypocrites do in the synagogues and in the streets, that they may be praised by men. Truly, I say to you, they have received their reward. But when you give alms, do not let your left hand know what your right hand is doing, so that your alms may be in secret; and your Father who sees in secret will reward you. And when you pray, you must not be like the hypocrites; for they love to stand and pray in the synagogues and at the street corners, that they may be seen by men. Truly, I say to you, they have received their reward. But when you pray, go into your room and shut the door and pray to your Father who is in secret; and your Father who sees in secret will reward you.

6:16-18   And when you fast, do not look dismal like the hypo-

> crites, for they disfigure their faces that their fasting
> may be seen by men. Truly, I say to you, they have
> received their reward. But when you fast, anoint your
> head and wash your face, that your fasting may not
> be seen by men but by your Father who is in secret;
> and your Father who sees in secret will reward you.

The references to synagogues sound as if Jesus is speaking to people who do not frequent those Jewish houses of prayer. That is indeed the situation in the Matthean community, but makes little sense in the ministry of Jesus who was clearly a pious and Torah-observant Jew. Plainly, these statements are borne out of controversy. If taken literally, the injunction about praying only in secret would virtually eliminate any community worship! Although Jesus was in conflict with different groups during his ministry, as will be explored later, Matthew's depiction of these conflicts is framed according to his disputes with the synagogue of the 80s.

This principle is also apparent in these passages:

12:30–32   [To Pharisees who accuse him of being in league
           with Satan Jesus replies:] He who is not with me is
           against me, and he who does not gather with me
           scatters. Therefore I tell you, every sin and blas-
           phemy will be forgiven men, but the blasphemy
           against the Holy Spirit will not be forgiven. And
           whoever says a word against the Son of Man will be
           forgiven; but whoever speaks against the Holy Spirit
           will not be forgiven, either in this age or in the age
           to come.

15:6–9   So, for the sake of your tradition, you have made
           void the word of God. You hypocrites! Well did
           Isaiah prophesy of you, when he said, "This people
           honors me with their lips, but their heart is far from
           me; in vain do they worship me, teaching as doc-
           trines the precepts of men."

Despite his emphasis on reconciliation and mercy, the evangelist writes that speaking against the Holy Spirit is forever unforgivable. The use of the term "Holy Spirit" in this way is a sign of the passage's post-resurrectional Church context. Those who are blaspheming against the Holy Spirit are Matthew's Pharisaic contemporaries, who, the evangelist asserts, are substituting their own traditions for God's will. Again, this is not to say that Jesus did not dispute with Jewish leaders during his ministry, but only that the writer's presentation is influenced by his own, later conflicts.

The level of the debate increases dramatically upon Jesus' arrival in Jerusalem. One Matthean peculiarity is evident in his presentation of the entry of Jesus into the city. Characteristically, the writer notes that Jesus' coming fulfills an Old Testament Scripture: "Tell the daughter of Zion, Behold your king is coming to you, humble, and mounted on an ass, *and* on a colt, the foal of an ass" (Mt 21:5, citing Zech 9:9). The evangelist apparently was using a Greek translation of the Old Testament because the original Hebrew does not include the word "and." Rather, the sentence is a typical example of Hebrew parallelism ". . . mounted on an ass, on a colt the foal of an ass." The evangelist, however, always has Jesus "fulfill" the Old Testament in a literal manner, and so he goes on to describe that "the disciples . . . brought the ass *and* the colt, and put their garments on *them*, and he sat thereon" (21:6–7). This somewhat humorous scene of Jesus somehow sitting astride two animals of different sizes is unique to Matthew. It illustrates how the evangelist's mind works, as well as being yet another indication of his scribal background.

More important, though, are the scenes which follow. In the temple, Jesus is accosted by the chief priests and elders who demand to know by what authority he is acting. After confounding them with a riddle, Jesus presents two devastating parables:

> "What do you think? A man had two sons; and he went to the first and said, 'Son, go and work in the vineyard today.' And he answered, 'I will not'; but afterward he repented and went. And he went to the second and said the same; and he answered, 'I will go, sir,' but did not go. Which of the two did the will of his Father?" They said, "The first." Jesus said to them, "Truly, I say to you, the tax collectors and the harlots go into the kingdom of God before you.
>
> "Hear another parable. There was a householder who planted a vineyard, and set a hedge around it, and dug a wine press in it, and built a tower, and let it out to tenants, and went

into another country. When the season of fruit drew near, he sent
his servants to the tenants to get his fruit; and the tenants took
his servants and beat one, killed another, and stoned another.
Again he sent other servants, more than the first; and they did the
same to them. Afterward he sent his son to them, saying, 'They
will respect my son.' But when the tenants saw the son they said
to themselves, 'This is the heir; come, let us kill him and have his
inheritance.' And they took him and cast him out of the vineyard, and killed him. When therefore the owner of the vineyard
comes, what will he do to those tenants?" They said to them, "He
will put those wretches to a miserable death, and let out the
vineyard to other tenants who will give him fruits in their
seasons." Jesus said to them…"Therefore, I tell you, the kingdom
of God will be taken away from you and given to a people
producing the fruits of it" (21:28-31, 33-41, 43).

In line with his earlier remark about the Pharisees substituting
their own traditions for God's will, Jesus informs the chief priests
and scribes that they are like a son who pays lip service to his father
but ignores his wishes. Even more pointed is the parable about the
wicked tenants. The Matthean belief that corrupt Jewish leadership
has been replaced is explicitly stated. The post-resurrectional perspective of the evangelist is clear. The son of the householder (Jesus,
Son of God) is killed by the wicked tenants (the Jewish leaders)
beyond the walls of the vineyard (outside Jerusalem). Consequently,
the evil tenants are put to death (the destruction of Jerusalem in
70?) and other tenants (Jewish believers in Jesus) are brought in.
Matthew's anger toward his fellow Jews who do not acknowledge
the Lordship of Jesus is apparent. In his eyes, the Pharisees at Jamnia
are no longer authentic Jews because they have refused to heed the
teaching of Jesus.

The evangelist's conviction that previous Jewish leaders have
been supplanted by believers in Christ is reiterated by the parable
which immediately follows:

And again Jesus spoke to them in parables, saying, "The kingdom of heaven may be compared to a king who gave a marriage
feast for his son, and sent his servants to call those who were
invited to the marriage feast; but they would not come. Again,
he sent other servants, saying, 'Tell those who are invited,
Behold, I have made ready my dinner, my oxen and my fat

calves are killed, and everything is ready; come to the marriage feast.' But they made light of it and went off, one to his farm, another to his business, while the rest seized his servants, treated them shamefully, and killed them. *The king was angry, and he sent his troops and destroyed those murderers and burned their city.* Then he said to his servants, 'The wedding is ready, but those invited were not worthy. Go therefore to the thoroughfares, and invite to the marriage feast as many as you can find.' And those servants went out into the streets and gathered all whom they found, both bad and good; so the wedding hall was filled with guests" (22:1-10).

Once more, the evangelist's outlook from the 80s is apparent. The italicized verse is clearly a reference to the destruction of Jerusalem in 70 by the Romans. The writer believes that the city's fall is a sign of God's wrath against those leaders who did not believe the words of his Son. The "unworthy" Jewish leaders therefore, lose their places at the banquet table to Jews and Gentiles from the streets and thoroughfares.

In the chapters which follow, the animosity between the Jewish leaders and Jesus intensifies. More will be said about these passages, especially chapter 23, when the historical ministry of Jesus is considered.

However, one important section in the Matthean trial of Jesus should be mentioned at this point. These verses occur only in the Gospel of Matthew, and again demonstrate the writer's feelings toward unbelieving Jews.

So when Pilate saw that he was gaining nothing, but rather that a riot was beginning, he took water and washed his hands before the crowd, saying, "I am innocent of this man's blood; see to it yourselves." And all the people answered, "His blood be on us and on our children!" Then he released for them Barabbas, and having scourged Jesus, delivered him to be crucified (27:24-26).

This passage again expresses the author's attitude toward the leaders of Judaism in the 80s. By having Pilate wash his hands of the affair, the evangelist removes any guilt for the death of Jesus from him and places it squarely on the shoulders of "all the [Jewish] people" who have been led astray by their corrupt leaders.

There are many serious reasons to doubt the historicity of this scene including its uniqueness to Matthew, the unlikelihood of that many people being on hand to make such statements, and known historical information about the character of Pilate. Such historical matters will be discussed in later chapters.

But it must be emphatically stated that Matthew does not intend to hold all the Jewish people guilty of the death of Jesus. Likening his contemporary Pharisaic rivals with the priestly leadership of Jesus' time, Matthew is depicting what happens when the people follow illegitimate leaders. He is arguing that Christian Jews, because of their Jesus-based interpretation of the Torah, are the only valid Jewish leaders in the post-Temple period. Matthew's language must be understood as emerging from this polemical context.

Gentiles in the Matthean Church

There is one other feature of Matthew's community which should be noted. Even though he feels that Pharisees are not legitimate leaders in Judaism, the evangelist still reveres the Torah, especially the perfected Torah of Christ. Consequently, it is likely he believes that Gentile Christians need to observe the Torah in some limited fashion. He seems to disagree with those who hold that the law of Moses is dead, and that Gentiles should ignore it. Consider these passages:

5:17-19   Think not that I have come to abolish the law and the prophets. I have come not to abolish them but to fulfill them. For truly, I say to you, till heaven and earth pass away, not an iota, not a dot, will pass from the law until all is accomplished. Whoever then relaxes one of the least of these commandments and teaches men so shall be called least in the kingdom of heaven, but he who does them and teaches them shall be called great in the kingdom of heaven.

5:46-47   For if you love those who love you, what reward

	have you? Do not even the tax collectors do the same? And if you salute only your brethren, what more are you doing than others? Do not even the Gentiles do the same?
6:7	And in praying do not heap up empty phrases as the Gentiles do; for they think that they will be heard for their many words.
7:6	Do not give dogs what is holy; and do not throw your pearls before swine, lest they trample them under foot and turn to attack you.
10:5–6	These twelve Jesus sent out, charging them, "Go nowhere among the Gentiles, and enter no town of the Samaritans, but go rather to the lost sheep of the house of Israel."
15:24–27	He answered, "I was sent only to the lost sheep of the house of Israel." But she [a Canaanite woman] came and knelt before him, saying, "Lord, help me." And he answered, "It is not fair to take the children's bread and throw it to the dogs." She said, "Yes, Lord, yet even the dogs eat the crumbs that fall from their masters' table."

These references indicate several things. First, the Matthean Jesus upholds the Torah even as he fulfills it. His ministry, and that of his disciples, was confined to Israel. Gentiles are generally regarded as dogs and swine whom Jews should never imitate. They do not deserve to receive holy teachings and sacred beliefs.

The evangelist believes that Gentiles have benefited from Jesus' coming because of the refusal of Jews to heed him. Throughout his Gospel, he has indicated that Jesus' coming was of universal significance. But that does not mean that Gentiles should ignore the holy law or trample it underfoot. Notice the ending Matthew has added to the parable of the guests invited to the wedding feast:

| 22:11–14 | "But when the king came in to look at the guests, he saw there a man who had no wedding garment; and he said to him, 'Friend, how did you get in here without a wedding garment?' And he was speechless. Then the king said to the attendants, 'Bind him hand and foot and cast him into the outer darkness; there men will weep and gnash their teeth.' " |

Even though Matthew holds that Gentiles should be admitted into the Church, they must come properly attired. They must observe the Torah in some fashion.

This idea makes great sense if the Gospel was indeed written in Antioch as many scholars suspect. We know from Gal 2:11-14 that Peter and Paul publicly argued in Antioch around the year 50 about whether Gentiles needed to observe dietary restrictions in order to share the Lord's Supper with believing Gentiles. It seems that Paul lost the argument because he quickly departed on a missionary journey. If the church in Antioch, then, has a practice of expecting Gentiles to follow minimal dietary standards, Matthew's Gospel continues that tradition. Although for Matthew former Jewish leaders have been supplanted, the law of God endures and it is not to be treated lightly by incoming pagans.

The Abiding Presence of Jesus

The writer concludes his Gospel by fulfilling one of his own opening passages. In 1:23 the writer declared that Jesus would be known as "God with us."

> Now the eleven disciples went to Galilee, to the mountain to which Jesus had directed them. And when they saw him they worshiped him; but some doubted. And Jesus came and said to them, "All authority in heaven and on earth has been given to me. Go therefore and make disciples of all nations, baptizing them in the name of the Father and of the Son and of the Holy Spirit, teaching them to observe all that I have commanded you; and lo, I am with you always, to the close of the age" (28:16-20).

The glorified Wisdom of God again speaks to his disciples on a mountain, instructing them that they must now teach to all the world the perfected law which he has given them. The Gentiles are to be included in salvation, and the Matthean community's baptismal formula is codified. The believers worship their Lord as divine, although there is doubt on the part of some. It is unclear to what this doubt refers: Do some doubt Jesus' divinity? That he has been raised? That Gentiles should be admitted? There is no agreement on this question.

Most significantly, the Matthean church is assured that Jesus abides with them, even though he has not yet returned in glory. This is in great contrast to the Marcan community which felt abandoned and eagerly awaited the Lord's imminent return. Matthew does not expect that Jesus will return shortly. There is work to be done. His law must be preached throughout the world. Jesus is with his followers as they undertake this task.

As a knowledgeable Jew, possibly a scribe, the writer of the Gospel of Matthew has produced a powerful image of Christ. Unlike Mark, who stressed that Jesus can only be understood by witnessing his suffering and death, Matthew emphasizes Jesus as the Wisdom/ Torah of God come to life. Those who carry out his teachings of forgiveness and mercy are truly children of God. They will spread the good news everywhere, confident that Jesus is with them as they observe his commandments.

QUESTIONS FOR REFLECTION AND DISCUSSION

1. What are some indications that the author of Matthew's Gospel was Jewish?

2. What would this evangelist have to say to people who mercilessly enforce the requirements of any system of laws, even the laws of Christ?

3. Is it better for modern readers to understand Matthew's notion of "fulfillment" as:
    (a) predictions which have come to pass; or
    (b) ancient themes embodied in the life of Jesus?
   What effect does your answer have on one's appreciation of the Old Testament Scriptures? Of Jesus' Jewish contemporaries?

4. Matthew's argument with Jewish contemporaries over correct interpretation of the Torah permeates his Gospel. Point to specific passages where this is evident. Why should modern Christians be able to distinguish polemical assertions from revealed religious truths?

5. The Gospel of Matthew contains several passages which relate to the writer's understanding of how the Church should be organized and how it should operate. Where do Matthew's ideas about the Christian community come from? How does he describe the role of leaders in the Church and the settling of disputes among Church members?

6. Matthew wanted his readers to believe that the Lord Jesus was present in their very midst. Why is this insight valuable for modern believers?

7. How does the Matthean Jesus show himself to be the perfect Jew, the fullest expression of what it means to be faithful son of God?

THE LUCAN JESUS:
HEALING SAVIOR

Preliminary Reading of the Gospel

As with the other two Gospels, it is advisable to begin our consideration of this evangelist by reading through his Gospel in its entirety. Using the outline which follows will assist in noting the various contrasts between this Gospel and those of Mark and Matthew. Also, it is worth noting that the Gospel of Luke is the first part of a two-volume work composed by the same author. Therefore, the reader may want to peruse Acts of Apostles, to which this chapter will also refer. Be alert to these characteristics of this writer:

1. differences with the Gospels of Mark and Matthew
2. usage of the words "Savior," "salvation," "saves," etc.
3. the role of the Holy Spirit
4. the author's attitude toward Judaism
5. the role of Mary in the Gospel
6. the "historical" quality of the writer
7. the role of the disciples in the Gospel

Rough Outline of the Gospel of Luke

I. PROLOGUE [1:1–4]

The evangelist declares his intention to compose an "historical narrative" about the events which have taken place.

II. BEGINNINGS IN JERUSALEM AND GALILEE [1:5—
    9:50]
    A. The Infancy Narrative [1:5—2:52]
       1. Annunciation of the birth of the Baptist.
       2. Annunciation of the birth of Jesus.
       3. Birth, circumcision, and naming of the Baptist.
       4. Birth, circumcision, naming, and presentation of Jesus.
       5. Jesus at twelve in the temple.
    B. Prelude to Jesus' Public Ministry [3:1—4:13]
       1. The message, ministry, and arrest of the Baptist.
       2. Baptism of Jesus.
       3. A genealogy of Jesus.
       4. The temptation of Jesus.
    C. Jesus' Activities in Galilee [4:14—9:50]
       Including Jesus' preaching, calling of disciples, miracles,
       and his acceptance by the people and rejection by the
       leaders.
III. THE JOURNEY TO JERUSALEM [9:51—19:27]
     Containing three references to Jesus' destination: 9:51–52;
     13:22; 17:11.
IV. JERUSALEM [19:28—24:53]
    A. Entry into Jerusalem, Temple-Cleansing, Preaching and
       Warnings [19:28—21:38].
    B. The Passion Narrative [22:1—23:56a]
       Conspiracy against Jesus, betrayal, Last Supper, arrest,
       trials, Jesus' crucifixion, death, and burial.
    C. The Resurrection Narrative [23:56b—24:53]
       1. The empty tomb.
       2. The disciples en route to Emmaus.
       3. Jesus instructs the Eleven and the disciples in Jerusa-
          lem.
       4. The ascension.

The "Historical Narrative" of Luke

The opening prologue of this Gospel reveals several interesting facts about the identity and the purposes of this evangelist:

> Inasmuch as many have undertaken to compile a "diegesis" ["narrative"] of the things which have been accomplished among us, just as they were delivered to us by those who from the beginning were eyewitnesses and ministers of the word, it seemed good to me also, having followed all things closely for some time past, to write an orderly account for you, most excellent Theophilus, that you may know the truth concerning the things of which you have been informed (1:1–4).

First, this Gospel is the only one addressed to a particular person. "Theophilus" is a Greek name which means "loved by God." Does this mean that the writer has composed his work for a person with that name, for someone bearing "Theophilus" as a nickname because of his curiosity to know more about Christianity, or for anyone who wants to learn about the saving actions of God and is therefore worthy to be called a friend of God? It is impossible to answer these possibilities.

More importantly, notice how the evangelist clearly distinguishes himself from those who "were eyewitness and ministers of the word." This passage confirms the main principles of the *Instruction Concerning the Historical Truth of the Gospels* discussed in chapter 1. Clearly the writer of the Gospel of Luke is not an eyewitness who was present during the ministry of Jesus himself, Stage One of the developing Gospel tradition. Nor was he a "minister of the word" who preached during Stage Two, the time of the apostles. Rather, he is a representative of Stage Three, the time of the evangelists.

Finally, the author uses an interesting term when he describes his work. Unlike the writer of Mark's Gospel, this evangelist does not refer to his composition as an "evangelion," as a "Gospel." Instead he says that he is seeking to compile a "diegesis" about Jesus. This Greek term is frequently used among Greek historians to describe a "narrative history" which they have written. Since Luke is in all likelihood a Gentile who is familiar with Hellenistic (Greek) literature, his choice of words indicates that he sees his work as comparable to the various Greek "histories" of the period. He is out to produce the definitive narrative recounting the meaning and significance of the life and ministry of Jesus.

This "historical" quality is apparent in several passages which are unique to the Gospel of Luke:

> In the days of Herod, king of Judea, there was a priest named Zechariah of the division of Abijah; and he had a wife of the daughters of Aaron, and her name was Elizabeth (1:5).

> In those days a decree went out from Caesar Augustus that all the world should be enrolled. This was the first enrollment when Quirinius was governor of Syria (2:1–2).

> In the fifteenth year of the reign of Tiberius Caesar, Pontius Pilate being governor of Judea, and Herod being tetrarch of Galilee, and his brother Philip tetrarch of the region of Ituraea and Trachonitis, and Lysanius tetrarch of Abilene, in the high priesthood of Annas and Caiaphas, the word of God came to John the son of Zechariah in the wilderness (3:1–2).

The same procedure can also be seen in Acts of Apostles:

> And one of them named Agabus stood up and foretold by the Spirit that there would be great famine over all the world; and this took place in the days of Claudius (Acts 11:28).

These sorts of passages give Luke's Gospel an historical veneer which is not as noticeable in any of the other Gospels. However, modern readers should not assume that this evangelist has been motivated by a twentieth-century definition of "history." His Gospel is as much the product of a post-resurrectional faith perspective as are the Gospels of Mark, Matthew, or John. The insertion of clauses which relate his narrative to the history of the Graeco-Roman world does not make his Gospel a modern historical study.

For example, in 1:5 and 2:2 the evangelist notes that Jesus was born during an imperial census, while Herod was king of Judea and Quirinius was governor of Syria. From many other sources it is known that Herod died in 4 B.C.E., whereas Quirinius did not become governor of Syria until 6 C.E.* Thus, there is a ten year gap between the reigns of these two officials, which Luke describes

---

*The terms B.C.E. and C.E., respectively meaning Before the Common Era and the Common Era, are an alternative way of denoting the time before Christ and after Christ which is inoffensive to non-Christians. In the spirit of ecumenical respect, this terminology will be used throughout this book.

as overlapping. In addition, there is no evidence that an empire-wide enrollment or census ever occurred. While Quirinius sponsored a census of Judea in 6–7 C.E., that enrollment would not have affected Galileans like Joseph and Mary, nor did it require people to migrate to their tribal homeland. It seems that the evangelist, writing eight decades after these events, has some vague and general information that Jesus' birth occurred near the end of Herod's rule. This same tradition is attested to independently in Matthew's birth account. Luke also has some knowledge about a census which had been taken, but he is unaware of either its geographical extent, the way in which it was conducted, or its exact date. For theological and literary reasons which will be discussed below, the writer has combined these two separate items in his infancy narrative.

Therefore, while Luke claims to be writing a "diegesis," his historical narrative should not be thought of as modern historical research. He believes that he is writing the latest chapters in the long history of God's dealings with humanity. He sees himself, as it were, composing the climactic segments of "biblical history." He is convinced that "the things which have happened among us" (1:1) have occurred in accordance with God's ancient plan to save all humanity. This overarching salvation-history perspective dominates both books of his two-volume work.

The Salvation of Israel

Volume One, the Gospel, stresses that God's salvation in Christ originates in the Jewish people. Jesus is the fulfillment of Israel's hopes and dreams, bringing forgiveness, reconciliation, and healing to a broken people. Luke's emphasis on the Jewish and Old Testament roots of Jesus manifests itself in several ways.

The first method used to situate Jesus in Judaism is the characterization of Jesus and his associates and listeners. Throughout the Gospel, Luke will describe those close to Jesus as pious, law-observant Jews. Note for instance these depictions of all of the major characters in the infancy narrative:

And they [Zechariah and Elizabeth] were both righteous before God, walking in all the ordinances of the Lord blameless (1:6).

And on the eighth day they came to circumcise the child [John] (1:59).

And at the end of eight days, when he was circumcised, he was called Jesus, the name given by the angel before he was conceived in the womb (2:21).

And when the time came for their purification according to the law of Moses, they brought him up to the temple to present him to the Lord (2:22).

Now there was a man in Jerusalem, whose name was Simeon, and this man was righteous and devout, looking for the consolation of Israel, and the Holy Spirit was upon him (2:25).

. . . when the parents brought in the child Jesus, to do for him according to the custom of the law . . . (2:27).

And there was a prophetess, Anna, the daughter of Phanuel, of the tribe of Asher. . . . She did not depart from the temple, worshiping with fasting and prayer night and day (2:36–37).

And when they had performed everything according to the law of the Lord, they returned into Galilee, to their own city, Nazareth (2:39).

Now his parents went into Jerusalem every year at the feast of the Passover (2:41).

These portrayals convey the essential righteousness of those Jews who figure in Jesus' infancy and childhood. "Blessed is she who believed that there would be a fulfillment of what was spoken to her from the Lord" (1:45) is a fitting description of each of these people. Despite his initial doubts, Zechariah eventually trusts the Lord's will (1:63); Elizabeth, filled with the Spirit, exclaims her joy at the realization of God's plans (1:41–44); Mary is the Lord's handmaiden who follows his word (1:38); Simeon recognizes that God has kept his promise to him (2:26,29–30); Anna speaks of the arrival of God's redemption of Israel (2:38). In one way or another they all "hear the word of God and keep it," an important Lucan concept from later in the Gospel (11:28).

A parenthetical comment might be added concerning the evangelist's ideas about Torah-observant Jews. In 2:22 he refers to Joseph and Mary going to the temple in Jerusalem for their purification in order to present their firstborn son to the Lord. Here the writer has made a few mistakes regarding Jewish practice. Two separate rituals have been combined into one; the purification of the mother who has been rendered unclean by the flow of blood accompanying birth is not the same as the offering of one's firstborn to the Lord. Furthermore, it was only the recently-delivered mother who required purification before temple worship. The father was not considered unclean and did not need to be purified. Luke's reference to *their* purification shows that his knowledge of Jewish observances is somewhat superficial. His lack of awareness of the particulars of these rituals is evidence of his own Gentile heritage. A Jewish writer would not commit such oversights.

The Lucan practice of depicting God's salvation commencing through devout Jews persists throughout the Gospel. In the Gospel of Luke the crowds at large are more positively portrayed than in the others. For example, in the scene which has come to be called "the rejection at Nazareth," Jesus' neighbors are at first pleased with what Jesus says in their synagogue, "and all spoke well of him and wondered at the gracious words which proceeded out of his mouth; and they said 'Is not this Joseph's son?' " (Lk 4:22). This is quite different from the parallel event in Mark and Matthew in which all the listeners immediately "take offense at him" (Mk 6:3; Mt 13:57).

[Even the Pharisees receive somewhat better treatment at Luke's hands than from the other evangelists. Jesus dines with Pharisees on three occasions (Lk 7:36; 11:37; 14:1), although the ensuing conversations are not very pleasant. Some Pharisees warn Jesus that Herod Antipas is seeking his life (13:31). Also, Luke preserves Mark's description of Jairus as a "ruler of the synagogue" (8:41—is he then a Pharisee?) which Matthew had edited to simply "a ruler" (Mt 9:18).]

The favorable portrayal of the people in general also manifests itself in the sheer numbers of people who follow Jesus. As the Gospel progresses Luke almost runs out of superlatives to describe their swelling ranks. He is the Cecil B. DeMille of the evangelists. These are only a few examples:

While the people pressed upon him to hear the word of God, he was standing by the lake of Gennesaret (5:1).

And he came down with them and stood on a level place, with a great crowd of his disciples and a great multitude of people from all Judea and Jerusalem and the seacoast of Tyre and Sidon, who came to hear him and to be healed of their diseases (6:17).

Now when Jesus returned, the crowd welcomed him, for they were all waiting for him (8:40).

When the crowds were increasing, he began to say, "This generation is an evil generation; it seeks a sign, but no sign shall be given to it except the sign of Jonah" (11:29).

In the meantime, when so many thousands of the multitude had gathered together that they trod upon one another (12:1).

Now great multitudes accompanied him (14:25).

It is noteworthy that in Luke the people are occasionally described as seeking Jesus to *hear* him. In Mark, the crowds simply sought Jesus to be healed. As will be discussed below, not all who hear Jesus respond appropriately by Lucan standards, but the overall impression one gets of the people at large is quite favorable. This is especially true during the passion narrative:

And there followed [Jesus being led to crucifixion] a great multitude of the people, and of women who bewailed and lamented him (23:27).

[After Jesus dies:] And all the multitudes who assembled to see the sight, when they saw what had taken place, returned home beating their breasts (23:48).

This is in marked contrast to Matthew, who, it will be recalled, laid the blood-guilt of Jesus' death on "all the people" who had exclaimed "his blood be on us and on our children" (Mt 27:25). Luke's theological approach is different from Matthew. He does not share Matthew's view that Christianity has replaced Judaism. Instead, Luke believes that Christianity is the divinely-ordained and intended offshoot of Judaism.

Luke's fondness for Jewish piety extends to his portrayal of Jesus. Luke pictures Jesus himself as a pious, observant Jew. Furthermore, Jesus is shown praying more often in this Gospel than in any of the others:

> Now when all the people were baptized, and when Jesus had also been baptized and was praying . . . (3:21).

> And he came to Nazareth, where he had been brought up; and he went to the synagogue, as his custom was, on the sabbath day (4:16).

> But he withdrew to the wilderness and prayed (5:16).

> In these days he went out to the mountain to pray; and all night he continued in prayer to God. And when it was day, he called his disciples, and chose from them twelve (6:12–13).

> Now it happened that as he was praying alone the disciples were with him; and he asked them, "Who do the people say I am?" (9:18).

> Now about eight days after these sayings he took with him Peter and John and James, and went up on the mountain to pray (9:28).

> He was praying in a certain place, and when he ceased, one of the disciples said to him, "Lord, teach us to pray, as John taught his disciples" (11:1).

> And he was teaching daily in the temple (19:47).

> [To Peter at the Last Supper:] ". . . but I have prayed for you that your faith may not fail; and when you have turned again, strengthen your brethren" (22:32).

> And he withdrew from them about a stone's throw, and knelt down and prayed, "Father, if thou art willing remove this cup from me" (22:41–42).

> And Jesus said, "Father, forgive them; for they know not what they do" (23:34).

> Then Jesus, crying with a loud voice, said, "Father, into thy hands I commit my spirit!" And having said this he breathed his last. Now when the centurion saw what had taken place, he

praised God and said, "Certainly, this man was righteous!"
(23:46–47).

By depicting Jesus in this way, as a sort of ideal Jew, Luke is clearly
presenting an example to be followed by his Christian community.
Just as Jesus prayed often, so, too, should his followers be in frequent communion with God. However, this characteristic portrayal
of Jesus also contributes to Luke's image of the rootedness of Christianity in pious Judaism. Like other holy people, Zechariah, Elizabeth, John the Baptist, Mary, Simeon, and Anna, Jesus, too, prays
often and observes Jewish customs.

This trait is also present in the Lucan early church, as these
few examples demonstrate:

[After Jesus ascended, the disciples] returned to Jerusalem with
great joy, and they were continually in the temple blessing God
(Lk 24:53).

All these with accord devoted themselves to prayer (Acts 1:14).

Now there were dwelling in Jerusalem Jews, devout men from
every nation under heaven (Acts 2:5).

And day by day, attending the temple together and breaking
bread in their homes, they partook of food with glad and generous hearts, praising God and having favor with all the people
(Acts 2:46). [Note the continuation of the favorable Jewish-
crowd theme as well.]

And as they were stoning Stephen, he prayed, "Lord Jesus,
receive my spirit." And he knelt down and cried with a loud
voice, "Lord, do not hold this sin against them" (Acts 7:59–60).

A *second technique* the evangelist uses to illustrate his belief that
salvation comes first to the Jews is his frequent invocation of Old
Testament themes and images. Whereas Matthew drew obvious
attention to the Hebrew Scriptures by means of his "this was to
fulfill . . ." passages, Luke does something similar in a more subtle
fashion. Compare these verses:

But [Zechariah and Elizabeth] had no child, because Elizabeth was barren, and both were advanced in years. But the angel said to him, "Do not be afraid, Zechariah, for your prayer is heard, and your wife Elizabeth will bear you a son, and you shall call his name John."
(Luke 1:7,13)
[The angel said to Mary,] "Behold your kinswoman Elizabeth in her old age has also conceived a son; this is the sixth month with her who was called barren. For with God nothing will be impossible."
(Luke 1:36–37)

The Lord said, "I will surely return to you in the spring, and Sarah your wife shall have a son." And Sarah was listening at the tent door behind him. Now Abraham and Sarah were old, advanced in age. . . . So Sarah laughed to herself, saying, "After I have grown old, and my husband is old, shall I have pleasure?" The Lord said to Abraham, "Why did Sarah laugh and say, 'Shall I indeed bear a child, now that I am old?' Is anything too hard for the Lord?"
(Genesis 18:10–14)

The theme of an elderly and/or barren couple receiving word of a divinely-favored birth is not restricted to these passages. It can also be found in the story of Manoah, his wife, and their son Samson (Jgs 13:2–21), and in the story of Elkanah, Hannah, and their son Samuel (1 Sam 1:1–28). The similarity with these two other couples is intensified by parallel comments about avoiding wine:

"he shall drink no wine or strong drink" (Lk 1:15)	"I have drunk neither wine nor strong drink" (1 Sam 1:15)	"and drink no wine or strong drink" (Jgs 13:4)

In all three cases the special child (John, Samuel, Samson) are instruments in God's unfolding plans for saving his people. By casting the birth of John the Baptist in these terms, the evangelist is demonstrating the history-shaping power of God at work once more. The Baptist, who "will go before the Lord to prepare his ways" (Lk 1:76), is closely associated by this writer with Jesus, the Savior of his people and of the whole world. By depicting John, through the use of Old Testament motifs, as an instrument of God, Luke also asserts that Jesus' coming is the goal of all this divine activity.

This Lucan trait of recurrent Old Testament patterns can be

seen further by considering the structure of his treatment of the births of John and Jesus. Note the arrangement of his infancy narrative:

I. Annunciations of Births
    A. Annunciation to Zechariah (1:5–23)
        concluding with Elizabeth's praise of God (1:24–25)
    B. Annunciation to Mary (1:26–38)
        concluding with Elizabeth's praise of Mary (1:39–45,56)
        [*later authorial addition: Mary's Canticle (1:46–55)*]
II. Births and Namings
    A. 1. Birth of the Baptist (1:57)
        2. Joy at his birth (1:58)
        3. Circumcision and naming of the Baptist (1:59–66)
            [*later authorial addition: Zechariah's Canticle (1:67–79)*];
        4. "The child grew . . ." (1:80)
    B. 1. Birth of Jesus (2:1–7)
        2. Joy at his birth (2:8–20)
        3. Circumcision, Naming, and Presentation of Jesus (2:21–27, 34–39)
            [*later authorial addition: Simeon's canticle (2:28–33)*]
        4. "The child grew . . ." (2:40)
III. Finding in the Temple [probable later authorial insertion] (2:41–52)
        concluding with "and Jesus grew . . ." (2:52)

When outlined like this the evangelist's intention to present parallel accounts of Jesus and John becomes clear. It is not an exact parallel in terms of the number of verses assigned to each person, nor is it ever forgotten that Jesus is markedly superior to John (compare 1:32 "Son of the Most High" with 1:76 "prophet of the Most High," for example). But there is little doubt that this arrangement underscores both the fruition of divine plans and the Jewish origination of Jesus' saving mission.

Within this structure many Old Testament resonances are noticeable. In particular, the terms chosen to describe Jesus' birth are very revealing:

The ox knows its owner, and the ass knows the *manger of the Lord*, but Israel does not know, my people do not understand. (Is 1:3)

[Solomon recounts:] I was nursed with care in *swaddling cloths*, for no king has had a different beginning of existence. (Wis 7:4–5)

O thou hope of Israel, its savior in time of trouble, why shouldst thou be like a stranger in the land, like a wayfarer who spends the night in *the lodgings?* (Jer 14:8)

Joseph also went up from Galilee . . . to the city of David which is called Bethlehem. And while they were there the time came for her to be delivered. And she gave birth to her first-born son and wrapped him in *swaddling cloths*, and laid him in a *manger* because there was no place for them in *the lodgings*. (2:4–7)

"And this will be a sign for you: you will find a babe wrapped in *swaddling cloths* and lying in a *manger*." (Lk 2:12)

And they went in haste, and found Mary and Joseph, and the babe lying in a *manger*. (Lk 2:16)

It is only by perceiving the Old Testament imagery which Luke employs that the full artistry of his birth account becomes apparent. The whole scene is shaped by the underlying question: Will Israel recognize the arrival of its salvation? The hope of Israel, its Savior, comes like an unknown traveler. Will Israel now perceive the "manger of the Lord," or will it repeat the ignorance of the generation bemoaned by Isaiah?

Shepherds who tend their flocks in the environs of Bethlehem, as David did hundreds of years before, arrive, having been divinely instructed to seek for a manger. The repetition of the word "manger" indicates the importance of this Old Testament reference for the evangelist. Like his famous and kingly predecessor Solomon, the child is wrapped in swaddling cloths. The utter humanity, and also majesty, through which salvation dawns is skillfully conveyed by the evangelist.

Do the Jews who witness this scene recognize the "manger of the Lord"? Do they perceive that God's unfolding plan is being realized before them? The reaction of the shepherds is ambiguous.

"All who heard it wondered" (2:18), a bewilderment-response which is often described unfavorably in the Gospels. On the other hand, the shepherds returned, "glorifying and praising God for all they had heard and seen" (2:20), a seemingly positive action on their part.

There is little doubt about the response of one participant in these events, though. "Mary kept all these things, pondering them in her heart" (2:19). These words do not convey a puzzled perplexity, but rather a profound reflection. They continue the Lucan portrayal of Mary as one who hears the word of God and keeps it (1:38; 11:27–28). In this Gospel, she clearly has recognized the salvation which has dawned (or the "manger of the Lord"), and is part of the initial gathering of believers after the resurrection: "All these with one accord devoted themselves to prayer, together with the women and Mary the mother of Jesus, and with his brothers" (Acts 1:14).

In any case, the birth account is framed in such a way, by use of Old Testament themes, to assert a basic Lucan conviction. God's salvation comes first, as promised, to Israel. But that coming presents a choice between belief and faithlessness because all Jews must decide for themselves whether or not they recognize the "manger of the Lord," the Lord's inbreaking salvation, in these events. As Simeon predicts in the same chapter, "this child is set for the fall and rising of many in Israel" (Lk 2:34).

It should also be pointed out that many of these scenes echo the birth of the prophet Samuel. Samuel's mother Hannah exclaims a canticle remarkably similar to Mary's (compare 1 Sam 2:1–10 with Lk 1:46–55). Samuel is presented at the Lord's sanctuary to the aged Eli just as Jesus is presented at the temple and the aged Simeon appears (1 Sam 1:24–28). Lastly, Samuel is described as continuing "to grow both in stature and in favor with the Lord and with men" (1 Sam 2:26) just as Jesus "increased in wisdom and in stature, and in favor with God and man" (Lk 2:52; see also 2:40 and 1:80).

The way the evangelist utilizes the Old Testament makes his perspective clear. God has fulfilled his promises to Israel of old. In accordance with the divine plan, salvation has come to the Jewish people, and, through them, to all the world. While his use of the Hebrew Scriptures might not be so obvious to today's readers, it must be remembered that Luke was writing to people who were much more familiar with the Old Testament than most modern Christians. This is true even if his intended audience was Gentile. Many of the Gentile Christians to whom Luke's work might be directed had previously been "God-fearing" pagans. These "God-fearers," before hearing of Christ, had admired much about Judaism, had to some extent observed Jewish customs and feasts, and were aware of the Jewish sacred writings. The evangelist himself was probably such a person. Their approach to the Old Testament is an unfamiliar one to twentieth-century believers, who might, therefore, miss the full impact of such expressions as "lying in a manger." This limitation would not be present for most Lucan readers in his first-century situation.

A *third approach* by which Luke conveys that salvation breaks into the world through the fulfillment of God's promises to Israel is the series of explicit statements to that effect made by various characters, especially in the infancy narrative. These pronouncements are most obvious in the canticles of Zechariah, Mary, and Simeon, and in the various angelic messages:

[the angel concerning John the Baptist:] "And he will be filled with the Holy Spirit, even from his mother's womb. And he will turn many of the sons of Israel to the Lord their God, and he will go before him in the spirit and power of Elijah . . . to make ready for the Lord a people prepared" (1:15–17).

[Mary proclaims:] "He has helped his servant Israel, in remembrance of his mercy, as he spoke to our fathers, to Abraham and to his posterity forever" (1:54–55).

[Zechariah said:] "Blessed be the Lord God of Israel, for he has visited and redeemed his people, and he has raised up a horn of salvation for us in the house of his servant David, as he spoke by the mouth of his holy prophets from of old . . . to remember his holy covenant, the oath which he swore to our father Abraham" (1:68–70,72–73).

[Simeon cried:] "Lord, now lettest thou thy servant depart in peace, according to thy word; for mine eyes have seen thy salvation which thou hast prepared in the presence of all peoples, a light for revelation to the Gentiles, and for glory to thy people Israel" (2:29–32).

All of these statements underscore the coming to fruition of God's eternal intention to save humanity. Zechariah, Mary, and Simeon recognize that in the occurrences which they witness, God's will is being furthered. Salvation has entered the world through the Jewish people, as God promised.

In addition, Luke emphasizes that these events are unfolding according to God's designs by the various "sign" assurances which are made. As a sign of God's involvement Zechariah is rendered unable to speak until the boy is named John (1:20,64). Mary is assured that her kinswoman Elizabeth is pregnant (1:36), which she subsequently discovers is indeed the case (1:40–45). The shepherds are told that they will find the infant wrapped in swaddling cloths in a manger as "a sign for you" (2:12). And Simeon had been promised that he would not die "before he had seen the Lord's Christ" (2:26). All these skillfully intertwined images and proclamations make it emphatic that God's will is being carried out in Jesus.

A Tale of Two Cities

The evangelist also communicates his ideas about salvation through his use of geography. Observe the locations of the major portions of Luke/Acts:

Jerusalem	the Gospel opens here and the events surrounding Jesus' birth occur here or in its environs (1:5–4:13).
Galilee	Jesus' ministry occurs only in this province (4:14—9:50).
to Jerusalem	Then he sets out toward the Jewish capital (9:51—19:27).
Jerusalem	All of the events at the end of Jesus' ministry happen here including his death and the Lucan resurrection appearances (19:28—24:53). There are no Galilean appearances as in other Gospels.
Jerusalem	Acts opens in the holy city. The ascension, Pentecost, the first church, Stephen's death, etc., all occur here (Acts 1:1—8:3)
to Samaria	After a dispersion from Jerusalem, preaching

and to Gentiles	begins in Samaria; Paul becomes a believer; Peter is divinely guided to baptize Gentiles (Acts 8:4—12:25).
"to the end of the earth"	Paul founds churches throughout Asia Minor and Greece with the Jerusalem church's blessing (Acts 13:1—19:20).
to Rome	Then Paul sets out for the capital of the Gentile 'global' empire (19:21—28:15).
Rome	The two-volume work ends at 28:31 with Paul in the center of the Gentile world, "preaching the kingdom of God and teaching about the Lord Jesus Christ quite openly and unhindered" (28:16–31).

This chart shows that Luke/Acts might reasonably be nicknamed a "Tale of Two Cities." Jerusalem plainly dominates the Gospel narrative, while Rome holds sway over the Acts account. This geographic arrangement corresponds to Luke's theological interests. The first volume, the Gospel, is primarily concerned with the inbreaking of salvation to the Jews. The Acts of the Apostles, the second volume, focuses on the spread of that salvation to all the world. This basic outlook, incidentally, is harmonious with two other New Testament writers. The Gospel of John indicates that "salvation is from the Jews" (Jn 4:22), and the apostle Paul writes that the Gospel is the power of God "for salvation to everyone who has faith, to the Jew first and also to the Greek" (Rom 1:16). Luke, however, develops this concept into a framework around which he has written his entire composition. A quick perusal of the Lucan Gospel will indicate the extent to which he has made his narrative conform to his theological/geographical interests.

The Gospel opens in Jerusalem. That city, which David captured from the Jebusites and where he enshrined the ark of the covenant as a means of consolidating his political power, is known throughout the Old Testament as the city of David. Strangely, Luke applies that title instead to Bethlehem (2:4,11), David's presumed birthplace (see 1 Sam 16:1), an attribution found in no other writing. Just as Matthew's infancy narrative had a preponderance of Mosaic parallels to Jesus, so Luke invokes a number of Davidic images for him. David, born in Bethlehem, became a sort of savior of his people when he fulfilled his destiny in Jerusalem. Jesus, likewise born in Bethlehem, became the Savior of his people when he fulfilled his destiny in Jerusalem. In any event, the entire birth account revolves around Jerusalem. Zechariah is a priest in the temple there (1:9); Mary visits Elizabeth in "the hill country, a city of Judah" (1:39), apparently near Jerusalem; Jesus is born in "the city of David," and is presented at the temple shortly thereafter (2:22).

The evangelist's geographic concern manifests itself just prior to Jesus' ministry. In the episode of the three temptations of Jesus by the devil (4:1–13), Luke alters the sequence of the temptations from that found in his "Q" sayings-source (compare with Mt 4:1–11). Now the final, ultimate temptation occurs on the pinnacle of the temple in Jerusalem. The climactic test to determine whether Jesus will remain faithful to his mission takes place in the city which is the focal point of salvation's commencement.

In line with his concern to portray Jesus as bringing the news of salvation only to his fellow Jews, Luke deletes Marcan accounts of Jesus' activities in Bethsaida, Tyre and Sidon, and the Ten Cities (Mk 6:45; 7:24,31). The Lucan ministry of Jesus is limited to Galilee and to Samaria, which he passes through on his way to Jerusalem.

Jesus' journey to his fate in Jerusalem and the events which take place there overshadow the latter two-thirds of the Gospel. The significance which the author places on the holy city is apparent from the three verses which specify it as Jesus' goal:

> When the days drew near for him to be received up, he set his face to go to Jerusalem (9:51).

> He went on his way through towns and villages, teaching, and journeying toward Jerusalem (13:22).

> On the way to Jerusalem he was passing along between Samaria and Galilee (17:11).

Finally, the climactic events of Jesus' crucifixion and resurrection occur in Jerusalem. Luke recounts appearances of the Risen Lord only in the vicinity of Jerusalem (24:13–32, the Emmaus incident, and 24:50–53, the ascension from Bethany), or in the city itself (24:33–49). The instruction found in Mark 16:7, "But go, tell his disciples and Peter that he is going before you to Galilee; there you will see him as he told you" (see also Mt 28:7), Luke alters to, "Remember how he told you, *while he was still in Galilee*, that the Son of Man must . . . on the third day rise" (Lk 24:6). A statement about the future has been transformed into a reference to the past. Any traditions which are not harmonious with Luke's geographical framework are deleted or adapted.

This geographical perspective continues in Acts of Apostles. The second volume opens just outside Jerusalem. The risen Jesus instructs his disciples to wait in the holy city for the bestowal of the Holy Spirit (Acts 1:4–5). He then, in effect, outlines the structure of the rest of the book:

> But you shall receive power when the Holy Spirit comes upon you; and you shall be my witnesses in Jerusalem and in all Judea and Samaria and to the end of the earth (Acts 1:8).

Acts then proceeds to describe the gradual, divinely-guided, spread of the Church from Jerusalem, to the rest of Judea, to Samaria, to Syria, Cyprus, Asia Minor, and Greece, and ultimately, to the capital of the world, Rome. Just as in the Gospel Jesus had set his sights on Jerusalem, so in Acts Paul declares that he must travel to Rome (Acts 19:21). The corresponding theological assertion is evident. Salvation has entered the world through Israel, especially at the Jewish capital of Jerusalem. Now God intends that the Gentile peoples should also be saved, the saved pagan nations being represented by the imperial seat of Rome. This perspective is visible in Paul's triple statements of purpose (which may parallel the three Jerusalem-destination phrases in the Gospel):

> And Paul and Barnabas spoke out boldly, saying, "It is necessary that the word of God should be spoken first to [Jews]. Since you thrust it from you, and judge yourselves unworthy of eternal life, behold we turn to the Gentiles. For so the Lord has commanded us, saying, 'I have set you to be a light for the Gentiles, that you may bring salvation to the uttermost parts of the earth' " (Acts 13:46–47).
> And when [Jews] opposed and reviled him, [Paul] shook out his

garments and said to them, "Your blood be upon your heads! I am innocent. From now on I will go to Gentiles" (Acts 18:6). [Paul, speaking to Jews in Rome:] "Let it be known to you then that this salvation of God has been sent to the Gentiles; they will listen" (Acts 28:28).

In the Lucan view of things, "going to the Gentiles" is physically expressed by "going to Rome." All of the narrative sweeps along to the penultimate scene of Paul preaching salvation in the heart of the pagan empire.

This, of course, corresponds to the situation of the evangelist's community in the mid-80s. The preceding decades have witnessed the gradual transformation of what had originally been a Jewish-sect into a distinct religion composed predominantly of Gentiles. Luke intends to show that this development was planned and guided by God. His fellow-believers should not feel that their faith is somehow invalid because of the separation from Judaism. Although he believes that universal salvation has sprung from God's covenant with Israel, Luke firmly asserts that the Church has progressed in accordance with God's eternal plan.

It should be pointed out that although Luke believes in the primacy of Israel—in other words, that salvation comes first to the Jews and then to the Gentiles—he also feels that the prime agent of salvation in the world is now the Gentile Church. This is especially apparent in Acts where Jews are often depicted as violently hostile to the Church and where there is not infrequent reference to "you" [Jews] who crucified Jesus (Acts 2:36; 5:30; 7:52; for example). The preeminence of the Church is also visible in the shift in geographical priority from Jerusalem to Rome.

This perspective naturally springs from Luke's situation. He writes when the majority of Christians are Gentiles, when the Jerusalem mother-church is no more, when there is opposition to Christianity from Jews (such as those at Jamnia—see chapter three), and when it is to the Church's interest to distance itself from Jews in the eyes of Rome (see below). Still, while Luke occasionally employs the strident polemic which also occurs in Matthew, his criticism of Judaism is tempered by an obvious reverence (not noticeable in Matthew) for the pious Jews from whom Christianity sprang. It is through the Jew Jesus, through his Jewish forebears, and his Jewish apostles that salvation has come to the Gentiles.

Luke has no desire to condemn those Jews who, in his time, have not come to believe that Jesus has brought salvation. Rather than a Matthean wrath, Luke tends to express both sorrow and hope about non-Christian Jews. Consider these three passages, which are unique to the Gospel of Luke:

> And he told this parable: "A man had a fig tree planted in his vineyard; and he came seeking fruit on it and found none. And he said to the vinedresser, 'Lo, these three years I have come seeking fruit on this tree, and I find none. Cut it down; why should it use up ground?' And he answered him, 'Let it alone, sir, this year also, till I dig about it and put on manure. And if it bears fruit next year, well and good; but if not, you can cut it down' " (Lk 13:6–9).

Besides being a comment on the need for productivity in an individual's life, this parable could, in the Lucan context, also be referring to those Jews who have not perceived the dawning of salvation in Christ. Instead of uprooting them, Luke counsels patience and hope.

Again, sadness and puzzlement seems to mark the evangelist's view of those who, having the Hebrew Scriptures, should have understood God's actions in Christ. "If they do not hear Moses and the prophets, neither will they be convinced if someone should rise from the dead" (Lk 16:31), says Abraham in the conclusion of the story of the rich man and Lazarus.

Finally, it is above all regret which characterizes the Lucan Jesus' lament over Jerusalem:

> And when he drew near and saw the city he wept over it, saying, "Would that even today you knew things that make for peace! But now they are hid from your eyes. For the days shall come upon you, when your enemies will cast up a bank about you and surround you, and hem you in on every side, and dash you to the ground, you and your children within you, and they will not leave one stone upon another in you; because you did not know the time of your visitation" (Lk 19:41–44).

Writing with some knowledge of the events of the siege of Jerusalem by the Romans in 69–70 C.E., the evangelist expresses sorrow, not glee, at the Jewish capital's destruction. This attitude would make sense if Luke is indeed a Gentile "God-fearer" who had much admired Judaism even before learning about Jesus. He regrets that by failing to recognize the bringer of true peace, the Jerusalemites doomed themselves to warfare and death. He prays that the "Father [will] forgive them" (23:34) their failure.

The Lucan reverence and esteem for Christianity's Jewish roots, however, does not distract him from his other strong conviction. The time of the Church is at hand and salvation must be spread to all the world.

The Salvation of the Nations

The geographical considerations underlying Luke/Acts might lead one to guess that the writer might be just as concerned with the significance of Christ for the Gentiles as he is with his rootedness in Israel. Being a Gentile believer himself, the evangelist is intensely interested in portraying Christianity in a way that will be appealing to his pagan kinfolk. This interest is seen in his genealogy of Jesus (Lk 3:23–38), which is significantly different from Matthew's (Mt 1:1–17). The Lucan family tree extends backward from Joseph all the way to "Adam, the son of God" (3:38). As the ideal descendant of the father of all humanity, Jesus will bring blessings to all of Adam's children.

However, Luke also wants to demonstrate to the authorities of the Roman Empire that Christianity is a legitimate religion and is worthy of imperial respect. Recall the historical circumstances in which Luke is writing. He is composing his work little more than a decade after the Jewish-Roman War. The Romans have little fondness for the rebellious Jews who proved to be such a troublesome opponent. So highly did the Romans esteem their eventual victory over the Jewish revolutionaries that they constructed a monument to it in the imperial capital. The Arch of Titus, depicting scenes of the sacking of Jerusalem, can still be seen in Rome today.

A Roman might find it difficult to distinguish between Gentile Christians and Jewish Christians and Jews. To him, they might all be classified as revolting troublemakers. Luke, therefore, wants to distance Christianity from Judaism, and to assure Romans that this religion is not a threat to Roman authority. His interest to gain Roman admiration and respect for Christianity is apparent throughout his Gospel. In addition, Luke also wants to bring salvation to as many Gentiles, Romans included, as possible.

References to Rome occur as early as chapter two of the Gospel. The evangelist describes a census of the whole world ordered by Caesar Augustus (2:1). As mentioned earlier, there is no evidence of such a census having ever taken place. Luke's dating of it while Quirinius was governor (2:2) and Herod king (1:5) is impossible since Herod died ten years before Quirinius assumed the governorship. The census serves the narrative purpose of getting Joseph and Mary to Bethlehem, where the evangelist's tradition locates Jesus' birth. (Remember that Matthew portrayed Joseph and Mary as residents of Bethlehem [Mt 2:1,10] and did not have this difficulty. He, however, had to bring the family to Nazareth where it was known Jesus had grown up [Mt 2:22–23].)

It appears that Luke may have some limited knowledge about a census of Judea ordered by Quirinius in 6–7 C.E. This census would not have affected the Nazarean Joseph and Mary as Luke describes, nor would it have required people to travel to ancestral townships. But although the evangelist did not know the exact date or details of this census, he may have been aware that Quirinius' order sparked the bloody revolt of Judas the Galilean. This revolt was the beginning of the Zealot movement which eventually triggered the Jewish-Roman War in 66. By depicting the Galilean couple, Joseph and Mary, obediently complying with the commands of the emperor Augustus, the evangelist is indicating that Christianity has been submissive to Rome from its earliest beginnings. It is not a revolutionary movement, but a peaceful, law-abiding tradition. The census thus serves the double purpose of meeting the geographic needs of the Lucan infancy account as well as furthering the evangelist's courting of Roman favor.

The fact that the writer has Caesar Augustus order the census is also significant. Under Augustus' reign, a protracted time of relative peace prevailed. Monuments to the Peace of Augustus were common throughout the Graeco-Roman world, many referring to him as "god" and "savior." His birthday, September 23, was widely celebrated, and was said to "mark the beginning of the good news, through him, for the world." There are undoubtedly echoes of these ideas in the angelic message to the shepherds at the birth of Jesus:

> "Be not afraid; for behold, I bring you good news of a great joy which will come to all the people; for to you is born this day in the city of David a Savior, who is Christ the Lord. . . . Glory to God in the highest, and on earth peace among men with whom he is pleased" (Lk 2:10,14).

Surely, the evangelist is expressing in terms familiar to his readers that the child born during the Peace of Augustus is the true savior of the world, whose coming is the ultimate good news for the world. In a sense he uses the terminology of Roman propaganda to further his own convictions. The Roman world should pay homage to the divine bringer of authentic peace.

A Roman centurion is the principal, though absent, character in a healing recounted in chapter seven. Unlike the Matthean parallel of this incident (Mt 8:5–13), the Lucan centurion does not come personally but sends intermediaries to ask Jesus to cure his dying slave:

> Now a centurion had a slave who was dear to him, who was sick and at the point of death. When he heard of Jesus, he sent to him elders of the Jews, asking him to come and heal his slave. And when they came to Jesus, they besought him earnestly, saying, "He is worthy to have you do this for him, for he loves our nation, and he built us our synagogue" (Lk 7:2–5).

After Jesus sets out, friends of the centurion appear bringing word that he considers himself unworthy to have Jesus come to him. He asks that Jesus only say the word and healing would occur. The centurion, as one in authority, recognizes others who possess authority (7:6–8).

It is interesting that Luke has the centurion approach Jesus through Jewish intercessors. This is apparently another manifestation of the Lucan principle that salvation comes to the Gentiles through the Jews. The characterization of the centurion (missing from Matthew's account) as one who loves Israel and is a patron of the local synagogue is also noteworthy. The evangelist is conveying to the Romans in his day that respect for Judaism, if not for Jewish rebels, is admirable. Any Roman who acknowledges the truth of the Jewish worship of one God will be quick to recognize the divine authority present in God's Christ.

Another Roman is mentioned in 13:1–3:

> There were some present at that very time who told him of the Galileans whose blood Pilate had mingled with their sacrifices. And he answered them, "Do you think that these Galileans were worse sinners than all the other Galileans because they suffered thus? I tell you, No; but unless you all repent you will all likewise perish."

Although it is impossible to relate with certainty the deaths discussed in this passage to any known historical event, this is probably the only description of Pilate in all the Gospels which conforms with extra-biblical characterizations of him. Such sources present the Roman prefect's policies as brutal and cruel. For reasons which will be explored below, the evangelists tend to portray Pilate in the passion narratives in a more favorable light than is probably valid historically.

It is notable in this passage that Jesus, a Galilean, does not react to the news by angrily denouncing Pilate as a bloodthirsty tyrant. Since Galilee was considered by the Romans to be a hotbed of revolution, Jesus' response is somewhat unexpected. Rather than issue a political statement, Jesus makes a religious point about the need for repentance and fruitfulness (13:4–9). Clearly, the Lucan Jesus is not an insurrectionist, nor should he be considered an enemy of Rome. He is the bringer of God's saving way of life.

Similarly, Jesus' answer to the question about paying taxes to Caesar is also unprovocative. "Render to Caesar the things that are Caesar's, and to God the things that are God's" (20:25) would not be considered rebellious by a Roman. Although in the Lucan trial before Pilate Jesus is accused of forbidding tribute to Caesar (23:2), the alert reader would recognize that charge as a falsehood.

The passion account plainly demonstrates Luke's concern to win the friendship of the Empire. After hearing the charges against

Jesus, Pilate asks him if he is the "King of the Jews," a title with obvious revolutionary connotations (23:3). Jesus' reply is hardly a denial of the charge. He really does not address Pilate's question at all, which, in Roman jurisprudence, is tantamount to an admission of guilt. Nonetheless, Pilate asserts that Jesus is innocent of the charges leveled against him. He will proclaim Jesus innocent a total of three times in the course of the proceedings:

> And Pilate said to the chief priests and the multitudes, "I find no crime in this man" (23:4).

> Pilate then called together the chief priests and the rulers and the people, and said to them, "You brought me this man as one who was perverting the people; and after examining him before you, behold, I did not find this man guilty of any of your charges against him; neither did Herod, for he sent him back to us. Behold, nothing deserving death has been done by him; I will therefore chastise him and release him" (23:13–16).

> A third time he said to them, "Why, what evil has he done? I have found in him no crime deserving death; I will therefore chastise him and release him" (23:22).

Despite the fact that Jesus is crucified by the Romans under the charge, "This is the King of the Jews" (23:38), Luke emphasizes that the Roman prefect himself declared Jesus innocent of the charge of rebellion. The likelihood of this actually happening historically will be discussed chapter nine, but from the point of view of the evangelist it is very important that Jesus not be considered a rebellious troublemaker by contemporary Romans. Jesus was admittedly crucified by Romans, yes; but he was executed undeservedly. He should not be thought of as a dangerous revolutionary, in spite of initial appearances.

This is forcefully stressed by Luke's alteration of the punchline of Mark's Gospel. There the commander of the Roman execution squad, after seeing Jesus die, exclaimed that truly he was Son of God (Mk 15:39). However, the Lucan scene is quite different:

> Now when the centurion saw what had taken place, he praised God and said, "Certainly, this man was innocent [or 'righteous']!" (23:47).

That the innocent, righteous Jesus was slain unjustly is recognized by a Roman soldier. Luke insists that the Church founded by this righteous Jesus is not a threat to the Roman Empire. It, too, is "innocent." That fact has been realized by those Romans who were present at Jesus' trial and execution.

This testimony by Roman characters continues in the sequel to the Gospel, the Acts of Apostles. A few brief references will demonstrate this. It is a Roman centurion, Cornelius, who is the first Gentile to be baptized into the community of Jesus (10:1–48). The Roman proconsul of Achaia, Gallio, refuses to hear charges that Paul has violated the law by preaching Christ (18:12–16). Roman soldiers rescue Paul who is being beaten by a Jewish crowd in the temple precincts (21:30–32). They rescue him again from a violent tumult in the Jewish council (23:10). The Roman tribune then sends Paul to the governor, Felix, writing that he has done "nothing deserving death or imprisonment" (23:29). Paul is spirited away by night to Caesarea in Roman protective custody (23:31–33). His case is eventually heard by King Herod Agrippa and the Roman governor Porcius Festus who declare, "This man is doing nothing to deserve death or imprisonment" (26:31).

Luke undoubtedly wants to convince the Roman authorities in his time that Christianity is a peaceable, legitimate religion. After all, the imperial authorities persecuted Christians in Rome in 64–66 C.E., and they could do so again. However, he also is motivated by his belief that Christ has brought salvation to all the world. Romans, as well as other Gentiles, must learn of the salvation that is theirs. We must now consider what the evangelist means by salvation and also how he feels Jesus has brought this salvation into the world.

The Bringer of Wholeness and Peace

The period of Jesus' ministry represents, for Luke, the pivotal moment in human history. Preceded by what might be termed the "Epoch of Israel" and followed by the "Epoch of the Church," Jesus' lifetime is that crucial period during which salvation appeared. Note the peculiarly Lucan presentation of this saying:

> The law and the prophets were until John [the Baptist]; since then the good news of the kingdom of God is preached, and every one is pressured to enter it (Lk 16:16).

Clearly, Luke considers the introductory activities of the Baptist to mark an epochal turning point. The preparation for universal salvation, which was, according to Luke, the purpose of Jewish history, has climaxed with the arrival of Jesus.

The concluding phase of Jesus' ministry appears in Acts immediately before Jesus ascends:

> So when they had come together, they asked him, "Lord, will you at this time restore the kingdom to Israel?" He said to them, "It is not for you to know times or seasons which the Father has fixed by his own authority. But you shall receive power when the Holy Spirit comes upon you; and you shall be my witnesses in Jerusalem, and in all Judea and Samaria and to the end of the earth" (Acts 1:6–8).

The time of the Church has begun. Believers in Jesus should not be preoccupied with thoughts of the ultimate end of things. Rather, they must spread the news of Jesus' salvation throughout the world.

What is it about Jesus that has caused such momentous consequences? Somehow the Lucan Jesus has brought to fulfillment and also inaugurated a process which affects all human history. What is the nature of the salvation which Jesus has introduced?

Insight into the evangelist's ideas about salvation can be gained by considering the effect that Jesus has on the various people he encounters in the Gospel. Consistently, Jesus is portrayed as bringing peace, in the sense of the Hebrew word "shalom." He brings a wholeness, a completeness which produces joy, contentment, and love.

Thus, Jesus' herald, John the Baptist, is described as a prophet who "will go before the Lord to prepare his ways . . . to guide our feet into the way of peace" (Lk 1:76,79). The angel announces to the shepherds that peace has dawned with the birth of Jesus (2:10–11,14). The very presence of the infant Jesus brings peace to the heart of Simeon (2:29–30).

The Baptist's ministry is portrayed as the curing of all the highs and lows, all the crooked and rough aspects of life (3:4–6). Jesus' ministry is characterized as the freeing of the poor, of captives, of the blind, and of the oppressed (4:16–21). Jerusalem is lamented for failing to recognize those "things that make for peace" (19:42). In summary, throughout the Gospel of Luke, both Jesus' preaching and his miracles heal physically and spiritually. Physical healings abound both in the Gospel, and also, through the agency of Jesus' disciples, in Acts. These cures, however, are only one aspect of the integral wholeness and inner peace which Jesus brings both to individuals and to relationships.

Three unique scenes in the passion narrative illustrate the various facets of the healing aura which surrounds the Lucan Jesus. All of the Gospels note that the ear of a slave of the high priest was removed by someone bearing a sword (Mk 14:47; Mt 26:51; Lk 22:50; Jn 18:10). However, it is only in the Gospel of Luke that one reads, "But Jesus . . . touched his ear and healed him" (22:51). The mere presence of Jesus is enough to produce this unlikely side-effect to his trial, a passage found only in Luke:

> And Herod and Pilate became friends with each other that very day, for before this they had been at enmity with each other (23:12).

Similarly, while the other synoptic Gospels assert that those executed with Jesus reviled him (Mk 15:32; Mt 27:44), only Luke presents this scene:

> One of the criminals who were hanged railed at him, saying, "Are you not the Christ? Save yourself and us!" But the other rebuked him, saying, "Do you not fear God, since you are under the same sentence of condemnation? And we indeed justly; for we are receiving the due rewards of our deeds; but this man has done nothing wrong." And he said, "Jesus, remember me when you come into your kingdom." And he said to him, "Truly, I say to you, today you will be with me in paradise" (Lk 23:39–43).

This repentant criminal, then, is made spiritually whole by the presence of Jesus. He joins the other witnesses, Pilate, the centurion, and the crowds, in recognizing Jesus' innocence. These three uniquely Lucan incidents demonstrate the extent of Jesus' saving presence. He heals physically, relationally, and spiritually. He brings a wholeness, a complete wellness and peace to all who permit themselves to be touched by his life. His death, in particular, brings about a "forgiveness of sins" which reconciles all people to each other and to God.

This emphasis on Jesus as the healing Savior manifests itself in many ways in Luke/Acts. Especially noteworthy is the Lucan concern for the poor and outcasts, for women, and for the disciples. Throughout the Gospel there are passages which denote a Lucan interest in the impoverished and the disabled, and the consequent responsibilities of the wealthy:

> "[The Lord] has filled the hungry with good things, and the rich he has sent empty away" (1:53).

> [John] answered them, "He who has two coats, let him share with him who has none; and he who has food, let him do likewise" (3:11).

> "The Spirit of the Lord is upon me, because he has anointed me to preach good news to the poor" (4:18).

> And he lifted up his eyes on his disciples, and said, "Blessed are you poor, for yours is the kingdom of God. . . . But woe to you that are rich, for you have received your consolation" (6:20,24).

> "Go and tell John what you have seen and heard: the blind receive their sight, the lame walk, lepers are cleansed, and the deaf hear, the dead are raised up, the poor have the good news preached to them" (7:22).

> "But God said to him, 'You fool! This night your soul is required of you; and the things you have prepared, whose will they be?' So is he who lays up treasure for himself, and is not rich toward God" (12:20–21).

> "But when you give a feast, invite the poor, the maimed, the lame, the blind, and you will be blessed, because they cannot repay you" (14:13–14).

"Go out quickly to the streets and lanes of the city, and bring in the poor and maimed and blind and lame" (14:21).

But when he heard this, he became sad, for he was very rich. Jesus looking at him said, "How hard it is for those who have riches to enter the kingdom of God!" (18:23–24).

And Zacchaeus stood and said to the Lord, "Behold, Lord, the half of my goods I give to the poor; and if I have defrauded anyone of anything, I restore it fourfold." And Jesus said to him, "Today salvation has come to this house . . ." (19:8–9).

There is little doubt that during his ministry Jesus was greatly concerned with the marginalized of Jewish society. But Luke has taken this tradition and clearly applied it to some issues in his church. Unlike Matthew, for instance, he does not spiritualize the beatitudes which he received from the "Q" source. He is more interested in blessing those who are "hungry" (Lk 6:21) than those who "hunger for righteousness" (Mt 5:6). The evangelist praises those who are generous to the poor, such as Zacchaeus, but is highly critical of those who hoard their wealth. Perhaps this reflects the situation of the Lucan church. It may be that Luke's is an affluent community which the evangelist believes is inadequately aiding the poor. Maybe wealthy Christians are discriminating against poor believers (a situation Paul faced in 1 Corinthians). In any event, the attention paid to the outcasts of society in Luke's Gospel is another reflection of the healing and restoration brought by the Lucan Jesus.

Women are also given special consideration in the Gospel of Luke. Besides the significant number of healings of women (especially 7:37–50) and parables involving women, there are also references to women performing discipleship roles:

Soon afterward he went on through cities and villages, preaching and bringing the good news of the kingdom of God. And the twelve were with him, and also some women who had been healed of evil spirits and infirmities: Mary, called Magdalene, from whom seven demons had gone out, and Joanna, the wife of Chuza, Herod's steward, and Susanna, and many others, who provided for them out of their means (8:1–3).

Now as they went on their way, he entered a village; and a woman named Martha received him into her house. And she had a sister called Mary, who sat at the Lord's feet and listened to his teaching. But Martha was distracted with much serving; and she went to him and said, "Lord, do you not care that my sister has left me to serve alone? Tell her then to help me." But the Lord answered her, "Martha, Martha, you are anxious and troubled about many things; one thing is needful. Mary has chosen the good portion, which shall not be taken away from her" (10:38–42).

These two passages are only found in the Gospel of Luke. The first plainly describes women as followers of Jesus, even if the word "disciple" is not directly employed. These women remain faithful in their loyalty to Jesus, for "the women who had followed him from Galilee" witness Jesus' death (23:49) and burial (23:55), and are the first to become aware of the resurrection (24:1–11,22–23). The practice of married and single women traveling about with Jesus and his male disciples would be scandalous to Jesus' Jewish contemporaries. The women's presence underscores Jesus' assertion that the peace of the kingdom is for all.

The second passage unambiguously portrays Mary in the posture of a disciple who sits at the master's feet and listens to his words. The incident forcefully claims that it is indeed proper for a woman to be a disciple of Jesus. She is not to be confined to "womanly" types of service. Her right to be a disciple "shall not be taken away from her." Do these verses indicate that the place of women in the Church is an issue in the Lucan community? There is not enough evidence to be certain, but surely the evangelist would be arguing for the inclusion of women in ecclesial activities. In this regard, notice that there are many women in Acts who are portrayed as disciples: there are women present when the Spirit arrives (Acts 1:14; 2:1), a woman "disciple named Tabitha" dies and is restored by Peter (9:36–42), a woman named Mary hosts persecuted believers in her house (12:12), a woman named Lydia is baptized and offers Paul and his companions hospitality (16:14–15,40), a woman named Priscilla, and her husband Aquila, travel about with Paul and teach Apollos the way of the Lord more accurately (18:1–3,18,26), and the four daughters of Philip, one of the seven, prophesy (21:8–9). Whether or not Luke is a proponent of women's discipleship, there is no doubt that he portrays women frequently healed and enabled by the presence of Jesus, and, later, by the apostles.

The presentation of the Twelve is also affected by the Lucan conception of Jesus as healing Savior. He completely suppresses the Marcan negative portrayal of the disciples. This is most obvious in the passion narrative. Whereas Mark showed Peter, James, and John three times failing to stay on watch while Jesus prays (Mk 14:33–34,37–41), Luke only recounts one dozing by the disciples and makes it quite understandable: "And when he rose from prayer, he came to the disciples and found them sleeping for sorrow (Lk 22:45). The Marcan pronouncement that "they all forsook him and fled" (Mk 14:50) is totally absent in Luke. In fact, Luke claims that the witnesses to Jesus' execution included the women "and *all* his acquaintances" (23:49)! This apparently means the male disciples and the Twelve, an assertion which flatly contradicts the traditions found in all the other Gospels. Luke, however, is not interested in the failings and controversies of the early believers. He is more concerned with showing how the healing presence of Jesus has touched their lives, making them powerful preachers and healers in their own right.

Similarly, in Acts Luke avoids referring to inner-Church conflicts and failings as much as possible. Although the letters of Paul make it clear that things were far from constantly harmonious, Luke would rather write:

> All who believed were together and had all things in common; and they sold their possessions and goods and distributed them to all, as any had need. And day by day, attending the temple together and breaking bread in their homes, they partook of food with glad and generous hearts, praising God and having favor with all the people. And the Lord added to their number day by day those who were being saved (Acts 2:44–47).

This depiction of a "saved" community reveals much. They are saved from all the destructive forces that alienate people from one another. They are healed of the divisiveness of financial status. They are freed from pangs of hunger, and none are in want. They are united in their gladness and joyfulness to God. They have been rescued from the domination of sin, a dominion which no longer afflicts them with disease, hunger, poverty, hatred, enmity, and unhappiness. Their loving peace is the salvation which has become theirs because of Jesus, the healing Savior.

The Lucan church can be assured that this salvation will continue to spread because the Holy Spirit has been the prime mover of all the events which Luke/Acts has related. Just as the Spirit guided and touched the Baptist (Lk 1:15), Mary (1:34), Elizabeth (1:41), Simeon (2:25–27), Jesus (3:22; 4:1,18; 10:21; Acts 1:2), the first believers (Acts 2:1–4; 4:31), the early missionaries (8:29, 39), Peter (4:8; 10:38–47; 11:12,15), the Apostolic Council (15:28), and Paul (13:2–4; 16:6–7; 19:21; 20:28), so, too, will the Spirit guide and touch the Christians of the Lucan church. God's divine plan to save humanity has been realized by Jesus, and its implementation is still being directed by the all-prevailing Holy Spirit. Those who live in the loving peace which brings wholeness and community will spread the salvation of God to all the world.

QUESTIONS FOR REFLECTION AND DISCUSSION

1. The author of the Gospel of Luke emphasizes the healing and wholeness brought by Jesus. What are the implications of his insight for humanity today? for the Church? for one's personal relationships? for the individual person?

2. Luke emphasizes that the followers of Jesus are not a threat to the Roman Empire. How does he convey this conviction in his Gospel? Do you feel that civil governments today should ever feel "threatened" by the Christian Church. Why or why not?

3. Luke believes that salvation has come to the world at large through Judaism. How does this belief manifest itself in his Gospel? How does it contrast with Matthew's assertions?

4. Although Luke reveres Judaism, in Acts he blames Jews for Jesus' death. What historical circumstances have motivated the author to write this way? Why should modern readers be aware of these circumstances?

5. Relate the Lucan understanding of life in the community of Christ to today's Church.

6. According to Luke, what place is prayer to have in the lives of faithful disciples of Jesus?

7. Many people who are concerned about the plight of the poor and the inequitable distribution of the world's resources find the Gospel of Luke very challenging. What features of Luke/Acts relate to these issues of social justice?

THE SYNOPTIC GOSPELS: REINTERPRETING THE JESUS-TRADITIONS

Reconstructing the Evangelists' Purposes

*H*aving explored each of the synoptic Gospels in their turn, it now remains to summarize and contrast our findings. The principal aim of Part I of this book, which this chapter concludes, has been to investigate the particular perspectives which originated in the situation of each evangelist—in other words, in Stage Three of the traditions found in the Gospels.

Several different techniques have been employed to accomplish this. In the case of the earliest written Gospel, Mark's, the overall structure of the Gospel provided clues to the writer's intentions. The concentration and manner of presentation of miracles in the first half of that Gospel contrasted markedly with the latter half's emphasis on the Son of Man's suffering and death. The Marcan treatment of the destruction of Jerusalem in 70 C.E. was useful in determining an approximate date for the Gospel's composition, and also offered insights into the events occurring in the Marcan church. The way in which Jesus was portrayed confirmed the likelihood of a community which has experienced suffering and violence. By comparing Mark's Gospel to the way in which Matthew and Luke edited it, it was possible to further identify those

Marcan concerns which were of less interest to the other evangelists. For example, the Marcan negative depiction of the disciples, which would serve to encourage the faltering and tested faith of Marcan church members, was pretty much eliminated by both Matthew and Luke who did not share this purpose of Mark's.

Matthew could be approached in different ways because of the overwhelming probability that he used Mark as one of his sources. Thus, contrasts between the two could be noted. For instance, Matthew's deletion of the Marcan reference to Jesus' family coming to take charge of him reflected a different understanding of Jesus. By comparing those parts of Matthew which seemed to be rooted in the "Q" sayings source with the "Q" parallels in Luke, Matthew's individual interests could again be determined. The Matthean presentation of the parable of the guests invited to a feast, for example, is noticeably different from Luke's version because of the reference to the king who "sent his troops and destroyed those murderers and burned their city" (Mt 22:7). Thus, Matthew's belief in the replacement of Judaism by Christianity was perceived. Finally, material which was unique to Matthew also shed light on his individual perspective. An illustration of this would be the exclusively Matthean passages in the Confession of Peter verses. By assigning Peter the rabbinic powers of binding and loosing, the evangelist's Jewish heritage and outlook was manifest.

Luke's Gospel provided similar avenues of exploration; it could be contrasted with its source, Mark, and also with the "Q" material in Matthew. However, Luke offered additional prospects in that the Gospel was only the first in a two-volume work. Lucan tendencies, which were observed by comparison with Mark and "Q", could be further examined by seeing if they continued into the Acts of Apostles. It was thereby possible to clearly perceive the Lucan usage of geography, historical epochs, and the priority of Israel.

It has become clear that each of the evangelists has reinterpreted the various traditions about Jesus which he possessed. They did this in order to convey their own unique understandings of Jesus (which were conditioned by their own cultural backgrounds and experiences) and in order to address the particular needs of their church communities. As a means of summarizing the insights garnered from these lines of investigation, it would be useful to graphically chart the main characteristics of each Gospel:

The Gospel of Mark

Date Composed: • around 70 C.E.

Place: • Rome is favored locale. Syria is a secondary site.

Author: • a Gentile or possibly a Hellenistic Jew because of the distant and occasionally inaccurate explanations of Jewish customs.

Sources: • oral and unknown written traditions, possibly including a miracles collection.

Notable Features: • "Immediately" is often used, giving the first half a rapid pace.
                  • Jesus' identity is proclaimed by demons, but secrecy is imposed.
                  • miracles are concentrated in the first half. They produce only confusion and awe.
                  • Jesus is rejected or not understood by everyone, including family, disciples, and various Jewish groups.
                  • although they receive private instruction, the disciples do not seem to understand Jesus better than anyone else.
                  • the second half focuses on Jesus teaching his followers that the Son of Man must suffer.
                  • Jesus is utterly abandoned and forsaken by everyone. News of his resurrection causes fright and confusion.
                  • No resurrection appearances.

Situation: • the Marcan church seems to be experiencing violent turmoil. It may be under systematic persecution. If composed in Rome in the late 60s, this church would have endured Nero's persecution, the deaths of Peter and Paul, and be currently hearing of the siege of Jerusalem and the dissolution of the mother-church.
                  • there may be "glory hounds" in the church who argue against enduring suffering, who assert that

performing wondrous feats is the best sign of being saved, and who claim that Jesus has privately given them secret knowledge of his present return in their glorified selves.

Author's beliefs:	• the true nature of Jesus cannot be perceived unless one has experienced his passion.
	• authentic disciples must be prepared to "take up their cross" and follow Jesus.
	• miracles and wondrous feats are not the critical components of real faith; nor are they the sign of authentic discipleship.
	• those who remain faithful to Christ despite suffering violence will be vindicated when Jesus returns as Lord.
	• Jesus the Lord will return soon, but he has not arrived yet.
	• the continuing validity of Judaism may be questioned, but it is not a major concern.

The Gospel of Matthew

Date composed:	• mid-80s.
Place:	• Antioch of Syria is widely favored.
Author:	• Jewish believer in Jesus, possibly a scribe.
Sources:	• the Gospel of Mark.
	• "Q" sayings source.
	• other special material.
Notable Features:	• begins with an infancy narrative.
	• has numerous "fulfillment passages," which quote Old Testament Scriptures and relate them to Jesus.
	• Jesus teaches often and is styled after Moses and other Jewish heroes.
	• Gentiles are prominently and favorably portrayed.
	• dreams are often used to convey divine messages.
	• has a threefold division: Jesus' beginnings; his public ministry; the journey to and events in Jerusalem.
	• the rejection of Jesus by his own people is given prominence. There is harsh anti-Jewish polemic.
	• Peter and the other disciples are given rabbinically-based authority over the community of Jesus.

- concludes with disciples being commanded to teach all nations.

Situation:
- the Matthean church seems to be a mixed Jewish-Gentile community.
- the Jewish members, including the author, are in bitter controversy with the Pharisaic leaders of Judaism who are meeting in Jamnia to restructure Judaism after the temple's destruction. Both groups accuse the other of understanding the law in a heretical manner.
- there may be disputes and bickering occurring within Matthean community.

Author's Beliefs:
- Jesus is the Living Wisdom of God. He is God's Way, God's Torah come to life. He teaches the ultimate and perfected law. As Wisdom is often rejected, so is Jesus.
- the law which Jesus brings is not to be paid mere lip-service. The law is to be done.
- the unity and harmony of the Church has the highest priority. The law is not to be used to dominate people. Authority is a service, not a power. Forgiveness, reconciliation, and mercy are the hallmarks of church life.
- Jews who follow the Torah taught by Jesus have replaced former leaders of the Jewish community. The destruction of Jerusalem is a sign of this replacement.
- Gentiles are meant by God to be part of the Church. However, they too must observe the law of Christ. Their admittance is subject to certain conditions.
- the return of Jesus in glory will not occur immediately. In the meantime, the church has the duty to "teach all nations."

The Gospel of Luke

Date Composed:
- mid-80s

Place:
- a wide variety of sites have been proposed. Somewhere in Greece or Asia Minor seems reasonable.

Author: • a Gentile believer, probably a God-fearer who ad-
                      mired Judaism before learning of Christianity.

Sources: • the Gospel of Mark.
                    • "Q" sayings source.
                    • other special material.

Notable Features: • is the first of a two-volume work. The second part
                      presents the spread of salvation to the nations.
                    • begins with an infancy narrative markedly different
                      from Matthew's.
                    • is patterned after a Greek "history."
                    • geography plays a major role. Jerusalem is the focus
                      of the Gospel as the site through which salvation
                      comes.
                    • many Old Testament themes are woven into the
                      Gospel and Acts, but the evangelist does not often
                      make obvious reference to the fact as Matthew did.
                    • an emphasis on Israel as first blessed by salvation,
                      as God had promised, is prominent.
                    • Jesus and his associates and followers are all de-
                      picted as pious, righteous, law-abiding Jews.
                    • frequent mention of the poor and of women occurs.
                    • Jesus is often depicted as praying.
                    • there is a major stress on Jesus as healer and peace-
                      bringer.
                    • the fact that Jesus was righteous and innocent is
                      emphasized.
                    • there is a tendency to smooth over conflicts, dis-
                      putes, and negative behavior among the disciples
                      and in the Church.
                    • huge crowds are prominent. They often are por-
                      trayed very positively.
                    • Romans are depicted favorably.
                    • a sad and melancholy attitude toward unbelieving
                      Jews is noticeable.
                    • there are frequent references to guidance by the
                      Spirit.

Situation: • the Lucan community is predominantly Gentile.
                    • Christians could be mistaken for Jews or Jewish

sympathizers by the Romans. There is danger in being perceived as revolutionaries by the Empire.
- some members of the Lucan community may be concerned about the disapproval of unbelieving Jews. Is the Church's separation from Judaism really what God planned?
- the Lucan community may be an affluent one, which the author feels is inadequately concerned with the poor.

Author's Beliefs:
- Jesus is the culmination of God's plan to save all humanity. His ministry marks the pivotal epoch in human history.
- salvation enters the world through Israel and is offered to Israel first.
- the salvation which Jesus brings is the very peace of God. It rescues people from hatred, sickness, conflict, and alienation from God and each other. Jesus brings interpersonal harmony, physical and spiritual wholeness, contentment, and joy.
- Christianity is the natural, divinely-intended offshoot of Judaism. It has not replaced Judaism, but grown out of it.
- Jews who have not recognized God's salvation in Christ are to be lamented. They are denying themselves the saving peace which Jesus brought.
- Christianity is a legitimate religion which should be respected by the Roman Empire. Romans are meant to share in the salvation of Christ.
- Jesus was innocent and righteous. His unjust death and resurrection was the ultimate sign of God's salvation.
- Jesus is not returning soon. The Holy Spirit, which has guided the fulfillment of God's plan, is present in the Church to orchestrate the spreading of salvation to "the end of the earth."
- the needs of the poor must be addressed.

The Origins of the Jesus-Traditions

Clearly, the evangelists freely adapted to their own interests and needs the Jesus-traditions which they received. Modern believers would hold that this adaptation took place under the Spirit's inspiration. All of the Gospels have their ultimate origins in the ministry of Jesus. Additional Jesus-traditions arose in the experience of the resurrection. These Stage One (Jesus' ministry) and Stage Two (apostolic post-resurrectional preaching) materials were the sources which the authors of the Gospels reinterpreted.

Information about the ministry of Jesus, then, must always be considered in the light of the later reinterpretation of the traditions by the Gospel writers. This does not mean that the Gospels do not contain historical information, but only that such information has been indirectly preserved. With this in mind, and having treated the evangelists' perspectives, we will now explore the historical ministry and purposes of Jesus.

QUESTIONS FOR REFLECTION AND DISCUSSION

1. After exploring each of the synoptic Gospels, what conclusions or insights have been the most significant or revealing for you?

2. Why can it be said that the historical Jesus is only indirectly preserved in the Gospels?

3. Why is it important for modern Christians to realize that the New Testament presents many different points of view?

4. Which of the three synoptic Gospels touches you most deeply? Why?

5. The Marcan church was persecuted and suffering. The Matthean church was actively teaching and disputing. The Lucan church was affluent and part of a rapidly expanding movement. How do these situations resemble or differ from your own church community?

6. If you were going to write a Gospel about Jesus, what would you want to emphasize? What current issues would you want to address?

Part II

JESUS

MAP

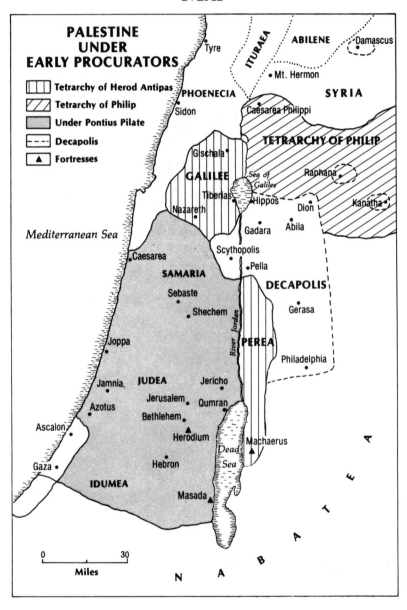

PALESTINE
UNDER
EARLY PROCURATORS

	Tetrarchy of Herod Antipas
	Tetrarchy of Philip
	Under Pontius Pilate
	Decapolis
▲	Fortresses

Tyre

ITURAEA

ABILENE

Damascus

Mt. Hermon

PHOENECIA

SYRIA

Sidon

Caesarea Philippi

TETRARCHY OF PHILIP

Gischala

GALILEE

Sea of
Galilee

Raphana

Tiberias

Hippos

Kanatha

Nazareth

Dion

Mediterranean Sea

Gadara

Abila

Caesarea

Scythopolis

Pella

SAMARIA

DECAPOLIS

Sebaste

Shechem

Gerasa

Joppa

River Jordan

PEREA

Philadelphia

Jamnia

JUDEA

Jericho

Jerusalem

Qumran

Azotus

Bethlehem

Ascalon

Herodium

Machaerus

Dead

Gaza

Hebron

Sea

IDUMEA

Masada

N A B A T E A

0   30
Miles

Chapter Six

A PROFILE OF THE MINISTRY OF JESUS

Jesus and John

By assessing the traditions found within the various Gospels and other New Testament books and by taking into account the particular purposes of the sacred writers, it is possible to construct an outline of the events and features of Jesus' ministry.

There is no question that the story of Jesus' activities must begin with his baptism in the Jordan by John the Baptist. The incident is found not only in the synoptic tradition but also in the Gospel of John. The strength of the memory is indicated by its unanimous mention, even though it is embarrassing to Christians who are in contention with advocates of the Baptist's messianic status later on in the first century. As discussed earlier, this embarrassment had caused Matthew, for example, to portray the Baptist as objecting to baptizing Jesus (Mt 3:14–16).

The Gospel of John, to which we shall refer occasionally in these chapters, relates some interesting things about Jesus and the Baptist:

> After this Jesus and his disciples went into the land of Judea; there he remained with them and baptized. John also was baptizing at Aenon near Salim, because there was much water there; and people came and were baptized. For John had not yet been put in prison (Jn 3:22–24).

And they came to John and said to him, "Rabbi, he who was with you beyond the Jordan, to whom you bore witness, here he is baptizing, and all are going to him" (Jn 3:26).

Now when the Lord knew that the Pharisees had heard that Jesus was making and baptizing more disciples than John (although Jesus himself did not baptize, but only his disciples), he left Judea and departed again to Galilee (Jn 4:1–3).

This picture of Jesus as, in effect, a disciple of the Baptist's is unique to John's Gospel. Jesus is shown as duplicating John's practices, although there is the inconsistent parenthetical statement that only Jesus' followers actually baptized (4:2). Does this depiction of Jesus preserve an early memory of Jesus' beginnings? It would certainly not be to the evangelists' interests to emphasize such a close connection between Jesus and the Baptist. Those who in the 80s and 90s held John to be the Messiah would make much use of a tradition that Jesus had once been a Baptist-disciple. Still, it is impossible to be certain about the accuracy of this account.

It is also difficult to capture the essence of the Baptist's preaching. The evangelists have all taken pains to show him as subordinate to Jesus and have expressed his message in the language of later Christian understanding (for example, ". . . he will baptize you with the Holy Spirit" [Mk 1:8]). The Baptist does seem to have a sort of "fire and brimstone" approach, however. He emphasizes the imminence of judgment and the resultant crucial need for repentance. (See the "Q" material in Mt 3:7–12 and Lk 3:7–9,15–17.)

There does seem to be a basis for believing that Jesus did not begin his own ministry, independent of whatever connections he had with the Baptist, until after John's arrest:

Now after John was arrested Jesus came into Galilee, preaching the gospel of God, and saying, "The time is fulfilled, and the kingdom of God is at hand; repent, and believe in the gospel" (Mk 1:14–15).

Now when he heard that John had been arrested, he withdrew into Galilee (Mt 4:12).

> But Herod the tetrarch, who had been reproved by [the Baptist]
> for Herodias, his brother's wife, and for all the evil things that
> Herod had done, added this to them all, that he shut up John in
> prison. . . . Jesus, when he began his ministry, was about thirty
> years of age (Lk 3:19–20,23).

Although the information is conveyed in different contexts, the
synoptic evangelists all link the beginnings of Jesus' ministry with
the imprisonment of the Baptist. John's Gospel, after noting that
he "had not yet been put in prison" (3:24), recounts the Baptist
stating that Jesus "must increase, but I must decrease" (3:30).

Table-Fellowship with Sinners

Whether or not he began as a follower of John, Jesus' independent activities seem to have had a markedly different tone. Rather
than emphasizing the prospect of rapidly-approaching judgment,
Jesus proclaims that God's mercy has come upon the world and
those who are especially blessed are sinners and outcasts.

Jesus' interest in the marginalized of Jewish society is apparent
throughout the synoptics. Two sayings are notable:

> "Those who are well have no need of a physician, but those
> who are sick; I came not to call the righteous, but sinners" (Mk
> 2:17).

> "I was only sent to the lost sheep of the house of Israel" (Mt
> 15:24).

Even taking into account the evangelists' adaptations of Jesus' sayings to their own purposes, it remains clear that Jesus was remembered as one who had a special involvement with the unrighteous.
This is perhaps most plain in the traditions which recount Jesus'
practice of sharing meals with such people.

It must be noted that in the Palestinian Jewish culture eating
with someone meant that you were on close personal terms with
that person. Fellowship-meals, at which a loaf of bread and a cup of
wine were shared among all present, were occasions celebrating
kinship or friendship. Yet it is apparent that Jesus acquired a reputa-

tion for engaging in such intimacies with people who were considered to be wicked:

> And as he sat at table in house, many tax collectors and sinners were sitting with Jesus and his disciples; for there were many who followed him (Mk 2:15).

> "For John the Baptist has come eating no bread and drinking no wine; and you say, 'He has a demon.' The Son of Man has come eating and drinking, and you say, 'Behold, a glutton and a drunkard, a friend of tax collectors and sinners!' " (Lk 7:33–34).

> Now the tax collectors and sinners were all drawing near to hear him. And the Pharisees and the scribes murmured, saying, "This man receives sinners and eats with them" (Lk 15:1–2).

The image of Jesus as friend of sinners is, by the time of the evangelists, a solidly established tradition. Luke makes use of it, in line with his interest in the poor and outcasts, in his Zacchaeus incident where bystanders murmur, "This man has gone in to be the guest of a man who is a sinner" (19:7).

People like tax collectors were considered to be traitors to Israel because they worked for the Roman overlords. Likewise, those of notorious repute, such as prostitutes, were also traitors to Israel because they had forsaken their covenant commitments to the Lord. In order for such persons to reenter the mainstream of Jewish community life, public repentance was required. Only then would it be possible for them to share in table-fellowship with those who were trying to live decent, law-observant lives.

Jesus' practice of sharing meals with sinners reversed that procedure. Instead of demanding repentance, Jesus broke bread with sinners first. Such direct, personal contact seems to have sparked the repentance ordinarily required as a prerequisite for friendship. Apparently touched by Jesus' openness, several of the unrighteous became part of Jesus' following (e.g., Mk 2:15), and a tax collector became one of the Twelve (Mk 2:14). The inclusion of sinful and marginalized Jews into the community of Israel must be seen as an important component of Jesus' mission.

The Choosing of the Twelve

There is no doubt that in the course of his ministry Jesus selected twelve men as his inner circle of followers. References to the Twelve occur in all the Gospels. It is difficult to ascertain their function, however. It has become commonplace to think of this group as the "twelve apostles," and to presume that they played an important formative role in the early Church. In actuality, there were other apostles than the Twelve (Paul, Barnabas, etc.), and the Twelve are mentioned as a group only a few times outside the Gospels.

In the letters of Paul, the earliest Christian writings which provide important information about the Church's development, "the Twelve" are mentioned only once: "[Jesus] appeared to Cephas [Peter], then to the Twelve" (1 Cor 15:7). In Acts, the Twelve summon the believers to settle a dispute (6:2), the Eleven select a replacement for the fallen Judas (1:15–28), and Peter, "standing with the Eleven" addresses a crowd (2:14). But other than those three passages, the Twelve do not appear again. Individuals such as Peter and John are frequently mentioned in Paul's letters and in Acts (see especially the accounts of the Apostolic Council in Acts 15 and Gal 2:1–10), but the Twelve as a unit seem to have played a minor role in the growth of the early Church. What seems to have been most remembered about them was their number.

This impression is confirmed by the Gospel accounts. Consider the various lists of the Twelve which appear:

first, Simon who is called Peter, and Andrew his brother; James the son of Zebedee, and John his brother;	Simon, whom he surnamed Peter; James the son of Zebedee and John the brother of James . . .	Simon, whom he named Peter, and Andrew his brother, and James and John,	Peter and John and James and Andrew,
Philip and Bartholomew; Thomas and Matthew the tax collector;	Andrew, and Philip, and Bartholomew, and Matthew, and Thomas,	and Philip, and Bartholomew, and Matthew, and Thomas,	Philip and Thomas, and Bartholomew and Matthew,

| James the son of Alphaeus, Thaddeus; Simon the Canaanean, | and James the son of Alphaeus, and Thaddeus, and Simon the Canaanean, | James the son of Alphaeus, and Simon who was called the Zealot, and Judas son of James, | James, the son of Alphaeus and Simon the Zealot and Judas son of James (Acts 1:13). |
| and Judas Iscariot who betrayed him (Mt 10:2–4). | and Judas Iscariot who betrayed him (Mk 3:16–19). | and Judas Iscariot who turned traitor (Lk 6:14–16). | |

The Gospel of John does not present a list of the Twelve, though these names appear: Andrew, Simon Peter, the sons of Zebedee, Thomas "one of the Twelve" (20:24), Philip, Judas Iscariot, "Judas (not Iscariot)" (14:22), and a Nathanael of Cana (21:2; 1:45–49).

It is striking that a group presumably as important as the Twelve is not remembered with greater precision. Matthew and Mark state that a "Thaddeus" was one of the Twelve, Luke/Acts asserts that a "Judas son of James" was part of the group, and John does not even attempt to name them all, but he does seem to speak of a "Nathanael" as if he also belonged to the inner circle. Over the years some have attempted to harmonize these discrepancies by declaring that Thaddeus = Judas son of James/not Iscariot (explaining why the betraying Judas is always surnamed Iscariot to distinguish him from Thaddeus/Judas), and Bartholomew = Nathanael (because both are mentioned alongside Philip [compare the lists with Jn 1:45]). These reasons seem more motivated by the desire to harmonize than by actual evidence, however. The simpler explanation is that there was no longer an accurate memory of the identities of the Twelve by the time the Gospels were written. Certainly the names of important figures like Peter and John were known. But although it was recalled that Jesus chose Twelve, the names of all of those selected have been forgotten. This is supported by the observation that most of those named are not ever mentioned again (Bartholomew, James son of Alphaeus, Thaddeus, Simon the Canaanean/Zealot), or appear on only one, or perhaps two, other occasions (Matthew, Judas not Iscariot, Nathanael).

We are left with these facts:

(1) the Twelve as a group are hardly ever referred to in those books which portray the post-resurrectional Church (Paul's letters, Acts);

(2) the evangelists are not aware of who exactly composed the Twelve, although they clearly know that twelve were chosen;

(3) many of the individuals named as belonging to the Twelve play quite minor roles in the evangelists' accounts.

It seems reasonable to conclude that the choosing of the Twelve was more significant for the historical ministry of Jesus than for the post-resurrectional Church. That is not to say that the testimony and witness of the Twelve and the other apostles (like Paul) was not of the greatest interest to later believers, but only that their number as Twelve, and whatever functions they were intended to perform, were more directly connected with Jesus' activities before his death than with the Church's mission afterward. In other words, the choosing of the Twelve is another feature of Jesus' ministry that must be considered in attempting to explore Jesus' aims and goals. Their intended purpose had to do with Jesus' mission, and not, it appears, with some unique role in the early Church. There are yet other aspects of Jesus' activities that must be discussed as well.

The Miracles of Jesus

The Gospels are unanimous in depicting Jesus as someone who performed wonderful deeds. These miracles may be classified into various groups, revealing much about their purpose and significance. The synoptic miracle accounts can be listed according to these simple categories:

Exorcisms [the casting out of demons]
* in the synagogue at Capernaum (Mk 1:21–28; Lk 4:31–37)
* the Gerasene demoniac(s) (Mk 5:1–20; Mt 8:23–34; Lk 8:26–29)
* the Syro-phoenician woman's daughter (Mk 7:24–30; Mt 15:21–28)
* the epileptic boy (Mk 9:14–29; Mt 17:14–21; Lk 9:37–43)
* the dumb man and Beelzebul (Mt 9:32–34; 12:22–24; Lk 11:14–15)

Healings [the cure of physical disorders sometimes including an account of sabbath controversies]

*Peter's mother-in-law (Mk 1:29–31; Mt 8:14–15; Lk 4:38–39)
* a leper (Mk 1:40–45; Mt 8:1–4; Lk 5:12–16)
* the paralytic (Mk 2:1–12; Mt 9:1–8; Lk 5:17–26)
* man with withered hand (Mk 3:1–6; Mt 12:9–14; Lk 6:6–11)
* Jairus' daughter (Mk 5:21–24a,35–43; Mt 9:18–19,23–26; Lk 8:41–42a,49–56)
* woman with hemorrhage (Mk 5:25–34; Mt 9:20–22; Lk 8:42b–48)
* a deaf mute (Mk 7:31–37)
* various blind people (Mk 8:22–26; 10:46–52; Mt 9:27–31; 20:29–34; Lk 18:35–43)
* centurion's slave (Mt 8:5–13; Lk 7:1–10)
* widow's son (Lk 7:11–17)
* crippled woman (Lk 13:10–17)
* man with dropsy (Lk 14:1–6)
* ten lepers (Lk 17:11–19)
* summaries of healings:
     -evening at Capernaum (Mk 1:32–34; Mt 8:16–17; Lk 4:40–41)
     -crowds from Tyre and Sidon (Mk 3:7–12; Mt 4:24; 12:15; Lk 6:17–19)
     -in Gennesaret (Mk 6:53–56; Mt 14:34–36)
     -many people (Mt 15:29–31)

Epiphanies [accounts which manifest presence of the divine]
* walking on the water (Mk 6:45–52; Mt 14:22–33)
* transfiguration (Mk 9:2–10; Mt 17:1–9; Lk 9:28–36)

Rescue [the saving from imminent disaster]
* stilling of the storm (Mk 4:35–41; Mt 8:23–27; Lk 8:22–25)

Gift Miracles [the bestowal of bounty]
* the catch of fish (Lk 5:1–11)
* feeding of five thousand (Mk 6:32–44; Mt 14:13–21; Lk 9:10–17)
* feeding of four thousand (Mk 8:1–10; Mt 15:32–39)

It is obvious that the vast majority of synoptic reports of Jesus' mighty deeds concern exorcisms and healings. Although in both cases a victim is relieved of physical abnormalities, there is a basic difference between the two types of miracles. By exorcising demons Jesus displays authority over what might be termed "cosmic evil." Afflictions that beset humanity from the outside are subject to Jesus' word. Healings, on the other hand, demonstrate the authority Jesus has over human failings. Recall that in the ancient world physical and moral sickness were understood to be integrally related. Jesus' actions denote authority over the brokenness of human beings which results in corporeal, emotional, and moral diseases. This is plain in the discussion about the paralytic who is told "Your sins are forgiven," even as his power of movement is being restored (Mk 2:1–12).

The miracles traditions were certainly presented by the evangelists according to their own desires and interests. For example, Matthew on occasion doubles the number of persons healed as in the case of the Gadarene demoniacs (compare Mt 8:28ff with Mk 5:1–5ff). Nevertheless, it seems certain that in his ministry an authority was displayed by Jesus' actions which caused much speculation about him. However, modern readers should be warned once more against projecting post-resurrectional insights back into the time of Jesus' ministry. No one witnessing a mighty deed by Jesus would conclude that he was God, even though modern Christians might expect such a deduction.

It is better to conceive of reaction to Jesus' deeds in two general ways. People might feel that God was working through Jesus as he had worked through other miracle-workers like Moses or Elijah. This is the logic of Peter's speech in Acts 2:22, thought by many to represent very early Christian thought, "Jesus of Nazareth, a man attested to you by God with mighty works and wonders and signs which God did through him in your midst . . ." Or Jesus might be perceived as some sort of sorcerer or pagan magician, consorting with sinister demonic forces. Such a viewpoint underlies the Beelzebul charge which probably dates from Jesus' ministry (Mk 3:22; Mt 9:34; 12:24; Lk 11:15). In either case, Jesus' miracles, in particular his healings and exorcisms, should not be thought of as proofs of his divinity. Both in the evangelists' reinterpretations and in Jesus' time the miracles were generally perceived as manifestations of authority for evil or for holiness.

Opposition to Jesus

Any account of the ministry of Jesus must reckon with the opposition to him which emerged. There is no doubt that he disputed with various groups about the proper interpretation of the

Torah, the law of Moses. Some accused him of disregarding the Torah, while he in turn charged opponents with twisting the law to their own purposes. Without doubt he won the enmity of the temple priests, who, as we shall see, were instrumental in arranging Jesus' execution.

It is also certain that after entering the holy city, Jesus caused a disturbance of some sort in the temple precincts. Combined with various sayings preserved somewhat confusedly in the Gospels, it appears that Jesus was convinced that the passing away of the temple in the light of the presence of some ideal temple was imminent. Such a belief would, of course, not endear Jesus to those who stood to lose the most should he be proved correct—namely, the temple leadership.

As with other aspects of Gospel interpretation, care must be exercised in jumping to conclusions about the identities of Jesus' chief opponents and the reasons for their opposition. Based on the Gospels as well as other sources, it is possible to describe the general characteristics of the various religious and political groups present in early first-century Judaism. All of the groups need to be understood in the context of the overpowering presence of the occupation forces of imperial Rome.

The Zealots were the "freedom fighters" of first-century Judaism. Believing that the Holy Land was polluted by the presence of the pagan Roman armies, they sought to incite an armed insurrection against them. Any Jews who were perceived as collaborators with the Romans were viewed as traitors worthy of death. By means of violence and threats of murder, the Zealots eventually succeeded in 66 C.E. in fomenting the devastating Jewish-Roman War. In the time of Jesus in the 30s, they were not an organized movement as such, but rather groups of scattered peasants forced into banditry by the economic predations of the Roman system. One of the Twelve is called a Zealot.

The Herodians were the descendants of Herod the Great and their supporters. After the death of the dynasty's founder, they were basically puppet-kings who ruled at the whim of the emperor. One of Herod's sons, Archelaus, was removed as sovereign of Judea and replaced by a Roman prefect. During Jesus' ministry, Herod Antipas, brother of Archelaus, reigned over Galilee. He was responsible for the death of the Baptist, and was apparently fascinated by and feared the reports he received about Jesus. Luke asserts that one of Jesus' women followers was the wife of Herod's steward (Lk 8:3). The Zealots, naturally, despised the Herodians as traitors and tools of the Roman oppressor.

Although one cannot simply equate them with the temple priests, there is little doubt that the Sadducees were closely identified with the priestly, aristocratic class centered in Jerusalem. These "tsaddiquim" or "righteous ones" saw the temple as the ultimate focus of Jewish spirituality and did all in their power to preserve its authority and ensure its prosperity. Therefore, they collaborated with the Romans in order to keep the peace, fearing the destruction that would result if the Empire used its full might against the Jewish people. The high priest, who oversaw the operations of the temple and probably the Sanhedrin or Jewish council as well, was appointed by Rome and was in all probability a Sadducee. The temple was the economic lifeblood of Jerusalem, providing income and sustenance for many of the residents who provided for the needs of Jews on pilgrimage to the holy city. In seeking to preserve the status quo, the Sadducees expressed a highly conservative philosophy, accepting only the five books of Moses as authoritative and tending to interpret them literally. They refused to acknowledge oral traditions, opposing those who felt that the Scriptures needed to be interpreted according to each generation's needs. The Zealots considered them to be traitors and conceivably aided in their total destruction during the Jewish-Roman War.

The Essenes were Jews who felt that the temple and Jerusalem were so corrupt and sinful as to be damnable. They established monastic communities along the shores of the Dead Sea where a true, faithful remnant of Judaism could survive. They developed a strict, austere lifestyle, writing rules of conduct on scrolls. When the Jewish-Roman War broke out in 66 C.E., they felt that the time of deliverance was at hand and took up the sword against both Romans and faithless Jews. They never returned to their Dead Sea communities, and their scrolls, carefully stored in caves, were not discovered until 1947. Although the Essenes are not mentioned in any of the Gospels, their writings have provided important information about the first-century Jewish world.

The Pharisees are a group whose complexity has become apparent to modern Scripture scholarship only fairly recently. Generally, the Pharisees, the origin of whose name is unknown, were a group of non-priestly Jews dedicated to the study of the Torah for the purpose of sanctifying all life. They sought to make everyday life as holy as if one were in the temple praying to the Lord. To accomplish this they relied much on their own traditions, and seem to have been particularly interested in purity and cleanliness practices related to table-fellowship. In addition, they believed that new understandings of God's wishes and plans were possible. For instance, they asserted that there would be a general resurrection of all the dead. Such a view was condemned by the Sadducees since it is not mentioned in the Torah. The Pharisaic movement, then, centered its attention on establishing ritual holiness among all the Jewish people, and viewed the temple in a lesser light. The Pharisees appear to have been popular with the people at large. They were respected for their knowledge of the law, for their piety, and for their criticism of the priestly aristocracy.

The picture becomes more complicated, though, because of the presence of various rival schools of Pharisaism during the ministry of Jesus. The school or house of Shammai seems to have been the dominant branch of Pharisaism in Jesus' day. According to rabbinic writings of later centuries, whose reliability about first century groups is highly contested in current scholarship, it was another Pharisaic group, Bet (house of) Hillel, which was eventually to prevail.

Although very little has been reliably ascertained about the differences between the Bet Shammai and Bet Hillel Pharisees, the Gospel portrayals of Jesus' opposition to the Pharisees might show evidence of Jesus advocating some Hillelite ideas against the then prevalent Shammaite teachings. Though heavily colored by the disputes in the 80s, Matthew 23, for example, presents Jesus castigating Pharisees for opinions apparently more characteristic of the Bet Shammai, a distinction to which the evangelist draws no attention.

Regardless of the differences between the rival Pharisaic groups, Jesus and the Pharisees probably had much more in common than is popularly realized. Above all, they shared the beliefs that God could be related to intimately, that the Torah must be internalized by the whole people, that the kingdom of God could be actively present in human history, that there would be a physical resurrection and final judgment, that the Messiah would not be identified with worldly politics, and, possibly with Bet Hillel, that the Gentiles were ultimately intended for salvation.

Although Jesus would have differences with all the groups discussed above, he would probably have been closest in outlook to Pharisees. He clearly had no interest in the violent purposes of the Zealots. They, in turn, would be displeased with any thoughts of rendering Caesar his due or of cures of Romans or their slaves. Jesus' attitude about the temple's impermanence would alienate him from the Sadducees. The Herodians appear to have opposed Jesus as another troublemaker like the Baptist. The Essenes, removed to their Dead Sea communities, played little discernible role in the Gospels, but would certainly have rejected Jesus' close association with sinners and outcasts.

It is ironic, then, that the Gospels present the Pharisees in such categorically negative terms. This is understandable when one realizes that the Essenes, Herodians, and Sadducees had all been swept from the scene as a result of the War, and so it was the Pharisees with whom the early Church was in conflict at the time the Gospels were written. Memories of Jesus' conflicts with particular Jewish groups, even if they were mostly with Sadducees for example, would be used by the evangelists against their current opponents at Jamnia. The fact that Jesus may have been closest in attitude to Bet Hillel was to be lost in the polemical situation between early Christianity and the Jamnia Pharisees.

Even though an assessment of Jesus' stance toward the law and the temple and the nature of opposition to him from various groups must be carefully nuanced, it is clear that Jesus felt authorized to definitively interpret Jewish traditions. While the Gospels, especially Luke, are undoubtedly correct in remembering Jesus as a pious, Torah-observant Jew, his understanding of the law was one which seemed to cause difficulty in varying degrees with all of the movements and groups described above. It was perhaps Jesus' attitude that the law, despite his reverence of it, was secondary in importance to his mission that was at the heart of religious disagreement with him. He interpreted sabbath customs, tithing regulations, social etiquette, and the commandments themselves all in the context of his mission and purposes.

What Was Jesus Doing?

And so, we come to the central question posed by this profile of Jesus' ministry: What was Jesus' purpose; what was his mission? Getting down to the details, what did his contact with the Baptist cause? Why did Jesus associate freely and enter into table-fellowship with sinners? Why did he choose the Twelve? Why did he promote a spirit of renewal among his fellow Jews? What was intended by his miraculous actions? Why did he feel it appropriate to relativize the importance of the temple and the interpretation of the Torah because of his own mission? What, in short, did Jesus think he was doing?

Although answers to these questions could already be partially discerned by the various components of this profile, for a clearer understanding we must turn our attention to the Gospels' memory of Jesus' preaching as presented in the parables.

QUESTIONS FOR REFLECTION AND DISCUSSION

1. Contrast the Baptist and Jesus. How were they similar? How were they different?

2. What may be some consequences of an awareness that Jesus disputed with one school of Pharisees, but seemed to hold views which were somewhat more compatible with another Pharisaic tradition? How might one's attitude toward Judaism be affected?

3. Are there modern groups which could be compared with the different movements in the Judaism of Jesus' time, namely, Sadducees, Zealots, Essenes, Herodians, and Pharisees?

4. What are some reasons why decent, God-fearing people might have found various features of Jesus' ministry offensive?

5. Does Jesus seem to have wanted to:
   (a) spark renewal within his Jewish heritage; or
   (b) start something completely new and separate from Judaism?
   What impact does your answer have on your understanding of Christianity?

6. Who would be the marginalized, "unrighteous" members of American society with whom Jesus would choose to share table-fellowship today?

7. Jesus appears to have entered into table-fellowship, a gesture of friendship and intimacy, with individuals who had not yet publicly repented of past wrongdoings. Can you devise a parallel situation in today's society or Church which would demonstrate how unsettling this practice was to some of Jesus' contemporaries?

Chapter Seven

PARABLES OF GOD'S REIGN

The Parables of Jesus

*T*here is little reason to doubt that Jesus, like other Jewish preachers of his time, conveyed much of his teaching in the form of parables. Modern educators are increasingly drawing attention to the instructive and penetrating power of story-telling, an awareness which was commonplace in the first-century culture. Stories have the ability to touch people's hearts, to challenge them in the deepest parts of their beings. Stories, metaphors and images are probably the only ways to effectively communicate the most profound aspects of human existence, to express concepts and feelings which words or formulae cannot convey. The apparent effectiveness of Jesus' words, regardless of whether they aroused support or opposition, must to a great extent be a result of his skills as a storyteller.

This is true despite the appalling notion in Mk 4:11–12 (and picked up in Mt 13:13 and Lk 8:10) that Jesus tells parables in order to confound his listeners and prevent them from comprehending his message:

> To you [disciples] has been given the secret of the kingdom of God, but for those outside everything is in parables, so that they may indeed see and not perceive, and may indeed hear and not understand, lest they should turn again and be forgiven.

140

By this logic Jesus is, in effect, speaking in riddles so as to thwart any possible repentance or reform. Certainly such an attitude makes little sense of Jesus' ministry. It will be recalled that one of Mark's purposes was to negate any claims that people in his church had received secret, private revelation from Jesus. By portraying the disciples as privately tutored by Jesus, and yet acting with even less comprehension than the supposedly parable-befuddled crowds, the evangelist cleverly undercuts any personal-revelation assertions by opponents in the 70s. For Mark, the news of the reign of God is not restricted to a few, nor is it something mysterious and incomprehensible, for "there is nothing hid except to be made manifest; nor is anything secret except to come to light" (Mk 4:22). The Marcan presentation of parables as confounding is done for his own reasons, and should not be deemed an accurate explanation of the purpose of parables. In reality, parables are powerful metaphoric stories whose soul-searing messages can forcefully challenge listeners.

Parables have certain unique qualities which should be noted. They always contain, at least in their original form, a surprising twist or unexpected turn of events which would shock and grab the attention of listeners. This feature is often difficult for twentieth-century Christians to appreciate because they have heard the parables countless times since childhood. The storylines have become too familiar and have lost their freshness and element of surprise. For example, it is startling to imagine that a father would so readily divide up his estate, prematurely bequeathing it to his younger son as the prodigal son parable indicates. Similarly, a farmer sowing seed so carelessly that only a fraction of it actually falls on arable ground is hardly standard practice.

Parables by their very nature are also stories which arise out of the life context of both the teller and the listeners. Farmers, vineyards, shepherds, and servants abound in Jesus' parables, indicating the rural and agricultural setting in which his ministry occurred. The cultural distance between modern readers and Jesus' first-century Palestinian world can make it difficult to fully relate to characters in the parables. For instance, the situation of the ten maidens awaiting the arrival of the bridegroom really has no present-day counterpart.

Occasionally, parables will have "cliff-hanger" endings. The final conclusion is not revealed because it is up to the listener to decide how to respond to the situation which the parable has presented. The best example of this is the ending of the parable of the prodigal son. Although the father pleads with his older son to join in the celebration of his younger brother's return, the story does not indicate what happens next (Lk 15:28–32). Does the older brother put aside his anger and come to the party? Or does he continue in his refusal to accept what is happening? It is, as we shall see, up to Jesus' listeners to wrestle with this decision in their own lives.

Parables are not allegories. In a parable the meaning of the story is not explained or defined. The multiple layers of significance are meant to grow in the minds and hearts of the story's listeners. People have a tendency to want to encapsulate the purpose of a parable, and this present chapter is no exception. In doing this, though, one runs the risk of limiting the possible effects that the story might have on listeners if they were left free to relate to the tale in their own personal ways. An allegory is a story in which all the elements and characters are defined and the ultimate purpose of the tale is clearly delineated. The evangelists, like anyone else, are drawn by the desire to put the parables into a box, so to speak. In doing so, they often transform what had once been a parable into an allegory.

The best illustration of this is Mark's allegorization of the parable of the sower. In attempting to apply the parable to his community's specific needs, the evangelist categorizes every element in the story. The seed = the word of God, the rocky ground = people whose faith has no depth, etc. (see Mk 4:14–20). By neatly defining things this way the evangelist not only compromises the power of the parable to touch different people in various, unique ways, he also skews the point of the parable away from its original purpose in the context of Jesus' ministry. All the evangelists do this to one degree or another, especially by tacking on summary, explanatory sentences to the end of the parable. These are sometimes other, one-line sayings of Jesus which are appended to the parable because the evangelist feels them appropriate. For example, at the end of the story of the servant given authority (Lk 12:42–48), Luke, on Jesus' lips, explains: "Everyone to whom much is given, much is required; and of him to whom men commit much they will demand the more" (12:48). Since Matthew has the same story from the "Q-source" (Mt 24:45–51) without the interpretative conclusion, it is obvious that Luke has inserted this comment for his own reasons. This concluding-sentence phenomenon is quite common, and readers should be careful of understanding the parable solely in the light of the evangelists' explanations. In the time of the ministry of Jesus the parable may have had a different purpose.

It is also true, as we have already seen, that the evangelists feel perfectly free to edit and rewrite the parabolic traditions which they have received from various sources in order to express their own, personal opinions or to meet the peculiar needs of their church communities. A vivid illustration of this point is the Matthean presentation of the parable of the great supper (compare with the version in Lk 14:16–24). Matthew has inserted:

> . . . while the rest seized his servants, treated them shamefully, and killed them. The king was angry, and he sent his troops and destroyed those murderers and burned their city (22:6–7).

This addition obviously emerges from Matthew's belief, not shared by Luke, that believers in Christ have replaced Judaism as God's chosen people. He considers the Roman destruction and burning of Jerusalem in 70 as a sign of divine wrath against the city where Jesus was executed. Certainly, the parable in its original context in Jesus' ministry could not have included such elements. In considering the message of Jesus by examining the parables, the later editorial activities of the evangelists must always be kept in mind lest subsequent issues and problems be inappropriately attributed to Jesus.

It is more difficult to reconstruct the original setting and context of some parables than others. A few parables are so heavily edited by the evangelists that it is almost impossible to recover their original sense. Indeed, there are some scholars who believe that most of the parables now preserved in the Gospels can shed only questionable light on Jesus' purposes and preaching. It is beyond the scope of this book to enter into the technical debate on this issue. However, although this or that parable might be suspected to have originated in the pen of the evangelist rather than the lips of Jesus, taken collectively the entire mass of parables surely reveals the substance of Jesus' message.

Even the most cursory glance at the parables shows that the vast majority of them concern what Jesus calls the reign or kingdom of God. Combined with other sayings of Jesus, it seems clear that the central theme of his preaching was the assertion that the reign of God was in the process of erupting into human history. The parables dramatically convey both the various consequences of the reign's arrival and also what God's people should be doing about it. Before turning attention to the parables, it is necessary to first consider what the term "reign of God" meant to first-century Palestinian Jews, including Jesus.

The Reign of God

One of the fundamental principles of Judaism, both ancient and modern, is the idea that creation is incomplete, that the world is not yet everything that God intends it to be. Warfare, the oppression of people, disease and hunger, natural calamities such as storms and earthquakes, violence in the animal kingdom, and especially the failure of all people to acknowledge the oneness of God are all signs that things are not the way they are meant to be. Constantly faced with this unfinished and unfulfilled state of affairs, especially when exacerbated by a series of conquests by other peoples, the inspired writers of the Hebrew Scriptures came to conceive of a time when God's will would prevail and his promises to Israel would be realized. Different prophets and writers pictured "the Day of the Lord" using various images: wars would cease, people would live in harmony with one another, animals would live in peaceful tranquility, illnesses and physical disorders would vanish, all injustices and oppression would be rectified, Israel would be restored to a position of glory, and all the pagan nations would stream to Zion to learn of the God of Abraham and to walk in his ways. On that day the reign of God would be established and his will would permeate all of creation:

> It shall come to pass in the latter days that the mountain of the house of the Lord shall be established as the highest of the

mountains, and shall be raised up above the hills; and peoples shall flow to it, and many nations shall come and say: "Come let us go up to the mountain of the Lord, to the house of the God of Jacob; that he may teach us his ways and we may walk in his paths." For out of Zion shall go forth the law, and the word of the Lord from Jerusalem. He shall judge between many peoples, and shall decide for strong nations afar off; and they shall beat their swords into plowshares, and their spears into pruning hooks; nation shall not lift up sword against nation, neither shall they learn war anymore; but they shall sit every man under his vine and under his fig tree, and none of them shall be afraid; for the mouth of the Lord of hosts has spoken (Mi 4:1–4; see also Is 2:1–4).

The wolf shall dwell with the lamb, and the leopard shall lie down with the kid, and the calf and the lion and the fatling together, and a little child shall lead them. The cow and the bear shall feed; their young shall lie down together; and the lion shall eat straw like an ox. The sucking child shall play over the hole of the asp, and the weaned child shall put his hand on the adder's den. They shall not hurt or destroy in all my holy mountain; for the earth shall be full of the knowledge of the Lord as the waters cover the sea (Is 11:6–9).

Then the eyes of the blind shall be opened, and the ears of the deaf unstopped; then shall the lame man leap like a hart, and the tongue of the dumb sing for joy (Is 35:5–6a).

In short, there would come a time when God as King of the universe would exert his authority and all creation would acknowledge his sway. In particular, Israel would be restored and the Gentile nations would find glory in her.

This, then, is a general description of the reign of God. It is important to stress that by the time of Jesus there were widespread variations on these basic themes. Many Jews believed that the commencement of the reign of God would be accompanied by the appearance of one anointed by God, in Hebrew "mashiah." There was a wide spectrum of views about what this mashiah would be like. Some Jews conceived of him as a perfect King, like David of old who was also known as the Lord's Anointed One, who would rule a restored Israel with justice and benevolence and whose throne would be eternal. Others thought of him as one who would inspire a perfect observance of the law. Still others pictured two mashiahs, a priestly one who would enlighten spiritual matters and a kingly one who would rule in the political sphere. And there were yet other Jews who really didn't dwell on the coming of a mashiah. No one at all imagined that the mashiah of God would suffer. Despite this disparity of expectations, the concept of the arrival of the reign of God is the undercurrent of all the various mashiah-related conceptions.

There were yet other ideas held by some. The Pharisees asserted that a general resurrection of the dead would occur when God's reign prevailed. There were also those who, motivated by the oppression of the Jews by the Greek kings and now by the Romans, believed that an ultimate time of persecution and suffering would occur before God intervened to establish his reign. This "ordeal," or "time of troubles" was thought to signal the beginning of the reign of God which would mark the vindication of the righteous and the downfall of the wicked.

What must be emphasized once more is the fact that there was no single, dominant expectation regarding how or when God's reign would arrive, although all Jews believed that God's supremacy would ultimately be revealed. Minimally, it can be stated that all would expect Israel to be restored and peace to prevail over all the nations, but beyond that little uniformity of opinion can be asserted. The conceptions regarding the mashiah were even more diverse.

That having been said, it now becomes possible to examine the parables of Jesus in order to determine what he thought about the subject he constantly proclaimed: the reign of God is at hand! By attempting to reconstruct the original setting and significance of the parables, it becomes evident that they can be grouped according to several overarching themes. These will be examined in turn. For the sake of simplicity, this treatment of the parables will assume that all of them originated in one form or another in the ministry of Jesus, although they have been heavily edited by the evangelists subsequently. Even if future research indicates that is not the case for a particular parable, or even for several, the conclusions reached by examining the parables in groups would still be substantially valid.

God Loves All People Even Though They Are Sinful

The Generous Employer (Mt 20:1–16)
The Two Sons (Mt 21:28–32)
The Lost Sheep (Mt 18:12–14; Lk 15:4–7)
The Two Debtors (Lk 7:41–43)
The Lost Coin (Lk 15:8–9)
The Prodigal Son (Lk 15:11–32)
The Wicked Tenants (Mk 12:1–11; Mt 21:33–44; Lk 20:9–18)
The Pharisee and the Tax Collector (Lk 18:9–14)

The manner in which Jesus announced the imminence of God's reign seems to have been one intended to promote joy rather than fear. Above all Jesus describes the reign's arrival as a consequence of the Father's love. God desires all his people to be part of this exciting event, even those who have heretofore been considered, either by themselves or by others, to be automatically excluded from God's grace. "The lost sheep of the house of Israel" are especially to benefit from the commencement of the reign of God.

This is made very evident in the parable of the generous employer:

For the kingdom of heaven [God] is like a householder who went out early in the morning to hire laborers for his vineyard. After agreeing with the laborers for a denarius a day, he sent them into his vineyard. And going out about the third hour (9 A.M.) he saw others standing idle in the marketplace; and to them he said, "You go into the vineyard too, and whatever is right I will give you." So they went. Going out again about the sixth hour (noon) and the ninth hour (3 P.M.), he did the same. And about the eleventh hour (5 P.M.) he went out and found others standing; and he said to them, "Why do you stand here idle all day?" They said to him, "Because no one has hired us." He said to them, "You go into the vineyard too."

And when evening came, the owner of the vineyard said to his steward, "Call the laborers and pay them their wages, beginning with the last and up to the first." And when those hired about the eleventh hour came, each of them received a denarius. Now when the first came, they thought they would receive more; but each of them also received a denarius. And on receiving it they grumbled at the householder, saying, "These last worked only one hour, and you have made them equal to us who have borne the burden of the day and the scorching heat." But he replied, "Friend, I am doing you no wrong; did you not agree with me for a denarius? Take what belongs to you, and go; I choose to give to this last as I give to you. Am I not allowed to do what I choose with what belongs to me? Or do you begrudge my generosity? (Mt 20:1–15).

As mentioned above, all parables have a surprising twist to them. Here the strange payment practices of the owner are unexpected and startling. The punchline of the story occurs after those who have been laboring since early in the morning protest being made equals of the late-comers. The owner of the vineyard inquires why they begrudge his generosity.

At the risk of allegorizing the story, it would be apparent to Jesus' listeners that God and Israel are being discussed. The fact that "the vineyard of the Lord of hosts is the house of Israel" (Is 5:7) is a well-known metaphor from the Hebrew Scriptures. What the day-long laborers are complaining about is the same thing that good, righteous people find upsetting about Jesus. How can you say that tax collectors and sinners are to be part of God's reign? Why should we who have striven since birth to live holy, Torah-observant lives be put on the same level as these lawless folk? Shouldn't we be considered greater than they who haven't seen the light until the last minute? The unbelievable generosity of the owner of the vineyard is Jesus' reply. God's reign is marked by graciousness because God is supremely gracious. Why should God's benevolence offend those who are good?

It seems clear that this parable, in its original setting, was addressed not to the outcasts, but rather to the law-abiding, decent people who had difficulty with Jesus' attitude toward sinners. The parable reminds them that they, too, became part of the vineyard (the people Israel) only as a result of the invitation of the owner (God's election of Israel). Now that God's reign approaches, God's generosity is being manifested even more powerfully. All who have benefited from God's kindness should rejoice at further instances of his graciousness.

It should be noted that this point is reiterated by the later evangelists who adapt the parable to refer to the admission of Gentiles, the new "latecomers," into the Church.

A similar message is conveyed by the parables of the lost sheep, the lost coin and the two debtors. Those who have wandered from their covenant with the Lord are eagerly sought by him. He desires their inclusion among his people so much that he pursues them, even when such action seems ridiculous (abandoning the ninety-nine sheep who should be guarded, for instance). The return of the lost is cause for tremendous celebration. Since they have so much to gain, the sinful naturally are more grateful for the opportunity which is now theirs than those who do not feel the need for such mercy.

It seems that Jesus desired that the good, decent, righteous people would join him in reassembling all of Israel into a united, loving oneness. These parables stress that God's mercy and generosity should also be manifested by those who claim to live by God's way. The parable of the prodigal son is a direct plea for the righteous to join in the party which must now be held to celebrate the restoration of all Israel as God's reign arrives. Will the righteous relent and celebrate? Or will they remain outside in anger? Will they imitate the boundless love of the father? Or will they follow the example of the angry, righteous older brother?

While Jesus courts the sympathies of the mass of decent, God-loving Jews, he appears less patient with those in authority who seek to use their power to keep the outcasts alienated from Jewish society. In the parable of the two sons one son refuses to do what his father commands but then changes his mind, while the other son who says he will obey does not act accordingly. Those in authority who reject the sinners are, in reality, disobeying the example of the limitless love of God. Those who eventually do turn to the Father are more dear to him than those who act hypocritically. Similarly, the parable of the wicked tenants who do not produce the fruits they should clearly is aimed at Jewish leaders. Although the parable in all three synoptics is heavily overladen with post-resurrectional perspectives, it is plain that in its original form it was a criticism of the caretakers of the master's vineyard who do not tend it properly. The parable of the Pharisee and the tax collector

(Lk 18:9–14) is likewise directed at those in power who feel that they are above needing the Lord God's mercy.

To which leaders, precisely, are these last three parables addressed? No certain answer is possible. However, they would seem to speak to those in authority who seek to maintain their status by limiting access to God's mercy. The temple leadership (in particular perhaps the Sadducees), who maintain a strict regulation of admittance to the temple precincts, would make likely candidates. The Pharisees of Bet Shammai, who tended to be more separatist than their Hillelian counterparts, would be secondary possibilities.

In any case, it is evident that Jesus understood the coming of the reign of God to require that all Jews be reunited and restored into the people of God. As a consequence of the limitless love and mercy of the Father, all could become part of the people of his reign. This message seems to have upset the righteous, whom Jesus sought to win over, and also those in authority, whom Jesus chastised for failing in their responsibilities to draw the people to God.

God's Reign Is at Hand Despite Outward Appearances

The Mustard Seed (Mk 4:30–32; Mt 13:31–32; Lk 13:18–19)
The Leaven (Mt 13:33; Lk 13:20–21)
The Sower (Mk 4:3–8; Mt 13:3–8; Lk 8:5–8)
The Patient Farmer (Mk 4:26–29)
The Friend Who Needed Help at Night (Lk 11:5–8)
The Unrighteous Judge (Lk 18:1–8)

Jesus' announcement that the reign of God was dawning gave joy to some, but provoked scorn from others. Expecting that the reign would be heralded by someone a bit more glorious than a carpenter from the backwash of Nazareth who was surrounded by fishermen, tax collectors, prostitutes, and other colorful characters, it would be hard to believe that God would be working through such riffraff. This unseemly gang was the reign of God?

Perhaps in response to such reactions, Jesus teaches that God's reign might be beginning inauspiciously, but it will have universal impact. Like the tiny mustard seed which explodes into an enormous, life-giving tree, or like leaven which transforms the entire loaf, so, too, will Jesus' activities produce cosmic consequences.

The parable of the sower dramatically expresses this conviction:

> Listen! A sower went out to sow. And as he sowed, some seed fell along the path, and the birds came and devoured it. Other seed fell on rocky ground, where it had not much soil, and immediately it sprang up, since it had no depth of soil; and when the sun rose it was scorched, and since it had no root it withered away. Other seed fell among thorns and the thorns grew up and choked it, and it yielded no grain. And other seeds fell into good soil and brought forth grain, growing up and increasing and yielding thirtyfold and sixtyfold and a hundred-fold (Mk 4:3–8).

As is characteristic of all parables, this story contains surprising twists. The sower is strangely inattentive to his task and wastefully scatters seed, not just on the tilled ground, but everywhere else as well. Consequently, only a small portion of seed actually will produce a crop. But that crop will be a tremendous one: thirty, sixty, and one hundred times more than what was first there! First-century agriculturalists would be shocked to hear of such yields. But that's the way God's reign is, Jesus asserts. It begins small but ends enormously. Despite the outward appearances of Jesus' ministry, God's reign is indeed commencing and it will have universal significance. As in the similar story of the patient farmer who waits for the seed he has planted to sprout and provide a harvest, so, too, God's reign once initiated will inexorably grow and blossom.

Taking a different approach, Jesus uses negative examples to assure his listeners that of course God will do what has been promised. If a harrassed man eventually assists his friend who needed help at night, will not God even more quickly vindicate his people by his reign? If an unrighteous judge will eventually do what is right, if only to be freed from a pestering widow, will not the righteous judge of the universe establish his reign much more speedily?

Despite outward appearances the reign of God is indeed breaking into the world, Jesus proclaims, and all of God's chosen people must be ready for it.

The Time of Decision Is Now!

The Children in the Marketplace (Mt 11:16–19; Lk 7:31–35)
Saying about the Signs of the Times (Mt 16:2–3; Lk 12:54–56)
The Budding Fig Tree (Mk 13:28; Mt 24:32–33; Lk 21:29–31)
The Great Supper (Mt 22:1–14; Lk 14:16–24)
The Servant Given Authority (Mt 24:45–51; Lk 12:42–46)
The Ten Maidens (Mt 25:1–3; see also Lk 13:24–28)
The Talents/Pounds (Mt 25:14–30; Lk 19:12–27)
The Useless Salt (Mt 5:13; Lk 14:34–35)
The Doorkeeper (Mk 13:33–37)
The Night Burglar (Mt 24:43; Lk 12:39)
The Rich Fool (Lk 12:16–21)
The Fig Tree (Lk 13:6–9)

Because of the imminent intervention of God in human history, Jesus exhorted all who would listen to realize that a time of decision, a time of crisis was upon them. They must commit themselves either to be a part of God's arriving reign or to be excluded from it. In either case, time is short!

Like the children in the marketplace who first want one thing and then another, Jesus' kinsfolk are failing to see the urgency of the matter. The signs of the times, such as wind, weather, or a budding fig tree, can be understood by all. Why, then, is it so difficult to accept that the reign of God clearly is approaching? Continuing to live as if things were always to remain as they are currently is comparable to a householder who doesn't take precautions against a night burglar, or a rich fool who believes his accumulated possessions will protect him from death, or a doorkeeper in danger of being asleep instead of watchful when his master returns.

Once more, Jesus has harsh words for those in authority who prevent God's Jewish people from perceiving the reign's significance. They are like a servant put in charge of the master's talents who buries the treasure with which they have been entrusted instead of using it to produce even more wealth. Just as a servant given authority will be punished for beating fellow servants when his Lord returns, so, too, leaders who oppress God's people will be treated similarly.

Jesus impresses on all who hear him, admirers, uncertain decent people, or contentious leaders, that God's reign is arriving whether they like it or not, whether they are ready for it or not. They must, therefore, decide how to respond. If they procrastinate too long, they might be too late, like the five of the ten maidens who didn't prepare and were not recognized by the bridegroom once he arrived. If they fail to make ready they will be like useless salt which is thrown underfoot. They will be like the expected guests who do not respond to the invitation to a great supper. Their places will be taken by those deemed unworthy. Just as a fig tree can be tended and fertilized and eventually produce fruit, Jesus prods his listeners to make up their minds in the short time remaining to them.

Decisive Action Is Needed

Going to Court (Mt 5:25–26; Lk 12:58–59)
Houses Built on Rock and Sand (Mt 7:24–27; Lk 6:47–49)
The Return of the Unclean Spirit (Mt 12:43–45; Lk 11:24–26)
Seeking the Place of Honor (Lk 14:7–11)
The Tower-builder and the King Planning a War (Lk 14:28–32)
The Corrupt Steward (Lk 16:1–7)
The Rich Man and Lazarus (Lk 16:19–31)
The Servant's Pay (Lk 17:7–10)

It appears that as Jesus' ministry progressed, his tone of urgency mounted. In ever more forceful images he warned that a well-considered, total commitment to God was called for by the crisis of the times. Vacillation could no longer be excused. One was either for God's reign or against it.

Failure to decide would be similar to someone going to court who loses the case and is imprisoned. Better to settle in advance than risk incarceration. There may be a certain exasperation on Jesus' part in some of these parables, particularly the parable of the corrupt steward. In this story, a fraudulent accountant, who is about to be exposed by an audit and dismissed, illegally halves the debts owed to his employer in order to have friends who will assist him once he is unemployed. The apparent point behind this hardly exemplary behavior (and unlike Luke's awful explanation of it in

16:8–9) is that at least this crook recognized a crisis when he saw one. At least he showed enough life to do something about it, even if it was illegal. Faced with the limitless consequences of the commencement of God's reign, how can anyone fail to react, even wrongly? How could anyone just sit there?

If a failure to take action is wrong, a half-hearted commitment to God is also unacceptable. It would be like someone who takes the easy way out and constructs a house built on sand. It will be washed away when disaster strikes, unlike the person who carefully erected a house built on rock. It would be like a tower-builder who runs out of materials halfway through, or a king planning a war who doesn't take stock of his own and the enemy's resources.

Unless Jesus' listeners would wish to receive the servant's pay of no praise for doing only their duty, they must now fully and enthusiastically dedicate themselves to God. There is no longer any excuse for delay. If they do not want to end up like the rich man (and presumably his five brothers), and wish to share in the heavenly bliss of Lazarus, then they must now pay heed to what Moses and the prophets announced: how God wants his people to live in the dawning of the reign of God.

Living in the Reign of God

The Treasure in the Field (Mt 13:44)
The Pearl of Great Price (Mt 13:45)
The Unmerciful Servant (Mt 18:23–35)
The Judgment of the Sheep and Goats (Mt 25:31–46)
The Good Samaritan (Lk 10:25–37)
Birds of the Air, Lilies of the Field (Mt 6:26–30; Lk 12:24–27)

What type of decision does Jesus want his fellow Jews to make? What sort of response does he expect from them? Since the arrival of the long-awaited reign of God is the most significant event in human history, the only adequate response is a total, uncompromised commitment to God's values.

Once one comes to accept that the reign of God is at hand, they must unswervingly pursue it, as if they had found a great treasure in the field or discovered a pearl of great price. To do this they must live and act the way God does; they must be merciful, and loving, and selfless as God himself. They must be constantly ready to forgive others' debts and to show mercy. If not, they would be like an unmerciful servant who fails to treat others the way his Lord has treated him. Whether or not they come to share in the completion of God's reign will be like the judgment of sheep and goats. Those to be included have been Godlike, while those to be excluded have acted in sinful, uncaring ways. People in the reign are those whose hearts have been permeated by God's law. One must not expect such holiness to be necessarily found in priests or temple leaders. All people, even a Good Samaritan, can reflect God's saving graciousness. The beneficence and empowering love of God is part of the very air that reign-people breathe. Like birds of the air or lilies of the field, they confidently trust their lives to the Creator of all.

Jesus' characterization of how God's chosen people are to live is rooted in a fundamental Jewish perception of God. In Judaism, God is probably best described by the Hebrew word "chesed." Unfortunately, this term has no direct English equivalent. It has several different aspects, and no one English word can capture all of them. Chesed denotes a permanent, irrevocable, unconditional, covenantal love. It often is rendered in English as "steadfast love." It also conveys a limitless mercy and forgiveness. Because God is God and Lord of all, he, by his very nature, constantly forgives and cherishes his chosen people. This nuance of chesed is frequently expressed in English as "boundless mercy" or "loving-kindness." Finally, chesed also contains the element of surprise, unexpected generosity, or undeserved graciousness. For the Jews, God's chesed is not anticipated, certainly unmerited, and always generous beyond the standards and expectations of human beings.

The significance of this profound notion of God is this: because God is a God of chesed, we, God's people, must relate to each other with the same sort of chesed that God has shown to us. The only acceptable response in gratitude to God's treatment of us is to treat one another the same way. We must share life together as God has shared his life with us. This conclusion underlies the great commandments to love God with one's whole heart and being (Dt 6:4–5) and to love one's neighbor as oneself (Lv 19:18).

Such a lifestyle is precisely what Jesus has described as living in God's reign. Those who have committed themselves totally to the way of God live a life intimately grounded in chesed, and the reign of God is operative in their lives. Jesus is calling upon his fellow Jews to be perfect Jews, to really be God's Jews, to live totally according to the values and nature of their God. In this manner, the reign of God will be present among a restored and reunited people of God, who will be prepared and assist in the imminent intervention of God in human history and in the establishment of his reign over all of creation. They will be a true light to the nations.

The Arrival of God's Reign

The Weeds Among the Wheat (Mt 13:24–30)
The Fishing Net (Mt 13:47–50)
The Days of Noah and Lot (Lk 17:26–30)
The Beatitude Sayings (Mt 5:3–12; Lk 6:20–26)

Jesus proclaims that the ultimate completion of all creation, and the universal acknowledgment of the reign of God, will see the vindication of the just and the downfall of the wicked. This idea is very much in tune with Jewish expectation, as described earlier. It is also a notion which was highly developed in the Book of Revelation, written at the end of the first century.

Since God is holy, his reign will also be holy, without stain of avarice or sin. The weeds among the wheat will be uprooted, the bad fish caught up with the good in the fishing net will be discarded, and, as in the days of Noah and Lot, the evil will be no more. Because Jesus emphasizes the golden opportunity for reinclusion into the people of God which the coming of his reign brings, it appears that the downfall of the sinful and arrogant must not be attributed to a lack of mercy on God's part. Rather, their demise is the natural and unavoidable consequence of their own decision to reject God's sovereignty. There is certainly a note of warning in these stories, but equally there is a message of hope. Hunger, thirst, mourning, and sorrow will vanish under God's reign. And, as long anticipated, the establishment of the reign of God will bring an ultimate wholeness and peace among all people.

They will be living lives reflecting the overwhelming chesed of the Lord of creation.

The Good News of Jesus

In summary, Jesus' message centered on his announcement that the long-awaited reign of God was soon to be realized. God was about to dramatically intervene in human history and, as a result, all the world would acknowledge his Lordship and live by his way. Jesus called for God's chosen people, the Jews, to recommit themselves to their covenant with God. The outcasts, the lost, the sinners—all must be lovingly embraced once more as God's own, because Israel must be restored. The honest, righteous Jews should rejoice and aid in this reconstituting of God's people. Those in authority, if true to their stewardship of the Lord's vineyard, must not only endorse but wholeheartedly participate in this renewal. A vibrant, palpable, and dynamic spirit of heartfelt chesed must unite all of the people of Israel in anticipation of the reign's arrival. On that day, all that is evil would perish, all the Gentile pagans would also come to be God's people, and all creation would be completed and at peace. In all of this, Jesus seems to have been motivated by a sense of urgency. He pressed his people to accept his message and to prepare in haste.

Having reconstructed the essential meaning of Jesus, it is now possible to relate this message to the principal features of his ministry. By doing so, some sense of how Jesus understood his own role and destiny will also be obtained.

QUESTIONS FOR REFLECTION AND DISCUSSION

1. Select a parable not discussed in detail in this chapter. Try to discern what Jesus' original listeners would have found to be a surprising twist in the story. How does the story relate to the overall picture of Jesus' message and ministry?

2. The synoptic Gospels portray Jesus' preaching to have been devoted exclusively to announcing the imminence of God's reign. The Gospel of John presents a Jesus who mostly talks about

himself. Which tradition is more rooted in the historical ministry of Jesus and which is more the result of the theological reflection of the author(s)? What impact does this have on your understanding of Jesus?

3. Describe the characteristics of the reign of God as portrayed by the parables of Jesus.

4. Is the reign of God proclaimed by Jesus something to happen in the afterlife or something occurring in the everyday world of human history? What implications does your answer have for the purpose of Christian life today?

5. What does Jesus seem to have wanted his listeners to do? How were they to respond to the news of the arrival of the reign of God?

6. What words would you use to describe the God depicted in Jesus' parables? What effect would a deep-seated, heartfelt faith in this sort of God have on your own life?

7. Visualize for yourself the kind of "mashiah" you would want to have appear today. What kind of world would you like this person to inaugurate? What would you have to do in your own life to live out this vision for the world?

Chapter Eight

GOD'S REIGN AND THE MISSION OF JESUS

Jesus and John

*O*ur rapid survey of the parables has served to demonstrate that the central focus of Jesus' ministry was the conviction that the reign of God was appearing in human history in a new and dramatic way. This realization provides tremendous insights into the meaning and purposes of the main features of that ministry as discussed in chapter six.

For instance, it was noted that early in his ministry Jesus had some association with the activity of John the Baptist. What little survives of the Baptist's preaching and actions seems to indicate that John believed a time of judgment was at hand. Those who were sinful would be swept away as chaff is separated from wheat. He called for his fellow Jews to be baptized as a sign of their repentance from sin and their determination to be accounted righteous when the day of judgment arrived.

It must be considered an historical fact that Jesus was baptized by John. Logically, he must have encountered the Baptist's view of the future. It seems reasonable to speculate that this contact with John's proclamation of the imminence of judgment prompted Jesus to announce his own views concerning what God was about to do. It seems clear that Jesus' own ministry was fully underway shortly after John's arrest.

As the parables have demonstrated, though, Jesus did not fully share the Baptist's view of things. For Jesus it was not primarily a day of judgment which was dawning, but the arrival of the fullness of God's merciful forgiveness and love. Instead of chastising the people of God to reform their sinful pasts, Jesus exhorted his kins-folk to be reconciled to each other and to reflect God's divine mercy and loving kindness in their daily lives.

This divergence between Jesus' and John's perspective may lie behind the scene in which John, ostensibly from prison, sends some of his followers to ask Jesus, "Are you he who is to come, or shall we look for another?" (Mt 11:3; Lk 7:20). Since John does not perceive Jesus as continuing his own "fire and brimstone" style of renewal, he questions whether Jesus is really an authentic pro-claimer of God's word. It seems that John has not anticipated the sort of proclamation of God's reign that Jesus has been undertak-ing. The invitation to a joyful celebration which Jesus continually offers to sinners and righteous alike has startled the Baptist as well as others.

Table-Fellowship with Sinners

The reign of God focus of Jesus' preaching provides enormous insights into all of Jesus' activities. His practice of sharing table with as yet unrepentant sinners is, in effect, a living parable. Jesus not only announces that the reign of God is like a feast to which all are invited, he actually lives out this conception by his own behav-ior. He is so convinced that the Father seeks out those who have strayed that Jesus himself especially searches for and addresses "the lost sheep of the house of Israel."

There is in his habit of engaging in social intimacies with the outcasts a remarkable consistency between Jesus' words and ac-tions. Just as the shepherd takes the initiative in hunting for the lost sheep, just as the king invites the uninvited to a great supper, just as the father has already forgiven his prodigal son, so, too, Jesus expresses his solidarity and communion with those who are es-tranged from Israel *before* they have repented. By his actions Jesus is calling for all God's Jews to act similarly because that is the way

God himself acts. Likewise, he defends his actions by insisting that he is only acting the way God does.

Clearly, the central conviction of Jesus that the reign of God was dawning, and that this reign was essentially a manifestation of God's boundless chesed, permeated both his preaching and his behavior. Jesus himself was beginning the reassembling and the restoration of scattered and divided Israel, a process which would be culminated when the reign was fully established.

The Choosing of the Twelve

The restoration of Israel appears to be the motive behind the selection of the Twelve as well. What better symbol of the people of God restored than the reappearance of the figures of the fathers of the twelve tribes of Israel? The Twelve were intended as yet another sign of the commencement of God's reign. They would preside over a reconstituted Israel, reminiscent of the ancient tribal organization of the people. This concept surely lies at the root of the Matthean saying in Mt 19:28:

> Jesus said to them, "Truly, I say to you, in the new world when the Son of Man shall sit on his glorious throne, you who have followed me will also sit on twelve thrones, judging the twelve tribes of Israel."

The Twelve as symbols of the twelve patriarchs explains several things. Since they were essentially representatives of the patriarchs, only men could be selected for this function, even though there were unquestionably women in the company of Jesus as well. Most significantly, since it was primarily their number which was important, it becomes apparent why the early Church neither remembered their identities accurately, nor assigned them unique roles in the post-resurrection period (see chapter 6). There was an interest in maintaining the number twelve, as Acts 1:15–28 demonstrates, but not in continuing their symbolic function. Once the Jesus-movement transcended its Jewish context and entered the Gentile world, the patriarchal significance of the Twelve became relatively unimportant.

In the context of Jesus' ministry, though, the selection of the Twelve is one more consequence of his mission to announce the impending reign of God to the Jewish people.

The Miracles of Jesus

Similarly, Jesus' healings, exorcisms, and other works of power should be understood as manifestations of the in-breaking reign of God. Recalling that God's reign was expected to rectify all injustices and remedy all afflictions of body and mind, Jesus' miracles are signs of the power of God beginning to complete a broken world. In this regard, Jesus' response to the Baptist's question about his identity is important:

> And Jesus answered them: "Go and tell John what you see and hear: the blind receive their sight and the lame walk, lepers are cleansed and the deaf hear, and the dead are raised up, and the poor have the good news preached to them. And blessed is he who takes no offense at me" (Mt 11:4–6; see also Lk 7:22–23).

Rather than fitting John's mold of an ardent reformer, Jesus sees his role as announcing and manifesting the merciful, loving generosity of God. The arrival of the reign of God means that creation is to be restructured according to God's gracious intentions. Jesus' miracles are the first signs of this restructuring. Jesus gives John a blessing, perhaps hoping that he will come to accept this unexpected manner of announcing God's presence. (Although this is the sheerest conjecture, one could argue that the presence of Baptist supporters in rivalry with the later evangelists indicates that John did not accept Jesus' ministry, and instructed his followers accordingly. This would be all the more reason for the Gospel writers to portray the Baptist solely as the herald of Jesus, with little stress on John's own independent, and divergent, activities.)

Be that as it may, the miracles of Jesus are not so much indications of Jesus' own identity as they are confirmations of his proclamation of the nature of God's imminent reign. As noted earlier, witnesses of these actions would conclude either that Jesus was a diabolical magician or an agent of God. If the latter, then they might be led to conclude that the reign of God was indeed at hand, although this conclusion is not inevitable. Since the writers of the Gospels of Mark and John both inveigh against a faith based solely on miracles, it is plausible that some in Jesus' own time simply understood him as a healer whom God had gifted, without perceiving the true significance of his miracles as signs of the imminence of God's reign. In any case, once more Jesus' word, deed, and mission are all inextricably rooted in his awareness of the arrival of the reign of God.

Jesus' Claims About Himself

In the synoptic Gospels, Jesus hardly ever speaks about himself. All of his energy is directed toward announcing the reign of God. The opposite is the situation in the Gospel of John in which statements beginning "I am . . ." abound. This feature seems to be a result of the theological reflection of the author of that Gospel, rather than a transcript of otherwise unknown sayings of Jesus. The synoptic tradition of Jesus being rather reticent to talk about himself is more likely historically accurate.

Although there are no explicit personal claims made by Jesus in the synoptics, there are certainly a number of implications discernible in his reign-oriented activity. First of all, Jesus, as the Gospels portray him, never shows any hesitancy about the accuracy or validity of his proclamation and his ministry. He is absolutely convinced that the reign of God is about to begin. He has no doubts at all about the nature of the God he calls his "Abba," his Father. God is merciful, loving, abounding in kindness—a God of chesed. His reign will cause these traits to permeate all creation. As far as modern scholarship is able to reconstruct, Jesus displayed no uncertainty that he had been appointed by God to herald the reign's commencement.

Now it could be argued, of course, that the evangelists have not preserved any such self-doubts on Jesus' part. This would not seem to be the case, however, because the synoptics have no difficulty in portraying Jesus as having to cope with temptation. If Jesus can be depicted as wrestling with temptation, why not have him question what his mission was? The synoptics all refer to a temptation of Jesus in the wilderness near the commencement of his ministry, and they likewise are unanimous in describing him as praying in the Garden of Gethsemane for an escape from impending disaster. While the historical details surrounding these events will never be fully known, in each case Jesus is tempted to deviate from his mission, to be unfaithful to his calling. He never seems to doubt what that calling is, but he must resist the impulse to abandon it.

It cannot be doubted that Jesus felt commissioned by God to announce the onset of the reign of God. Equally, it is certain that Jesus felt impelled to describe that reign as one of reconciliation, mercy, friendship, and love. Since Jesus clearly envisioned the beginning of a new age, the conclusion is unavoidable that Jesus understood his mission to be that of the "mashiah." He was the Jew anointed by God to announce the beginning of his reign. By his words and actions Jesus actually inaugurates the reign, albeit in embryonic form, and the power of God's completing and creative love is manifest.

The Jewish context of this perspective must be strongly emphasized. The term mashiah, for all its varied interpretations, was never equated in Judaism with divinity. The mashiah was to be a human person, a Jew, chosen by God to herald his reign. Only in the light of the resurrection experience did Jesus' followers begin to identify Jesus as divine, and the term "messiah" (the anglicized form of "mashiah") took on previously absent divine connotations. The two words will be carefully differentiated in these paragraphs in order to distinguish the pre-resurrectional Jewish conceptions of mashiah from the post-resurrectional Christian understandings of messiah (or Christ).

Jesus' whole ministry hinges on his apparently certain self-awareness of his role as mashiah. He is unshakeably persuaded that the reign of God is near at hand and that he has the God-appointed duty both to announce this tremendous news and to ready his people for the reign's arrival. Nonetheless, the synoptic Gospels do not portray Jesus as naming himself mashiah. He may have deliberately discouraged that title's usage because of its resonances with military or dynastic expectations, whereas Jesus saw himself as a mashiah reflecting God's healing reconciliation. This might be preserved in the Marcan Jesus' silencing of Peter after his exclamation about Jesus' identity (Mk 8:29–32). A term that would mislead people into thinking of a return of the Davidic monarchy would distract people from Jesus' true message.

Other titles may or may not have been applied to Jesus in the course of his ministry. He may have been called "lord" in the sense of "sir." The word's reference to the Lord transcendently enthroned at the right hand of God would not arise until after the resurrection. In any case, Jesus did not call himself "lord." He could conceivably have been called a prophet. Jesus certainly would fit the definition of a prophet as someone who speaks on behalf of God. The title, however, would be an insufficient designation for the herald of the new age, and, once again, Jesus does not seem to have employed it about himself. It is possible that Jesus may have been called "son of God," meaning one beloved of God as David and Israel were called sons of God. The title would, of course, assume even more significance after the resurrection when Jesus would be described as Son of God in a very unique sense. And although the term would be very appropriate for one who often called God his Abba-Father, it does not appear that Jesus ever referred to himself as uniquely Son of God.

The only term which Jesus may have used to describe himself is "son of man." In the common usage of the Aramaic which Jesus spoke the expression has a couple of colloquial meanings. It can refer either to the speaker ("the son of man is tired," rather than "I am tired") or to a third person who is being discussed ("the son of man [over there] is tired"). Certainly Jesus could have used the expression in either of these senses on many occasions. In addition the phrase may also have a reign of God connotation:

> I saw in the night visions, and behold, with the clouds of heaven there came one like a son of man, and he came to the Ancient of Days and was presented before him. And to him was given dominion and glory and kingdom, that all peoples, nations, and languages should serve him; his dominion is an everlasting dominion, which shall not pass away, and his kingdom one that shall not be destroyed (Dan 7:13–14).

This symbolic conception from the Book of Daniel refers to the ultimate establishment of God's reign. The "son of man" figure probably represents the people of Israel as a whole and, therefore, is consonant with the tradition that eventually all the nations would acknowledge the sovereignty of Israel and of Israel's God. It is hotly debated among scholars whether this "son of man" might also have been related to the mashiah-figure by the time of Jesus. If so, then Jesus' usage of the expression would be quite harmonious with his apparent mission.

Whether or not Jesus used the term son of man to refer to himself as the anointed herald of God's reign, there can be little doubt as to how Jesus understood the purposes of his ministry. Although he never explicitly claimed specific titles, he clearly acted as a mashiah with the duty to usher in the gracious and peaceful reign of God.

Opposition to Jesus

Perceiving Jesus as herald of the New Age also clarifies the reasons why various peoples and groups opposed him. As a consequence of his conviction that the reign of God was dawning, Jesus would anticipate that his mission was of significance for Gentiles, too. Although not addressing them directly, Jesus' preparation of Israel for the reign's arrival would ultimately mean the salvation of the Gentiles. When the reign fully commenced, Gentiles would acknowledge the sovereignty of God and, therefore, would be accounted righteous. With this universalistic dimension in mind, Jesus seems to have been just as sympathetic to the few Gentiles who crossed his path as he was to his fellow Jews. His preaching about the reign of God promised a global reconciliation of all humanity. God's Jews should now treat even the oppressor Romans with the same mercy and love they were to show to one another.

This attitude would quickly win the enmity of the Zealots and the Essenes. The Romans were to be destroyed, not befriended. The pagans were to be shunned, avoided, and finally defeated. If there is any reliability in later rabbinic descriptions of them, the Bet Shammai Pharisees would also be offended. According to rabbinic characterizations of their view, Gentiles were categorically unrighteous and would not be saved in the world to come.

Sadducees would be displeased with Jesus' attitude toward the temple and the priesthood. As will be seen in chapter nine, even the temple was to give way before the onset of God's reign. In Jesus' view, a perfected people of Israel would form a new, more fitting, dwelling place for God.

In varying degrees, Pharisees were evidently critical of Jesus' perspective on the law. Jesus seems to have asserted that even the law, which he himself venerated and observed, was to be practiced in the light of the emerging reign of God. Jesus' attitude relativized the Torah's importance, making it subordinate to the in-breaking reign. Thus, Jesus could call for an intensification of those Torah-principles which the reign would see perfected (such as an attitude of mercy toward all), while at the same time ignoring those (possibly Shammaitic-) Pharisaic interpretations which were contrary to the reign's values (such as shunning the wicked). It is unclear to what extent the Bet Hillel Pharisees disagreed with Jesus, mainly because it still remains next to impossible to isolate the divergent Pharisaic traditions. At the least, it seems that they held views which were somewhat compatible with Jesus' application of the Torah, but they did not share his conviction in the imminence of the reign of God. They would, therefore, also question whether the law could be relativized before a reign whose imminence was debatable.

In any event, the opposition which Jesus faced can largely be understood in the context of his proclamation of the reign of God, and, in particular, with the demands which Jesus declared that reign imposed on God's people. Still unclear, though, is why some opponents finally decided to assist in arranging Jesus' execution. The events leading up to the death of Jesus must now be considered. These include not only the occurrences in Jerusalem, but also Jesus' own awareness of the likelihood of his death should he bring his ministry to the holy city.

Jesus' Attitude Toward His Death

All of the Gospels indicate that Jesus predicted that he would die in Jerusalem. The synoptics and John differ in their presentation of this tradition—the synoptics providing precise details while John speaks in very general terms. As mentioned in chapter two, it seems reasonable to deduce that Jesus warned his disciples that his death would be all but inevitable once they arrived in Jerusalem. As we will see, he probably also indicated in general terms that God would ultimately vindicate him even in the face of death. The synoptic evangelists, knowing what had transpired after the fact, added the details regarding the passion and resurrection to what had originally been less precise statements. The original, imprecise predictions were more closely preserved, though with theological overlays, in John.

How would Jesus know he was likely to die? Being an intelligent man, he was doubtless aware that his message would be most challenging to the leadership of the temple. Furthermore, Jerusalem was the site of one of the residences of the Roman prefect, Pontius Pilate. With his reputation for crucifying potentially incendiary Jews with great dispatch, Jesus would certainly see Pilate as dangerous. Since Pilate also appointed the high priest, the temple authorities and the Sadducees were known to act to please their Roman overlords and to keep the peace. Faced with such facts, it would be difficult to imagine that Jesus would *not* foresee the almost inevitable outcome of his Jerusalem mission. It is very plausible, in fact, that Jesus predicted that he would be crucified. Since Jews in Jerusalem were under the authority of the Romans, and since Romans executed Jews by torturing them to death in crucifixion, any death sentence of Jesus would take an unavoidable form.

Knowing these things, why did Jesus go to Jerusalem? How would Jesus come to deal with the practically certain knowledge of his own anguished death? What significance or purpose would such a death have?

The answer to the first question is obvious. Jerusalem, the capital of the Jewish people, the site of God's temple, would have to receive the good news of God's approaching reign. If all of God's chosen people were to be prepared to further the in-breaking of God's reign of justice and peace, then the Jews of Jerusalem must also be summoned. Those in the highest positions of authority, the temple-leaders, must be called forth to use their power in the reign's behalf.

Since Jesus is convinced of his mission as mashiah, a proclamation to Jerusalem is a necessary aspect of that mission. Even if a horrible death is to be the likely outcome of such a venture, Jerusalem must be addressed with the good news. Still, it is unthinkable that Jesus would have simply marched into the holy city on a futile and suicidal mission. Could Jesus, who unquestionably had an intimate understanding of God as a loving, empowering Father, possibly have imagined a God who would send him on a mission doomed to end only in failure and disgrace? Could any human being, especially a pious Jew like Jesus, be at peace with the notion that God would assign someone a fool's errand with no possible hope of success or accomplishment? Since Jesus plainly foresaw his own death, it is necessary to presume that he would have had to assign it some meaning, some purpose in God's plan. Furthermore, the significance attributed to his approaching death most likely would be related to Jesus' goals in heralding the reign of God.

It was mentioned earlier that some Jews in Jesus' time expected that there would be a time of troubles, an ordeal or a trial, that would precede the climactic intervention of God in human history. This period of ultimate crisis would test severely the faithfulness of God's people. Only the remnant who remained true to God would be vindicated. There is evidence that this train of thought was present in Jesus' ministry as well. Although the synoptic passages which preserve Jesus' teaching about the ordeal (Mk 13:3–37; Mt 24:4–36; Lk 21:8–36) are heavily colored by the evangelists' concerns and post-70 situations, it seems likely that Jesus spoke of an impending trial for those faithful to God: "For there will be such tribulation as has not yet been from the beginning of the creation which God created until now, and never will be. And if the Lord had not shortened the days, no human being would be saved . . ." (Mk 13:19–20). Jesus' disciples must expect to be tried and beaten (Mk 13:9–11), and families will betray their own members to death (13:12), but "he who endures to the end will be saved" (13:13). It is plausible that Jesus deduced that the temple and Jerusalem would be destroyed by the Romans should the hatred of the Zealots come to prevail (13:2). Such destruction would mark the supreme crisis and trial of God's people.

Given this expectation of an ordeal to precede the full arrival of the reign of God, it would seem logical to conclude that Jesus saw his own imminent death as the commencement of that time of troubles. His personal sufferings would test his own faithfulness to God. By challenging Jerusalem to accept the beginning of God's

reign of reconciliation and mercy, Jesus would either spark a wonderful renewal among God's people or precipitate the ordeal, beginning with his own testing, which would set the stage for God's
intervention.

This perspective is visible in several synoptic passages:

> But Jesus said to them, "You do not know what you are asking.
> Are you able to drink the cup that I drink, or to be baptized
> with the baptism with which I am baptized" (Mk 10:38)?

> "I came to cast a fire upon the earth; and would that it were
> already kindled! I have a baptism to be baptized with; and how
> I am constrained until it is accomplished" (Lk 12:49).

> And as they were eating, he took bread, and blessed, and broke
> it, and gave it to them, and said, "Take, this is my body." And
> he took a cup, and when he had given thanks he gave it to
> them, and they all drank of it. And he said to them, "This is my
> blood of the covenant, which is poured out for many. Truly, I
> say to you, I shall not drink again of the fruit of the vine until
> that day when I drink it new in the kingdom of God" (Mk
> 14:22–25).

> And he said, "Abba, Father, all things are possible to thee;
> remove this cup from me; yet not what I will, but what thou
> wilt" (Mk 14:36).

The first two passages use the metaphors of cup, fire, and baptism
all in reference to Jesus' ordeal. The fire which Jesus will set will
spark the climactic trial of all the world. The cup that he will drink
is not an easy one to receive, yet it is something in which he is
ready to immerse (baptize) himself. (It might be noted that this
latter image of Jesus' death as his baptism is developed by later
writers in reference to Christian initiation: "Do you not know that
all of us who have been baptized into Christ Jesus were baptized
into his death?" [Rom 6:3].)

At the Last Supper, it has become clear that the leaders of
Jerusalem have rejected Jesus' message and that his death is inevitable. Jesus identifies bread and wine with his body and blood which
will be broken and poured out for many. Yet, ultimately Jesus will
be vindicated and will feast with the faithful in the reign of God.

Nonetheless, Jesus' approaching suffering is his greatest trial, which he wishes could be avoided.

An important perspective in this regard can be garnered by examining the passages which have been traditionally titled the Lord's Prayer. This prayer appears in differing forms in Mt 6:9–13 and Lk 11:2–4. The Lucan version is shorter and probably more closely approximates the length of Jesus' own prayer. However, while the Matthean form has additions supplied by the evangelist, the source material may be closer to the setting of Jesus' ministry. By taking these factors into account, as well as considering the Jewish conceptions which underlie the evangelists' usage of Greek, this reconstruction emerges:

> Father,
> may your name be sanctified,
> may your reign come;
> give us today the bread-of-tomorrow,
> and forgive us our debts as we have forgiven our debtors,
> and do not bring us to the trial.

Clearly, an expectation and a longing for the reign of God dominates the prayer. In typically Jewish fashion, God is called upon to sanctify his name, to show forth his sovereign glory, by bringing his reign into existence. He is requested to bestow today the "bread-of-tomorrow," a metaphor for the life of his reign. The petitioner asks God for the merciful bounty of the reign, for he, too, has tried to be true to the merciful values of that reign.

Finally the hope is expressed that the ordeal before the reign's onset might be avoided, and, if not, that the petitioner will not fall into faithlessness during it. The force of this request for Jesus might be captured by paraphrasing this line in the first person, and by imagining it on Jesus' lips: "And do not bring *me* to the trial." Perhaps, the Lord's Prayer dates from a point in Jesus' ministry when there was still a possibility that Jerusalem might accept his message. Maybe the ordeal could yet be forestalled. Whether this is true or not, Jesus' prayer certainly is a plea for God to establish his reign as speedily, and as painlessly, as possible.

And so, Jesus sets his face toward Jerusalem. It is his destiny as mashiah to proclaim the reign of God in the holy city. Although death is the most probable, if not inevitable, outcome of his activities there, Jesus resolves to remain faithful to his mission. His death will be in the service of the approaching reign and for the many who will be saved by the reign's arrival. His own, personal ordeal will trigger the calamitous time of troubles which might cause suffering for his followers and the destruction of the holy city, but which would lead inevitably to the glorious intervention of the reign of God. Jesus himself, by remaining faithful to his mission, trusts that the God who loves him ultimately will vindicate him. Israel will be restored, the dead will be raised, the Gentiles will turn from idolatry, and all of creation will be united in the loving embrace of the Creator of all. Thus, while Jesus does not desire to die, and hopes it might be avoided, he accepts its increasing likelihood as something necessary to bring the reign of God into being.

QUESTIONS FOR REFLECTION AND DISCUSSION

1. Jesus extended friendship to sinners *before* they repented. Why would Jesus' belief in the imminence of the reign of God cause him to act this way? What implications does this have for today's believers?

2. If his miracles provoked either a belief that God was working through Jesus or that Jesus was in league with demonic forces, what caused people to eventually conceive of Jesus in divine terms? What significance did his miracles have in terms of his proclamation of the reign of God?

3. What was Jesus' mission?

4. What was the reason, in the context of Jesus' ministry, for the selection of the Twelve? Does this reasoning explain the less frequent mention of the Twelve in the post-resurrectional Church? How?

5. Jesus' belief in the coming and in the nature of the reign of God caused him to relativize the importance of some of the religious structures of his day, such as the temple and the Torah, even though he personally revered them. How would such an attitude manifest itself in today's Church? What things might seem of less importance in the light of a conviction that the reign of God was in the process of permeating all of creation?

6. Discuss the meanings of the pre-resurrectional Jewish term "mashiah" and the post-resurrectional Christian term "messiah." Why is it important to make distinctions between these concepts?

7. What example does Jesus' attitude toward his all but inevitable execution in Jerusalem give to modern Christians as we ponder our own inevitable deaths?

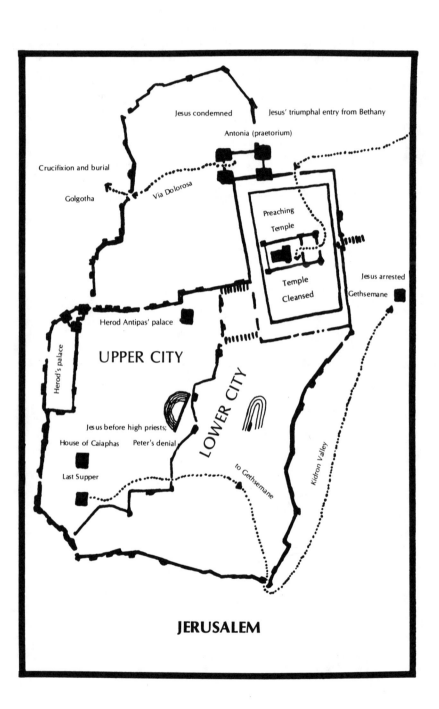

Jesus condemned   Jesus' triumphal entry from Bethany

Antonia (praetorium)

Crucifixion and burial

Golgotha   Via Dolorosa

Preaching

Temple

Temple   Jesus arrested
Cleansed   Gethsemane

Herod Antipas' palace

Herod's palace

UPPER CITY

LOWER CITY

Jesus before high priests;

House of Caiaphas   Peter's denial

to Gethsemane   Kidron Valley

Last Supper

JERUSALEM

Chapter Nine

THE DEATH OF JESUS

The climactic events of Jesus' ministry began with his arrival in Jerusalem. Despite the various dangers confronting him, Jesus brings his message of the commencement of God's reign to the holy city. This chapter will explore the Gospel accounts of the events which transpired in Jerusalem, particularly focusing on the passion narratives. A reading of all four passion narratives before proceeding may be helpful. Refer to Mk 14:32—15:47; Mt 26:36—27:61; Lk 22:39—23:56; Jn 18:1—19:42.

The Temple

All four of the Gospels indicate that Jesus entered Jerusalem riding on a colt amid the cries of onlookers who cheer the arrival of a king (Mk 11:7-10; Mt 21:7-9; Lk 19:35-40; Jn 12:12-15). The scene is related to Zech 9:9:

> Rejoice greatly, O daughter of Zion!
> Shout aloud, O daughter of Jerusalem!
> Lo, your king comes to you,
> triumphant and victorious is he,
> humble and riding on an ass,
> on a colt, the foal of an ass.

Since this tradition is found in all the Gospels, and since Jesus' entire ministry has been directed at proclaiming an approaching reign, this manner of entry seems quite plausible. Whether Jesus deliberately patterned his arrival after the Zechariah passage is not clear, but it is certain that within a week's time he was executed as a pretender "King of the Jews." The conclusion that Jesus reached the holy city intending to announce dramatically the inauguration of the reign of God is difficult to escape. This notion is borne out in the events which followed.

Once more, the Gospels are unanimous in relating a disturbance caused by Jesus in the temple precincts (although John's Gospel situates the event at the beginning of Jesus' ministry; see Mk 11:15–19; Mt 21:12–13; Lk 19:45–48; Jn 2:13–22). However, as occurs frequently, all of the evangelists interpret this event according to the circumstances of their own era. Their interpretations do not necessarily coincide with the event's original significance or purpose in the ministry of Jesus. Consider the Marcan account:

> And they came to Jerusalem. And he entered the temple and began to drive out those who sold and those who bought in the temple, and he overturned the tables of the money-changers and the seats of those who sold pigeons; and he would not allow anyone to carry anything through the temple. And he taught, and said to them, "Is it not written, 'My house shall be called a house of prayer for all the nations'? But you have made it a den of robbers." And the chief priests and the scribes heard it and sought for a way to destroy him; for they feared him, because all the multitude was astonished at his teaching (Mk 11:15–18).

The evangelist has understood Jesus' actions in the light of Jer 7:11, "Has this house, which is called by my name, become a den of robbers in your eyes?" He asserts that Jesus enables all the world to have access to God by using the words of Is 56:7, "for my house will be called a house of prayer for all peoples."

This interpretation, as valid as it might be for the Marcan church, does not seem suitable for the ministry of Jesus. It must be remembered that in Jesus' time more Jews lived outside Palestine than within it. For Jews living elsewhere, a pilgrimage to Jerusalem to pray in the temple was a wonderful and infrequent occurrence. Coming from great distances, such pilgrims would not haul along with them the animals to be used in the temple sacrifices. They would purchase them on the spot. In addition, to make these purchases they would not be able to use the money minted in Alexandria or Rome, but they would have to convert them into the local currency. This was the function of the money-changers. Hence, the merchants and money-changers were an absolutely vital part of the temple's existence. Their operations in the outermost courts of the temple were not considered to be scandalous or unsightly. On the contrary, the temple provided an essential economic-base for the city's residents. Attempts to accuse the money-changers of fraudulent business practices as an explanation for Jesus' actions miss the point. Jesus would not have expected people who earned their livelihood by selling and money-changing to abandon their source of income. They would be expected to be back in operation within five minutes of Jesus' departure. His actions must be seen as prophetic signs. They were meant to deliver a symbolic message to those on hand, a message not clearly conveyed by the evangelists' presentations.

It is possible to perceive two general symbolisms in Jesus' behavior. First, his actions may relate to Zech 14:21, "And there shall no longer be a trader in the house of the Lord of hosts on that day." If, however briefly, the merchants have been driven from the temple precincts, then a symbolic statement has been made that the day of the Lord has arrived. The hour of the in-breaking of the reign of God is at hand. And if that epochal moment has come, then Jesus must be seen as the mashiah of that reign. He has, in effect, presented his credentials to the Jerusalem community. The reign of God is beginning because it has been proclaimed by God's anointed agent.

Second, the action of overturning tables and driving folks away has a more physical, more violent significance. It is a sign of destruction. Jesus has symbolically asserted that the temple is doomed to destruction, or, at the very least, to obsolescence. With the coming of the reign of God, the temple would be unnecessary because God will dwell directly with his people. Jesus may have seen his own role as building a living temple composed of the restored and reunited people of Israel among whom God will reside in intimate unity. This temple of the reign of God would be the perfect and ultimate dwelling place of the Lord of hosts.

That Jesus also intends to warn that the temple will be destroyed is very likely when one recalls the explicit words to that effect in Mk 13:2 (see also Mt 24:2; Lk 21:6). In addition, all the Gospels preserve in a somewhat confused manner that Jesus was accused of threatening to destroy the temple:

> And some stood up and bore false witness against him, saying, "We heard him say, 'I will destroy this Temple that is made with hands, and in three days I will build another not made with hands' " (Mk 14:57–58; see also Mt 26:60–61).

> Jesus answered them, "Destroy this temple, and in three days I will raise it up" (Jn 2:19).

In both the synoptic and the Johannine traditions, the original setting has been overlaid with post-resurrectional perspectives, as the key words "in three days" reveal. Nonetheless, they both preserve the concept from Jesus' ministry that the temple was to be destroyed, and that Jesus himself was building another, more perfect temple.

Whether Jesus' actions were seen as only noting the temple's relative unimportance next to the imminence of God's reign, or if they were understood to denote the temple's approaching doom, the temple leadership would be threatened. In either case, the authority of the priestly, aristocratic class of Sadducees was imperiled. Furthermore, when one compares Jesus' actions with a similar situation in the Old Testament, it becomes clear that Jesus' deeds would provoke a lethal retaliation.

> "Thus says the Lord, 'If you will not listen to me, to walk in my law which I have set before you, and to heed the words of my servants the prophets whom I send to you urgently, though you have not heeded, then I will make [the temple of Solomon] like Shiloh, and I will make this city a curse for all the nations of the earth.' " The priests and prophets and all the people heard Jeremiah speaking these words in the house of the Lord. And when Jeremiah had finished speaking all that the Lord had commanded him to speak to all the people, then the priests and the prophets and all the people laid hold of him, saying, "You shall die!" (Jer 26:4–8).

Jesus, by symbolically demonstrating that the reign of God was at hand and that the temple's days were numbered, has issued a direct challenge to the authority of the temple leaders. Perhaps considering him a dangerous rabble-rouser, they seem to have quickly decided, in the words of Mark, "to seek for a way to destroy him" (Mk 11:18).

Jesus Before the Authorities

It would appear that within a few days time the authorities made their move by taking Jesus into custody while he was praying at night in a garden outside the city. Although there are variations of detail among the Gospel accounts, the overall outline of the events in the garden is fairly consistent. An armed force is led by Judas to the secluded spot. It is not clear if the arresters are "from the chief priests, scribes, and elders" (Mk 14:43; Mt 26:47) or are "soldiers and some officers" (Jn 18:3) which could only refer to Romans. Some sort of collaboration between the temple leadership and the Roman prefect seems most likely.

In addition, there appears to have been some measure of violent resistance. All the Gospels report the severing of an ear of a slave of the high priest, although they each offer different embellishments. Mark and Matthew simply assert that someone cut off the slave's ear (Mk 14:47; Mt 26:51). Luke informs us that the slave's right ear was amputated (Lk 22:50), and John relates that Peter was the sword-slinger and that the slave was named Malchus (Jn 18:10). Similarly, all the Gospels show Jesus reacting to the violence in different ways. The Marcan Jesus ignores what has occurred (Mk 14:48), the Matthean Jesus declares that the violent will perish in violence and that he could summon twelve legions of angels to his defense if he so desired (Mt 26:52–53). Since the Roman Empire had only four legions in the environs of Palestine, an attack by twelve angelic legions could certainly be considered as overkill. The Lucan Jesus declares "no more of this!" and heals the wounded slave (Lk 22:51), and the Johannine Jesus instructs Peter to sheath his sword because Jesus must drink the cup which the Father has given him (Jn 18:11). While this scene clearly shows the individual perspectives of the later evangelists, the overall tradition seems clear. Jesus was arrested in the garden and taken away, apparently abandoned by all his followers.

In a related fashion, all the Gospels recount that shortly after Jesus' arrest, Peter denied him three times (Mk 14:66–72; Mt 26: 69–75; Lk 22:54–62; Jn 18:15–18,25–27). Once more there are individual variations: the cock crows twice in Mark but only once elsewhere (Mk 14:72); somehow the Lucan Jesus who is inside turns and sees Peter outside in the courtyard just as the cock crows (Lk 22:61); and the denials in John's Gospel do not occur one after the other, but are interrupted by Jesus' questioning by the high priest (Jn 18:19–24). Despite these particular alterations, the tradition that Peter denied Jesus is undoubtedly a solidly established tradition by the time the Gospels were composed and should be understood as an historical event.

The reason why the happenings in the garden and the denials by Peter are preserved with relative unanimity seems plain. There were followers of Jesus who witnessed both of these events and so were able to recount what had happened later. In subsequent decades when the evangelists wrote, these two traditions were widely known and were incorporated into their Gospels, albeit with individual modifications and additions.

The same cannot be said of Jesus' hearing either before Jewish authorities or before Pilate. There is no harmony at all in the Gospels' presentation of these occurrences. In Matthew, Jesus is led to the house of Caiaphas, the high priest (Mt 26:57), but in John he is brought instead to the house of Annas, Caiaphas' father-in-law (Jn 18:13). In Mark and Matthew "the chief priests and the whole council" condemn Jesus to death at a clandestine night meeting (Mk 14:55–65; Mt 26:59–68). In Luke a hearing before "the assembly of . . . both the chief priests and scribes" does not occur until dawn (Lk 22:66), while in John Jesus is questioned only by "the high priest," not an entire council, and then, strangely, he is sent by Annas to "Caiaphas the high priest" who apparently had already interrogated him (Jn 18:19,24). The various charges brought against Jesus are similarly discordant.

The reason for this confusion is obvious. There were no disciples of Jesus present at his hearings who could subsequently launch traditions about what had happened. All that Jesus' followers knew was that he was taken away by force in the night and that by nine o'clock the next morning he was being publicly displayed in crucifixion outside the city walls as a pretender king. The details of what transpired between those two points had to be guessed at both by Jesus' friends and by the later evangelists.

In reconstructing the actions and motives of the participants in these events, it is extremely important to bear in mind the theological nature of the Gospels. As has been repeatedly stressed, the evangelists all are writing from the perspective of their experience of the resurrected Christ. Their accounts of Jesus before the authorities are dominated by their own theological insights into the significance of Jesus' death. Furthermore, as has been seen elsewhere in the Gospels, their presentations are colored by the debates and arguments taking place at the time their works are being composed. This becomes very evident when the various charges brought against Jesus are listed and examined, particularly in this passage from Mark:

> Again the high priest asked him, "Are you the Christ, the Son of the Blessed?" And Jesus said, "I am; and you will see the Son of Man seated at the right hand of Power, and coming with the clouds of heaven." And the high priest tore his garments, and said, "Why do we still need witnesses? You have heard his blasphemy. What is your decision?" And they all condemned him as deserving death (Mk 14:61–64; see also Mt 26:63–66; Lk 22:67–71).

This "trial scene" may be the one most familiar to modern-day Christians. That Jewish leaders wanted to see Jesus dead because he had blasphemed is a common opinion. However, this passage is dominated by post-resurrectional ways of thinking about Jesus, and, therefore, must not be taken to represent an entirely accurate account of what occurred before Jesus' death. In particular, the high priest's question, "Are you the Christ, the Son of the Blessed?" (or in Mt 26:63: ". . . tell us if you are the Christ, the Son of God"), certainly originates in that time after the resurrection when Christians have come to understand Messiah/Christ as synonymous with divinity. We have seen that the synoptic Gospels contain no claim to divinity on the part of Jesus, although he certainly saw his mission to be that of the mashiah, the herald of God's reign. While some might have doubted that assertion, it is hard to imagine how anyone would have considered Jesus as divine before the resurrection. The high priest's question thus becomes unlikely, if not impossible, in the context of Jesus' ministry.

In addition, Jewish tradition does not consider claiming to be the mashiah as blasphemous. Jesus acting as mashiah would not provoke cries of blasphemy. It is blasphemy to assert that there is more than one God, thereby denying that God is one. Again, we have seen no hint of such an assertion in the synoptic accounts of Jesus' ministry.

It might be noted that similar points could be made about another incident in which the blasphemy charge arises. In Mk 2:5–11 Jesus is accused of blasphemy when he declares that a paralytic's sins are forgiven. In fact, Jesus has simply announced the forgiveness of the man's sins, just as the priests in the temple did daily. He does not claim to have made himself equal to God. In the context of Jesus' ministry, some might have questioned his right to make such pronouncements, but would not see him as committing blasphemy. By the time of the evangelists, however, the debate about blasphemy would be occurring. Christians, claiming to forgive sins in the name of the Lord Jesus, would be offensively blasphemous to non-Christian Jews. Jesus' reference to the Son of Man figure from the Book of Daniel in both the healing of the paralytic and the trial scene should be understood as declarations about the imminent future. Since the reign of God is arriving, the time for the forgiveness of all sins is at hand, and with the reign's arrival the power of the Son of Man would be clearly manifested to all. Such assertions would certainly be debatable during Jesus' ministry, but would not be blasphemy.

However, debates about blasphemy were clearly in progress at the time the Gospels were written. Christians were arguing that Jesus was the unique and divine Son of God, while Jews were perceiving that claim as a blasphemous violation of monotheism. The high priest's question represents the issues being fought about later in the first century, not ones current in the ministry of Jesus. Having no traditions about what happened once Jesus was taken into custody, the evangelists have filled in the gaps by imagining the scene in terms of their own situations. It must be concluded that the charge of blasphemy, in the strict sense of the term, was not the reason for Jesus' execution. Jesus may have been opposed for the things he had done and said in his role as mashiah, but not, it would appear, because he had claimed to be divine.

Charges brought against Jesus in other passages may provide more insight into his appearances before the authorities:

> Now the chief priests and the whole council sought testimony against Jesus to put him to death; but they found none. For many bore false witness against him, and their witness did not agree. And some stood up and bore false witness against him, saying, "We heard him say, 'I will destroy this temple that is made with hands, and in three days I will build another, not made with hands.' " Yet not even so did their testimony agree (Mk 14:55–59; see also Mt 26:59–61).

> "If we let him go on thus, everyone will believe in him, and the Romans will come and destroy both our holy place and our nation." But one of them, Caiaphas, who was high priest that year, said to them, "You know nothing at all; you do not understand that it is expedient for you that one man should die for the people, and that the whole nation should not perish" (Jn 11:48–50).

> Then the whole company of them arose, and brought him before Pilate. And they began to accuse him, saying, "We found this man perverting our nation, and forbidding us to give tribute to Caesar, and saying that he himself is Christ a king." And Pilate asked him, "Are you the King of the Jews?" (Lk 23:1–3a).

The Marcan passage, which occurs just before the mention of blasphemy discussed above, might be more deeply rooted in the actual events surrounding Jesus' death. While the confused testimony against Jesus may echo the evangelist's own confusion about what really happened, the charge of threatening the destruction of the temple is apparently based on something Jesus actually did and said. Although this temple-tradition is far from clear, it seems certain that Jesus discussed the temple's fate, and his own symbolically destructive deeds in the temple precincts indicate what that fate would be. Whether Jesus asserted that the temple was doomed because of the onset of the reign of God or because of violent devastation wrought by the Romans, he had attacked both the status quo and the authority of the priestly aristocratic class. Inciting or even predicting such upheaval would invariably be viewed as dangerous. Thus, the Johannine verses may well be grounded in historical reality. Some of the temple leadership could very plausibly have argued that Jesus must be eliminated lest he provoke a disastrous Roman retaliation against all the Jewish people. As collaborators with the Romans in keeping the peace, the Sadduceic aristocracy moved to crush an incipient threat against both stability and their own power. They had enough trouble dealing with the criticisms of the Pharisees, Essenes, and Zealots. The frequent mention in all accounts of the high priest confirms this perspective. As an appointee of the Roman prefect, his involvement in an effort to remove potential disrupters of the peace is only natural. His presence in all the Gospels confirms that Jesus was regarded principally as a threat to peace, to the security of the temple, and to political stability.

Romans, of course, would not be concerned with the niceties of Jewish spiritual tradition. Someone who proclaimed the imminence of the reign of God would not be understood in Jewish religious terms, but as a political revolutionary. For a Roman, the reign of God would represent the restoration of a Davidic, independent Israelite monarchy and the overthrow of Roman sovereignty. Pontius Pilate must be understood from this point of view. The Lucan passage above presents three charges leveled against Jesus in the presence of Pilate. They all have political resonances which would make Pilate regard Jesus as dangerous.

While "perverting our nation" has the religious meaning of teaching falsely, and no doubt temple authorities regarded Jesus' views on the temple's destruction as falsehoods, spoken on the lips of collaborators with the Roman occupation it could also describe one who disturbs the peace. Obviously "forbidding tribute to Caesar" and claiming to be "Christ a king" are tantamount to inciting revolt. It is certainly no accident that Pilate's question "Are you the King of the Jews?" appears in all the Gospels (Mk 15:2; Mt 27:11; Lk 23:3; Jn 18:33). He is assessing if Jesus is an incendiary Zealot.

Again, the Gospel writers have no eyewitness testimony on which to base their presentation of this scene. They know that

Jesus had to have been brought before Pilate because he plainly had to have ordered Jesus' crucifixion. Since it was known that Jesus was crucified under a sign proclaiming him as "King of the Jews" (Mk 15:26; Mt 27:37; Lk 23:38; Jn 19:19), then the subject of kingship must have been part of Pilate's questioning. Believing through their post-resurrectional awareness that Jesus was indeed a king, the evangelists all show Jesus to some extent affirming the title. But, amazingly, Pilate immediately proceeds to seek to release Jesus.

This depiction of Pilate is quite unrealistic. Here is a Jew who has been brought before him by his own temple subordinates. They have declared this Jesus to be hostile to Rome. Upon examination Jesus asserts his kingship, an arrogance that would have quickly provoked a crucifixion without a second thought. Extrabiblical sources confirm that Pilate was not slow to crucify Jews who were deemed dangerous to Roman interests. Pilate was eventually removed from his office because he ordered the massacre of a group of Samaritans in 35 C.E. The reality of what happened to Jesus seems quite simple. Presented as a potential or actual troublemaker, who has talked about a reign, and who caused a disturbance in the temple, Jesus was quickly and efficiently dispatched to the cross. Since it is likely that Jesus was brought to Pilate sometime after dawn and was crucified at around 9 A.M., during which time Jesus was scourged and forced to carry his crossbeam out of the city, the decision before Pilate must have been resolved fairly quickly.

Why then do the Gospels present Pilate in such a favorable light? It is widely agreed that there is a tendency in the Gospels to shift the burden of the guilt for Jesus' death from Pilate onto the Jewish people. The later the writing of the Gospel, and the wider the distancing of the Church from Judaism, the more pronounced this tendency becomes. Thus, while Mark and Luke describe crowds stirred up by chief priests calling for Jesus' execution (Mk 15:11; Lk 23:18–21), Matthew has "all the people" cry "his blood be on us and on our children!" (Mt 27:25), and John depicts "the Jews" exclaiming the most implausible "We have no king but Caesar!" (Jn 19:15). The evangelists seem to be motivated by two interests: (1) they desire to present the Romans and their treatment of Jesus in as positive a light as possible in order to be favorably regarded by the Empire in which the Church is developing; (2)

they wish to dissociate themselves in Roman eyes from the rebellious Jewish nation which revolted against Rome in the war of 66–70 C.E.

Into this discussion must be brought the strange episode of Barabbas. All the Gospels, in one form or another, portray Pilate giving the people the opportunity to choose between Jesus and Barabbas. The synoptics indicate that Pilate had the custom to release a Jewish prisoner to honor the Passover (Mt 27:15), but John asserts that it was a Jewish custom (Jn 18:39). There is no extra-biblical evidence for any such practice among the Romans. In fact, it runs against common sense. Why would the Romans put known Zealot revolutionaries back into circulation? Is it likely that Pilate, known for his swift punishment of the enemies of Rome, would kindly offer to release a man "among the rebels in prison, who had committed murder in the insurrection" (Mk 15:7)? Furthermore, the very name Barabbas is puzzling. Bar-abbas means "son of the Father," a title remarkably appropriate for Jesus. Add to this the baffling fact that some Matthean manuscripts identify him as "Jesus Barabbas." The crowd is then left with the confusing choice between "Jesus 'Son of the Father' " and "Jesus who is called the Christ" (Mt 27:17). It almost sounds as if they must select between two ways of understanding the same individual! In any case, this episode remains most problematic for modern Scripture scholarship. Nevertheless, it seems reasonable to suggest that the entire scene is a further manifestation of the evangelists' inclination to exonerate the Romans from guilt and attribute it to the Jewish people. The terrible consequences of this polemically-based maneuver will be discussed further in the Epilogue.

However, such a pro-Roman tendency cannot conceal the historical facts: Jesus was executed by Roman soldiers in the manner reserved for seditionists, he was crucified with other insurgents, and the charge of "King of the Jews" refers to the crime of insurrection. The conclusion is inescapable. Jesus was arrested by the temple authorities, either on their own initiative or at the behest of the Romans. He was deemed by them to be dangerous to the stability of Israel and to the well-being of the temple. He was brought to Pilate for execution as an enemy of Rome and a threat to the peace. He was promptly ordered by Pilate to be crucified as the standard penalty for one found guilty of the charge of insurrection.

The Execution of Jesus

The Gospel writers felt little need to graphically describe the details of Jesus' death. Their readers were all too familiar with the horrors of a Roman crucifixion. Instead, they were more concerned to present Jesus' death in a religious perspective and patterned their accounts especially around Psalm 22.

Modern Christians, who are well aware of the subsequent joyous event of the resurrection, seem to find it difficult to relate to the utter despair and desolation which befell Jesus' followers at his death. They suffered the trauma of witnessing a loved one slowly tortured to death and experienced the agonized end of all their hopes and dreams. Understandably, subsequent artistic portrayals sanitize the crucifixion scene, leaving believers out of touch with the absolute shame and degradation which afflicted crucifixion victims and their associates.

From what the Gospels reveal, it is safe to assume that Jesus was executed according to fairly standard Roman practice. After being sentenced, the condemned was scourged with a Roman flagellum. This preliminary torture would essentially skin the victim alive if not closely supervised. In a way this punishment benefited the prisoner, who, weakened by the flagellation, would expire that much more quickly upon the cross. Unscourged victims could linger in the agony of crucifixion for almost a week. In addition, the flaying of the person began the process of his degradation and dehumanization. The whole point of Roman crucifixion was to reduce the victim to the status of a thing, stripping him of every vestige of human dignity, in order to discourage any challenging of the might of Rome.

The criminal was then usually attached by ropes, possibly by nails, to a crossbeam. He was paraded through the city streets via a circuitous route, still naked from his scourging, to the execution site. A sign hung about his neck or carried in front of him indicated the person's crime. The victim was thus subjected to further degradation by having to endure the taunts and derision of passers-by. Spectators would not only learn the nature of the victim's offense, but would gather to witness the conclusion of the spectacle at the place where the uprights of the crosses were permanently mounted. In the case of Jesus and other Jews executed in Jerusalem, the condemned were apparently redressed in their clothing after being scourged for the march through the streets so as not to defile the holy city. Since Jesus' execution had to be hastened because of the approaching holyday, the most direct path out of the city was probably taken.

Romans executed Jews outside of the city walls on a small hill alongside a major road. Crucifixions were always carried out in a prominent place so that as many people as possible would witness the scene. The public torture of criminals was intended to act as a deterrent to crime and revolt. It also made their deaths even more shameful. Jews were crucified beyond the walls of the holy city because the place of execution was accursed ground.

Upon reaching the execution site, a condemned Jew like Jesus was stripped and laid on the ground on top of the crossbeam. Four- to five-inch nails were then driven through the bones of the victim's wrist. The cross beam with the prisoner attached was raised up onto the vertical beam. The victim sat astride a peg which was placed just beneath his buttocks. The person's feet were pushed up on the vertical beam so that the legs protruded outward and were nailed to the cross. The procedure was complete.

A person hanging in crucifixion was forced to constantly try to raise himself up on his impaled feet in order to breathe freely. As his strength waned and the pain in the feet became unbearable, the victim's body would slowly sink, redistributing the weight onto his arms and causing his lung muscles to cramp from the strain. Only by raising himself up again could those cramps be alleviated and breathing be restored.

Thus, the torture of the crucified was manifold. The relentless pain from the nails caused a constant writhing in agony. The continual see-saw motion to maintain breath resulted in the wrist bones grinding around the nails as they rotated. A terrible thirst consumed the victim as he gradually lost bodily fluids through tremendous sweating and constant bleeding. Pinioned helplessly on the vertical cross, the tortured person was assaulted by the scorching sun and by myriads of insects attracted by the sweat and blood. Unable to control his bodily functions and exposed naked to the gaze of spectators, a crucified man was utterly humiliated and dehumanized. No longer a human being, the victim was reduced to a screaming mass of writhing pain. Unless his death was hastened by breaking his legs to prevent the lifting up needed to breathe, his agony could endure for several days.

Jesus apparently suffered in this manner for about six hours. Completely degraded and publicly displayed alongside other criminals, his death seemed to testify to the fraudulence of his ministry. All his actions and words about an arriving reign were a sham. His tortured body was buried in a nearby tomb—a dishonorable burial for an executed criminal. Jesus' ministry had ended in evident disaster.

QUESTIONS FOR REFLECTION AND DISCUSSION

1. Should Jesus' actions in the temple be understood as a condemnation of Judaism or as a prophetic declaration about the reign of God and his own role as mashiah? Which view is more common among modern believers? Why?

2. The temple authorities could not have desired to kill Jesus because he had allegedly claimed to be divine since such assertions did not arise until after the resurrection. If blasphemy was not their motive, then why did they collaborate in a scheme to execute Jesus? Were their reasons religious concerns, issues of power and authority, or both?

3. In view of what we know happened, how did Pontius Pilate most probably regard Jesus?

4. For what reasons do the Gospel writers tend to portray Pilate more favorably than is likely historically?

5. It seems certain that neither the Pharisees nor the residents of Jerusalem were involved to any significant degree in the execution of Jesus. Why is this awareness so important in the light of subsequent historical developments?

6. What conclusions about the future would the disciples be likely to draw after experiencing the events surrounding Jesus' execution?

Chapter Ten

THE RESURRECTION AND THE
MESSIANIC AGE

Despair and Disbelief

*I*t often comes as a surprise when one realizes that the Gospels do not present uniform accounts of the events after Jesus' burial. Refer to the resurrection narratives found in Mk 16:1–20, Mt 28:1–20, Lk 24:1–53, and Jn 20:1—21:25 for the passages to be discussed below.

Despite the differences in the accounts, it seems possible to deduce some of the actions of Jesus' followers at that time. Although the Gospels do not dwell on this, it is evident that Jesus' friends were crushed by what had occurred. The terse Marcan statement that "they all forsook him and fled" (Mk 14:50) is probably an accurate description of the behavior of the male disciples at least. It may be that a good number of them escaped northward back to Galilee after the disaster in Jerusalem (Mt 28:7, for example).

The prevailing mood appears to have been one of utter defeat, despair, and terror. This is apparent in the Lucan story of two disciples returning home to Emmaus (Lk 24:13–33). While the episode has certainly been embellished by the evangelist, it may well be based on an historical event since a primitive form of the same tradition can be found in one of the appendices to Mark's Gospel: "After this he appeared in another form to two of them, as they were walking into the country" (Mk 16:12). What should be noted about the Lucan account is the description of the travelers' states of mind:

> And they stood still looking sad. Then one of them, named Cleopas, answered him, "Are you the only visitor to Jerusalem who does not know the things that have happened there in these days?" And he said to them, "What things?" And they said to him, "Concerning Jesus of Nazareth, who was a prophet mighty in deed and word before God and all the people, and how our chief priests and rulers delivered him up to be condemned to death, and crucified him. But we *had hoped* that he was the one to redeem Israel" (Lk 24:17b–21a).

This passage nicely summarizes the probable thoughts of Jesus' associates. Having seen the friend through whom God's reign had been powerfully announced so ignominiously executed, it could only be concluded that Jesus had failed and that an exciting prophet had been viciously destroyed. There was nothing else to do but go back home, full of sorrow and regret. Even though Jesus had indicated to his disciples that he would probably be killed, and even though he conveyed a deep trust in the Father to ultimately vindicate his mission, now all such assurances faded before the awful reality of Jesus' agonizing death.

This despair can also be seen in the virtually unanimous reaction to the news that Jesus' tomb was empty and to the assertions by some that angelic messengers had announced that Jesus was raised. Note particularly the italicized verses in these passages:

> And entering the tomb, [Mary Magdalene, and Mary the mother of James, and Salome] saw a young man sitting on the right side, dressed in a white robe; and they were amazed. And he said to them, "Do not be amazed; you seek Jesus of Nazareth, who was crucified. He has risen, he is not here; see the place where they laid him. But go, tell his disciples and Peter that he is going before you to Galilee; there you will see him, as he told you." And they went out and fled from the tomb, *for trembling and astonishment had come upon them; and they said noth-*

ing to anyone, for they were afraid (Mk 16:5–8, the original Marcan ending of the Gospel).

Now when he rose early on the first day of the week, he appeared first to Mary Magdalene, from whom he had cast out seven demons. She went and told those who had been with him, as they mourned and wept. But when they heard that he was alive and had been seen by her, *they would not believe it.* After this he appeared in another form to two of them, as they were walking in the country. And they went back and told the rest, *but they did not believe them.* Afterward he appeared to the Eleven themselves as they sat at table; *and he upbraided them for their unbelief and hardness of heart, because they had not believed those who saw after he had risen* (Mk 16:9–14, the longer appendix to Mark's Gospel).

Now the eleven disciples went to Galilee, to the mountain to which Jesus had directed them. And when they saw him they worshiped him; *but some doubted* (Mt 28:16).

Now it was Mary Magdalene and Joanna and Mary the mother of James and the other women with them who told this to the apostles; *but these words seemed to them an idle tale, and they did not believe them* (Lk 24:10–11).

[The disciples en route to Emmaus continued:] "Yes, and besides all this, it is now the third day since this happened. Moreover, some women of our company *amazed* us. They were at the tomb early in the morning and did not find his body; and they came back saying that they had *even* seen a vision of angels, who said that he was alive" (Lk 24:22–23).

To this list could be added the doubting Thomas cycle from the Gospel of John (20:19–29) and the difficulties experienced by the Lucan Jesus in Lk 24:37–38. There seems to have been a universal rejection of the notion that Jesus, who had been hideously tortured to death, had somehow been brought back to life. The conclusion is unavoidable that the personal resurrection of Jesus was something that was entirely unexpected. (This confirms the assertion that the passion predictions were originally not as detailed as the later evangelists made them.) Nevertheless, within a brief space of time personal experience seems to have convinced Jesus' friends that he had indeed been resurrected and that a new age was dawning for the world.

He Has Been Raised!

The Gospel writers have preserved these personal experiences of the raised Jesus in the form of "appearance" narratives. While there are several of them in the Gospels, no two are identical:

Mark (there is no resurrection appearance in the original ending of the Gospel, but in the longer appendix are found):

(1) 16:9–11   appearance to Mary Magdalene
(2) 16:12–13   appearance "in another form" to two disciples
(3) 16:14–20   appearance to the Eleven at table in Jerusalem

Matthew

(1) 28:9–10   appearance to the women leaving the tomb
(2) 28:16–20   appearance to the Eleven in Galilee

Luke

(1) 24:13–33   appearance to the two on the road to Emmaus*
(2) 24:34   reference to an appearance to Simon Peter
(3) 24:36–53   appearance to the entire Jerusalem group; Jesus eats with them and ascends*

John

(1) 20:14–18   appearance to Mary Magdalene*
(2) 20:19–29   appearances to group with and without Thomas
(3) 21:1–23   appearance by Sea of Tiberius*

While there is great disparity among these narratives in terms of location, persons involved, and words exchanged, there are a few commonalities that are very revealing. First, Jesus is only perceived by those who already possessed some amount of faith in his ministry. There are no appearances to Pilate or Caiaphas, for instance, to persuade them of the futility of their homicidal actions. Only those who were already close to Jesus become aware of his presence. Only through the eyes of faith is Jesus' abiding presence discernible.

Second, several of the appearances (those asterisked above)

contain the element of an initial lack of recognition. When the
Marcan appendix appearances, which are only related in the most
basic fashion, are discounted as narratives, it becomes clear that
about half of the appearance narratives include this non-recognition
element. The disciples en route to Emmaus suppose Jesus to be a
fellow traveler (Lk 24:29), the assembly in Jerusalem doesn't seem
to know quite what they are experiencing (Lk 24:37), Mary Magdalene thinks Jesus is a gardener who has somehow lost the missing
body (Jn 20:15), and the disciples in the boat only perceive an
unrecognizable figure on the shore (Jn 21:4). It would appear that
an awareness of the resurrection involved a gradual process of recognition. Once recognized, however, there was no doubt that the
same Jesus who had been known and loved during his ministry had
now miraculously been raised to a new type of life.

   Third, a few of the appearance accounts relate the awareness
of Jesus' presence to the sharing of a fellowship meal. This is most
clearly seen in the climax of the Emmaus story when Jesus "took
the bread and blessed, and broke it, and gave it to them and . . .
they recognized him" (Lk 24:30–31). Similarly, he is manifested to
the Eleven "at table" (Mk 16:15) and proves who he is by eating
before the Jerusalem company (Lk 24:42–43). These accounts are
apparently rooted in the early Church's celebration of the Lord's
Supper. This meal quickly took on a ritual significance among
Jesus' followers. It was a reminder of all the fellowship meals that
had been shared together during Jesus' ministry. It recalled Jesus'
words that his broken body and poured-out blood would further the
reign of God (see Paul's comments in 1 Cor 11:26, "For as often as
you eat this bread and drink this cup you proclaim the Lord's death
until he comes"). And it celebrated the abiding presence of the
raised Jesus in and among the fellowship-community. Thus, it may
well be that the presence of the resurrected Jesus was strongly felt
when his followers came together and celebrated his supper. There
is a strong connection between the resurrection and the life of the
community in the Gospel appearance accounts, and it is apparent
elsewhere in the Gospels as well, for instance, "where two or three
are gathered in my name, there am I in the midst of them" (Mt
18:20).

   The Gospels preserve in various ways, then, the growing
awareness that death had not conquered Jesus. The realization was

not based solely on the empty tomb, which the evangelists take pains to show as producing confusion and bafflement, not faith. This is also apparent in Paul's testimony about the resurrection in 1 Cor 15:3–8, where the empty tomb is not even mentioned. The empty tomb may have confirmed the suspicions of some regarding Jesus. But it was personal, and almost indescribable, experiences of the raised Jesus, both individually and communally, that convinced the disciples that God had intervened in human history and had raised Jesus of Nazareth to new and glorious life. In mounting excitement and enthusiasm, they began to ponder the significance of this unexpected and unique event. They burst with the desire to spread the news about what God had done. They started to wonder if the reign of God might have commenced in an unimaginable and startling way.

Jesus Christ, Lord and Son of God

The most immediate problem facing the earliest believers was the disgraceful death of Jesus. Being Jews, they were all aware that someone crucified was considered to be accursed. Further, there was no Jewish expectation that the mashiah of God would suffer. Jesus' execution seemed to conclusively mark the end of his mission. As Paul would put it about two decades later, the crucifixion of Jesus was "a stumbling block to Jews and folly to Gentiles" (1 Cor 1:23).

Yet, the believers had become passionately convinced that God had raised Jesus. This action was conceived of in the Pharisaic terms of resurrection. But instead of being the general resurrection of all the dead, God had first raised one individual, his messiah, "the first fruits of those who had fallen asleep" (1 Cor 15:20). In coming to grips with this fantastic event, the disciples of Jesus scoured the Jewish Scriptures, searching for passages which would help them make sense of what had occurred.

They found resonances with their experiences particularly in the suffering servant passages in Isaiah, especially 52:13—53:12. While these verses pertained to the suffering of Israel during the Babylonian captivity and contained no reference to a future mashiah, those who had experienced the resurrection found in them answers to the paradox which confronted them. God's servant was to suffer so that salvation might dawn for the world. For believers in the resurrection, Jesus was the messiah, the Christ, who was destined to suffer: "Was it not necessary that the Christ should suffer these things and enter into his glory?" (Lk 24:25–26).

In their excitement to share the resurrection experience with their fellow Jews, the believers attempted to use Old Testament texts to show that the crucifixion of Jesus was all part of God's eternal plan. Jesus' death was not a tragic mistake that God had to step in to rectify. They felt that events had unfolded as God had intended. A portion of Peter's speech in Acts 2, believed by many to represent an early way of preaching about Jesus, illustrates this divine perspective:

> "Men of Israel, hear these words: Jesus of Nazareth, a man attested to you by God with mighty works and wonders and signs which God did through him in your midst, as you yourselves know—this Jesus, *delivered up according to the definite plan and foreknowledge of God,* you crucified and killed by the hands of lawless men. But God raised him up, having loosed the pangs of death, because it was not possible for him to be held by it" (Acts 2:22–24).

In addition, it quickly became apparent to the disciples that the act of God in raising Jesus also constituted a divine approbation of all that Jesus had said and done. Jesus had said above all else that the reign of God was at hand and that God was about to dramatically intervene in human history. Had not that, in fact, occurred? Was not the reign breaking-in as Jesus had said? Was his own resurrection not proof of this?

The excitement of the resurrection experience also shifted the focus somewhat from the reign which Jesus proclaimed to the person of Jesus himself. Had not Jesus always called God his Father? Did not the resurrection prove that Jesus was indeed God's Son with whom he was well pleased (a sentiment expressed at the baptismal scene when the Gospels were written decades later; see Mk 1:11)? Was it not ironically true that Jesus was indeed "King of the Jews" as the title on the cross had announced? Had not God himself confirmed this in the act of raising Jesus? Referring to the

Daniel son of man passage, had not Jesus "been presented to the Ancient of Days [God] and given dominion, glory, and kingdom"? Would he not soon return "with the clouds of heaven" to firmly establish "his dominion which shall not pass away" (Dan 7:13–14)? Should not every knee bend and "every tongue confess that Jesus Christ is Lord, to the glory of God the Father" (Phil 2:11)? "Let all the house of Israel therefore know assuredly that God has made him both Lord and Christ, this Jesus whom you crucified" (Acts 2:36).

In short, the experience of Jesus' resurrection triggered a process in which Jewish traditions were redefined to make sense of what had happened and in which Jesus was recognized as deserving the titles Messiah, Christ, Lord, and Son of God. The resurrection event convinced his followers that they had somehow been touched by the presence of God himself. Note the excellent example provided by Matthew 28:9, "And behold Jesus met [the women returning from the empty tomb], and said, 'Hail!' And they came up and took hold of his feet and worshiped him." The perception that the raised Lord is divine and deserves worship is a function of the resurrection experience. As we have seen, such ideas did not occur during the ministry of Jesus of Nazareth.

As time passed, the emphasis on the divinity of Jesus increased and was clarified. Rather than being designated Lord at his resurrection, Jesus came to be presented in divine terms at earlier and earlier points. The Gospels themselves illustrate this developing awareness. The first Gospel, Mark, begins with Jesus' baptism in the Jordan with a divine voice announcing him as "beloved Son" (Mk 1:11). Matthew and Luke, both written a decade or more later, commence with the story of Jesus' birth, emphasizing his conception by the power of God's Holy Spirit (Mt 1:20; Lk 1:35). The last Gospel composed, John, starts its account in the primeval ages before the dawn of time, when "in the beginning was the Word, and the Word was with God, and what God was the Word was" (Jn 1:1). As the first century progressed, Christians came to retroject their resurrection faith in Jesus as Son of God further and further back into his ministry and, indeed, even back before the beginning of human history.

Thus, the perception of Jesus as divine, which permeates all the Gospels, originated in the resurrection. Other ramifications were perceived as well. The first preachers about Jesus stressed the importance that his death and resurrection had for the entire world.

The Return of the Lord

It will be recalled that the Jewish definition of God's mashiah, in very general terms, was that God would call forth a Jew to be his agent in heralding and ushering in the reign of God. With that reign it was thought by many that universal peace would arrive, that the general resurrection of the dead would take place, and that all the Gentile nations would come to learn of the ways of the God of Israel.

Believers in Jesus as Lord held that the resurrection of Jesus marked the beginning of the age to come, of the messianic age. This was the intent of the writer of Matthew's Gospel when, in a unique passage, he indicated that with Jesus' death "the tombs also were opened, and many bodies of the saints who had fallen asleep were raised, and coming out of the tombs after his resurrection they went into the holy city and appeared to many" (Mt 27:52–53). The death and raising of Jesus denoted the commencement of the reign of God as demonstrated by the Matthean "mini" general resurrection of the dead.

Given their conceptions of the arrival of God's reign, it seems only natural that the disciples concluded that Jesus, enthroned as Lord, would quickly return to usher in the new age in all its fullness. God's dramatic intervention in human history had begun. After a brief interval when the good news of the reign's arrival could be spread for one last time, and perhaps after a brief time of troubles such as Jesus had to endure, Christ the Lord, the Son of Man and Son of God, would inaugurate the reign of God.

This expectation of the imminent return or "parousia" of the Lord in triumph and judgment was widespread in earliest Christianity. It seems to be a direct result of the urgency with which Jesus announced the reign's coming during his ministry, and the conclusion of the believers that the resurrection of Jesus marked the final days of the present age. The expectation can be seen in many New Testament books.

The earliest New Testament writer, the apostle Paul, composed his letters between 50 and 60 C.E. He originally preached that Jesus was returning so soon that he later had to console the church in Thessalonica who feared that those who died before the parousia were lost forever (1 Thes 4:13–18). He wrote to the church in Corinth that "the appointed time has grown very short" because "the form of this world is passing away" (1 Cor 7:29,31). Later in his ministry, Paul came to suspect that he might die before the Lord's return (Phil 1:19–26), but he believed that those reading his letter would be alive to see it (2:14–18). This belief that the Lord was coming soon no doubt motivated Paul to travel far and wide in his preaching of the good news.

As was noted in chapter two, the Marcan community, persecuted in the mid-60s, eagerly awaited the return of the Lord to save them. The evangelist urged his church to remain steadfast in their faith because "this generation will not pass away before all these things take place" (Mk 13:30).

Once peace was restored following the destruction of Jerusalem in 70 C.E., the expectation that the Lord would return soon seems to have dwindled. Writing in the mid-80s, Luke/Acts describes a Church being guided by the Spirit to spread the Gospel throughout the earth (Acts 1:8), and the Matthean Jesus instructs his followers to "make disciples of all the nations" (Mt 28:19). The Gospel of John, composed in the mid-90s, contains no mention of the return of Jesus. The expectation of an imminent parousia appears to have understandably resurged in times of persecution, as evidenced by the Book of Revelation, written during the persecution of Christians by the Emperor Domitian in the early 90s. However, it generally was a by-product of the early enthusiasm surrounding the resurrection. The delay in Jesus' return caused a modification of original views, especially by the switching of emphasis to the work of the Church among the pagan nations.

Salvation for the Nations

One expectation concerning the reign of God was that the pagan Gentiles would come to learn about the God of Israel and would forsake their sinful, idolatrous lifestyles. Believing that the new age had commenced with the resurrection of Jesus, it might well have also been thought that the time of the Gentiles was at hand. When disciples of Jesus preached him to Jews outside of Palestine, they were amazed to find their words eagerly received among some of the Gentiles. It seems that by the early 40s, pagans in the city of Antioch were seeking admission to the Church, and some believers baptized them without requiring conversion to Judaism as a preliminary step. This eventually led to the first great controversy in the early Church: the debate over the admission of the Gentiles.

It should be noted that there is no evidence that any believer argued that Gentiles should categorically be denied membership in the community of Jesus. Some wanted to circumcise them as Jews first, others expected them to observe some minimal Jewish dietary standards, and others wanted them admitted without any reservations whatsoever (see Acts 15; Gal 2:1–10). But it seems that no one felt they should be excluded. This unanimity must be rooted in the proclamation of Jesus that the reign of God was dawning, in the expectation that the reign would include salvation for the Gentiles, and in the belief that the resurrection marked the beginning of the messianic age.

Many Jewish believers in the Lordship of Jesus appear to have been motivated by the thought that pagan idolaters were not to be part of the reign of God. They would first have to acknowledge the oneness of the God of Israel and to begin to walk in his ways. People like Paul believed that, through Christ, God had provided Gentiles with the opportunity to become his adopted children. And they could become part of a saved people independently of the Mosaic law because of the dramatic new action which God had done in raising Jesus. God's unbelievable generosity had paved the way for all peoples to be saved:

> Now the righteousness of God has been manifest apart from the law, although the law and the prophets bear witness to it—the righteousness of God through faith in Jesus Christ for all who believe (Rom 3:21).

By sharing in the life, death, and raising to the new life of Christ, Paul believed that all peoples would begin living ethical and moral lives. Gentiles were called upon to abandon the idolatrous habits which had led to all types of sinfulness (Rom 1:28–31) and to imitate Christ (1 Cor 11:1) who "is the likeness of God" (2 Cor 4:4). By following the example of Christ "who humbled himself and became obedient to death, even death on a cross" (Phil 2:8), believers would lead God-like lives founded upon mutual love and selflessness.

Paul's assertion that the dawn of the messianic age meant that Gentiles could now be accounted children of God without becoming Jews was a controversial one. After much debate it eventually became the accepted belief of the entire Church. It is important to realize, though, that this viewpoint is rooted in Jesus' original proclamation of the reign of God, even though reign of God language is not often used after the resurrection to express it.

The same merciful and welcoming openness that Jesus of Nazareth displayed toward the sinners and outcasts in his ministry was subsequently manifested by believers in Jesus the Christ toward pagan Gentiles. Jesus taught that the reign's arrival would begin an age marked by the abundant overflowing of God's merciful and reconciling love. Christians held that this messianic age had clearly been inaugurated by God at the resurrection, who therefore desired to have the graciousness of his reign extended to the whole world.

All of the various strains of traditions in the New Testament reflect this awareness. The messianic age of the reign of God had decisively begun with God's action of raising Jesus to Lordship. Consequently, the lifestyle of that reign must now be lived by all who had come to recognize the reign's commencement. In whatever particular metaphors and images they chose to express themselves, all the Christian preachers seem to have sought to establish and maintain communities which embodied the values of the reign of God as proclaimed by Jesus:

> For as in one body we have many members, and all the members do not have the same function, so we, though many, are one body in Christ, and individually members one of another. . . . Let love be genuine; hate what is evil, hold fast to what is good; love one another with brotherly affection; outdo one another in showing honor (Rom 12:4–5,9–10; written around 58 C.E.).
>
> You know that those who are supposed to rule over the Gentiles lord it over them, and their great men exercise authority over

them. But it shall not be so among you; but whoever would be great among you must be your slave, and whoever would be first among you must be slave of all (Mk 10:42–44; written around 70 C.E.).

So if you are offering your gift at the altar, and there remember that your brother has something against you, leave your gift there and go; first be reconciled to your brother, and then come and offer your gift. . . . You must be perfect as your heavenly Father is perfect (Mt 5:23–24,48; written around 85 C.E.).

Now the company of those who believed were of one heart and one soul, and no one said that any of the things which he possessed was his own, but they had everything in common. There was not a needy person among them (Acts 4:32,34a; written around 85 C.E.).

I do not pray for these only, but also for those who believe in me through their word, that they may all be one; even as you, Father, are in me, and I in you, that they may also be in us, so that the world may believe that you have sent me. The glory which you have given me I have given to them, that they may be one even as we are one, I in them and you in me, that they may become perfectly one, so that the world may know that you have sent me and have loved them even as you have loved me (Jn 17:20–23; written around 95 C.E.).

To this small sampling many other passages could be added. It seems undeniable that whether Pauline, Marcan, Matthean, Lucan, or Johannine, all the Christian traditions emphasized that the values of love, reconciliation, unity, equality, service, and selflessness must prevail in the Church. This is so because of the new, messianic age, begun in Christ's resurrection, which is founded upon those qualities of God himself as revealed by Jesus.

The excitement shared by the earliest believers in the Lordship of Christ is obvious. Like Jesus' parable of the yeast in the dough, they were spreading outward from Jerusalem, transforming the previously idolatrous world into a united community reflecting the graciousness and loving kindness of God. All this was to be done because of God's ultimate intervention in raising his most obedient Son, Jesus, to new life.

The Power of the Resurrection

To summarize, the awareness of the resurrection had many profound effects on the friends and disciples of Jesus of Nazareth. Most immediately, it reversed the depression and despair which had oppressed them after experiencing the torturous death of their leader. Such a direct intervention by God could only mean that everything Jesus had proclaimed about the imminent reign of God was true. Since that reign was expected to reverse all the evils and injustices in the present age, God's swift reversal of the greatest of injustices, the death of Jesus, demonstrated that the reign had indeed commenced.

This realization, however exciting, would not be shared by others until some explanation could be devised for Jesus' degrading execution. Being Jews by birth, Jesus' followers instinctively consulted the Jewish sacred writings for insight. As the Gospels show, the Old Testament provided several possible ways to come to grips with the crucifixion. By applying these texts to their experience of Jesus' death and raising, the disciples redefined the traditional understandings of the mashiah to their new situation. Thus, while it was thought that the mashiah would usher in the reign of God swiftly and triumphantly, Jesus Messiah (Christ) had commenced the reign of God by being vindicated as suffering servant. Old Testament passages which had never been thought of in a messianic context before could now be seen to resonate with the resurrection event. The redefinition of messianic expectations (denoted in this book by the differing usages of mashiah/messiah) and the use of Old Testament verses as proof-texts to make sense of the tragedy of Jesus' death were early consequences of believers' personal experiences of the raised Jesus.

A similar shift in emphasis occurred regarding the person of Jesus himself. Throughout his ministry and apparently shortly thereafter (Acts 2:22–24, for example), Jesus was perceived by some as a great prophet, perhaps the final mashiah-prophet, through whom God was announcing the commencement of his reign. The resurrection, however, sparked new insights into Jesus' identity. Clearly, in experiencing Jesus his friends had encountered God himself. Although the inherent Jewish awareness of monotheism made it difficult to express such profound concepts, the titles of Lord, enthroned Son of Man, and Son of God became increasingly meaningful. As time passed, greater and greater emphasis was to be placed on who Jesus was (see Mk 1:1) rather than on the reign which he proclaimed. This is seen quite clearly in the last Gospel to be written, the Gospel of John, in which the term "reign of God" appears only twice and in which Jesus constantly talks about his own identity. The messenger had become the message.

The resurrection also prompted the expectation that the raised Jesus would soon return transcendently enthroned as Lord of both the living and the dead to definitively establish his perpetual reign. The urgency with which Jesus had proclaimed the reign's imminence and the evidence provided by his resurrection fired the belief that events were rapidly moving to their divinely-ordained climax. When later developments showed that the age to come might not be fully inaugurated for some time, a concern for the Church's mission in the meantime became prominent.

Finally, the resurrection as proof of the messianic age (or the age of God's reign) triggered the belief that the time had come for the pagan Gentiles to be included as people of God. While Jesus' ministry had been confined to readying the Jewish people for the arrival of the reign of God, followers of Jesus the raised Christ came to understand that this mission now extended to all the world. The view that Gentiles were to be saved as Gentiles and not as Jews eventually came to prevail. Preachers of the good news traveled far and wide establishing church communities which were to live out the values of the reign inaugurated by Jesus. The peace promised by the reign of God was felt to be spreading throughout the world. Disunity and enmity between peoples was coming to an end. All this was possible because of the revelation of the nature of God and his reign as embodied in the ministry and death of Jesus, and as divinely authenticated by his resurrection.

QUESTIONS FOR REFLECTION AND DISCUSSION

1. It appears that it was difficult for Jesus' friends to accept that he had been raised. Why was this so?

2. Why was Jesus' crucifixion a cause for embarrassment? What did the early believers try to do to offset this scandal?

3. Why did the resurrection cause many to believe that Jesus would be returning in glory very soon?

4. Why was a realization of Jesus as divine a consequence of the experience of Jesus' crucifixion and resurrection? What impact did this realization have on Jesus' original proclamation?

5. Why did the early Church believe that Gentiles should be admitted into the people of God? What were the consequences of this belief?

6. How do you experience the raised Lord in your life?

CONSEQUENCES OF A CRITICAL AWARENESS OF THE SYNOPTIC GOSPELS

The Critical Approach to the Bible

*T*he Church has always considered the Bible to be norma-
tive for its preaching and practice. In particular, the witness of the
generation of eyewitnesses to Jesus' ministry and their immediate
successors, the apostles and evangelists, has served as the basis for
ecclesial self-definition for centuries. The enthusiastic support
which the Roman tradition has given to the critical approach to the
Scriptures has provided a wealth of new and challenging insights
into Christian origins, as well as recovering to some degree the
perspectives and attitudes of the earliest believers in Jesus as Lord.

The Pontifical Biblical Commission's 1964 *Instruction Concerning the Historical Truth of the Gospels* defined the broad categories of
Gospel development which critical research had revealed. The
three stages of Gospel tradition have proven to be of crucial importance in understanding not only the evangelists' works, but the
historical ministry of Jesus himself. It has been the purpose of this
book to present the fruits of exploring the Gospels along these
lines. This presentation of the Gospel writers' situations and of
Jesus' historical ministry has, by and large, represented the synthesis of broad-based scholarly consensus. The principal perspectives
contained herein have also been recently reiterated in the Pontifical
Biblical Commission's 1984 statement entitled *The Bible and Christology*, excerpts of which will be cited in these concluding pages.

This final chapter intends to offer some personal reflections on the consequences of a modern, critical awareness of the Gospels and of Jesus' ministry. It has been my experience that this perspective provides liberating and challenging realizations about the nature of Christianity and the responsibilities of all the baptized.

The Death of Jesus and the Nature of God

One of the most important conclusions of modern scriptural research is that the New Testament represents a very diverse spectrum of opinions about the significance of Jesus' life and death. "The New Testament authors . . . bear witness indeed to the same Christ, but with voices that differ in the harmony of one piece" (*The Bible and Christology*, 2.2.2.2.b) and this ". . . variety is to be greatly esteemed" (1.2.10).

At times in Christian history, one or another of these diverse perspectives on Jesus has become so predominant that an unbalanced or exaggerated viewpoint resulted. In particular, it seems to me that understanding Jesus' death exclusively according to the biblical conception of "expiation" has led to grave distortions. Appearing in only four New Testament verses (Rom 3:25; Heb 2:17; 1 Jn 2:2; 4:10), the term biblically refers to God's perpetual willingness to forgive offenses once the sinner takes steps to correct the wrongdoing. In this sense, some New Testament writers theologically understood Jesus' death as an act of ultimate faithfulness and obedience to God which resulted in divine mercy exploding throughout the earth.

However, by failing to balance this perspective with other New Testament insights, the understanding came to be misconstrued over the centuries to signify that God somehow had to be appeased for the sins of the world. The only adequate recompense had to be the bloody and supremely painful death of his divine Son. God thus becomes a vengeful and bloodthirsty sadist, whose eagerness to destroy and torment sinners has been forestalled by Jesus' horrible death. Unquestionably, this portrayal is diametrically opposed to the image of God as loving Father who yearns for the lost to return—an image which dominates the entire Old Testament and was clearly the hallmark of Jesus' preaching. Nonetheless, I am constantly startled to see how many people still are burdened by the fear that God is a vindictive tyrant. The historical reconstruction of Jesus' ministry would seem to be the ideal antidote to this unfortunate conception.

There can be no doubt that the God of Jesus was (and is!) a God whose passionate love for his people far surpasses human expectations. He is a God who seems almost ludicrously generous and beneficent. I suspect that it was his intimate experience of the love of the God he called Father that enabled Jesus to face the prospect of the terrible death which awaited him in Jerusalem. There is not the slightest trace of evidence that Jesus preached that God had to be "paid back" or "appeased" for sins. In fact, there are mountains of indications to the contrary.

Modern reconstruction makes it most plausible that Jesus saw his death as a personal sacrifice which would trigger the inbreaking of God's reign. Referring to his death as his personal "trial," Jesus may have seen his own commitment to the selfless love characteristic of God and of his reign being tested. Subsequent Christian writers described this fidelity of Jesus to his mission in terms of obedience and faithfulness. Their reflections led to further theological assertions which could be interpreted ambiguously and, ultimately, in a warped and twisted fashion. The following chart illustrates one way in which this contortion may have developed:

Ministry of Jesus:
    Jesus sacrificed himself for the sake of God's reign.
                ↓
[Early reflection:]   ↓
    Jesus' resurrection commenced the reign of God
      which enabled all people to become God's children
        and be saved from enslavement to sin
[Later developments:]   ↓
    Jesus' death brought the forgiveness of the world's sins.
                ↓
    Jesus died for our sins.
                ↓
    The punishment which we deserved fell upon Jesus (?).
                ↓
    Jesus died to pay back the world's sinful debt to God (??!).

In any case, it seems to me that later theological explanations of the significance of his death should never obscure the utter trust and love which Jesus felt toward the God whose reign was imminent. To the extent that such explanations promote a fear of God in people's hearts, they have departed from the witness of the sacred Scriptures. Christians who believe that they must imitate Jesus their Lord can never conceive of God in the bloodthirsty and vindictive terms which seem to have become widespread. The God of Jesus is a God of surpassing love.

Jesus, the Ultimate Human Person

Two related tendencies which were noted in the Gospels eventually developed into extreme and exaggerated forms to the detriment of the Christian message. Once more, a critical and historical awareness of the Gospels can remedy this situation.

They both involve the person of Jesus. As has been seen, the resurrection experience prompted a recognition of Jesus as divine, and the ever-increasing attribution of the titles Lord and Son of God to him. Yet as time passed a distinction failed to be made between the historical Jesus and the Christ revealed as Lord. Post-resurrection insights were assumed to be both the substance of Jesus' preaching and the ways in which people understood him during his ministry. As a consequence, the humanity and the Jewishness of Jesus tended to be overlooked in practice. However, it is of great importance that the pivotal role of the resurrection be realized. It sparked a radical redefinition of the Jewish traditions of Jesus' earliest followers. "This faith had its origin and progressive growth in Jesus' resurrection; it was an event of salvation introduced among people who already shared the religious experience of diverse Jewish communities" (*The Bible and Christology*, 1.2.3.1).

Jesus as divine Son of God has been so stressed in Christian history that his deep humanity was little considered. Although the Church always asserted that Jesus was indeed "true God and true man," that belief apparently had little effect on popular preaching or piety. The divinity of Jesus became so supremely important that I believe most Christians became functional docetists (a heresy which denies the humanity of Jesus). As a result it was difficult to relate to Jesus as a real person. He was elevated beyond the reach of human beings, and others, especially his mother, were used as intermediaries to appeal to him. As one catechist in a Bible study group I facilitated recounted, children who had been taught about Jesus as God suddenly were unable to speak to him in the friendly, personable way that they had before his divinity had been stressed. This was a sad and ironic fate to befall him who "reconciled to himself all things, whether on earth or in heaven . . ." (Col 1:20). Furthermore, the Pauline directive to imitate the life of Jesus became impossible. How can a person imitate one who was perfect because he was God?

Pushed far enough, even the resurrection loses its importance because all it demonstrated was that God can't be killed (a notion found in heretical Gnostic gospels written in the second and third centuries). Clearly, neither Jesus nor his friends thought in such terms. So far removed from conceiving of Jesus as divine were his disciples that their faith "was completely shattered at his death." That Jesus would be raised from the dead was "in no way expected by the disciples, with the result that they accepted the truth of his resurrection only with hesitation" (*The Bible and Christology*, 2.2.2.1).

The historical-critical reconstruction of the ministry of Jesus shows how utterly human, in the best sense of the word, he really was. Like any human person he experiences frustration, temptation, and moments of crisis. Like any human person "he grows more and more in the awareness of the mission entrusted to him by the Father, from his childhood up to his death on the cross. Finally, he experiences death in as cruel a fashion as any other human would; or as the Epistle to the Hebrews puts it, 'Son though he was, he learned obedience from what he suffered' [Heb 5:8]" (*The Bible and Christology*, 2.2.1.3.b).

To me, one of the most profound insights garnered from the critical exploration of the Gospels is the awareness of Jesus' complete trust in the Father. Even though he foresaw the probable outcome of his mission to Jerusalem, and even though he shrank from the awful death that was in store, he nevertheless put his very life at the service of God's reign. He trusted that ultimately God would not forsake him. Significantly, he may have done this without necessarily knowing precisely how things would turn out. Since his followers had no inkling that a resurrection of Jesus was imminent, it seems to me conceivable that Jesus himself had no such expectation. His commitment to God thus becomes even more total and even more awesome. Most importantly, it is an attitude rooted in the limitations of the human condition *which we are capable of emulating*. Jesus becomes a flesh-and-blood human person, a beloved friend, whose perspectives and lifestyle we are challenged to imitate. We are no longer let off the hook, so to speak, by dismissing Jesus' life as the consequences of his divinity. No, it is Jesus' *human* intimacy with his Father which confronts us. It is Jesus' *human* love for the people he encounters and the very *human* way in which he touches them which challenges us to pattern our relationships and friendships on his example. It is his willingness to surrender his very life for the sake of the reign of God that causes us to imitate his selflessness and faithfulness.

All of these thoughts are certainly not meant to deny the "true God" which was revealed in Jesus. However, my experience in facilitating scores of Bible study groups has shown how difficult it is for many people to let go of the divine straitjacket in which Jesus has been imprisoned and really appreciate and identify with his humanity. I have found two scriptural perspectives to be helpful.

First, a recovery of the Jewish understanding of humanity is necessary. As heirs to the Greek metaphysical view of the universe, we tend to compartmentalize and pigeon-hole things. We tend to conceive of human and divine as polar opposites, diametrically opposed to one another. This outlook makes it practically impossible to imagine how two such disparate realities could be unified in the person of Jesus. Because of our propensity to categorically segregate the human from the divine, people have had to functionally disregard one or the other in Jesus. Over the course of Christian history, it is Jesus' humanity which has usually been slighted.

However, the Jewish tradition is that humanity has been created in the image of God (Gen 1:26–27; 5:1–3; 9:6). Human beings have been made to be like God, to be reflections of him in some way. It is probably when people are lovingly oriented toward concern for others that they most reflect the very nature of God. Paul perceived that Jesus was "the image of God" (2 Cor 4:4) into whose likeness Christians were being transformed (2 Cor 3:18). Thus, imagining Jesus as the ultimate embodiment of what it means to be in the image of God can help bridge the Hellenistic chasm between the human and the divine. After the resurrection, the disciples came to realize that in Jesus they had had a direct encounter with the loving essence of God himself. Because of that experience, they had to reorient and repattern their lives according to that supremely God-like way of living. They had to be "perfect as their heavenly Father is perfect" (Mt 5:48).

A second Pauline perspective also helps to come to grips with the humanity/divinity of Jesus. In Philippians 2:5–11, Paul discusses how the pre-existent Christ "emptied himself" and became a human being, subject to all the limitations of the human condition. So consonant with his Father's will was he, and so truly limited by his human estate, that he even endured a terrible death. Therefore, God exalted him to Lordship over all creation. This viewpoint asserts the divine origins of Jesus and yet carefully preserves his essential humanity. It was his human fidelity to God which Paul believes resulted in his resurrection and in the dawning of salvation for a world previously enslaved to ungodly lifestyles.

The critical awareness of the historical development of the Gospel message, then, recovers and makes real the humanity of Jesus of Nazareth. It challenges modern believers to pattern their lives after him who was the ultimate revelation of God's love.

Jesus, the Jew from Nazareth

In a similar vein, as Christianity became a religion distinct from the Judaism from which it had emerged, there was an ever-increasing tendency to overlook or to deny the historical reality that Jesus was a Jew. Jesus was portrayed as one who opposed a Judaism which was caricatured and stereotyped by subsequent Christians as a cold, joyless, legalistic religion. Judaism was presented as the perfect foil for Jesus. Everything that was good about Christianity was denied to Judaism, which Jesus was seen to have terminated. Jesus' preaching of the reign of God was taken to represent the coming of Christianity, the authentic religion which supplanted its perverse predecessor.

Most dangerously, the Gospel writers' tendency to shift blame for Jesus' death from the Romans to the Jews led to the charge of deicide against the Jewish people. From the earliest centuries of Christian history, Jews were vilified as evil, satanic, enemies of God whose innate wickedness led them to kill the Son of God. Christianity was thus separated from its Jewish roots and became the breeding ground of ungodly hatred against God's chosen people. Ultimately, this distortion of the Christian message would lead to the awful events of the holocaust in this century.

Presently, the Roman Catholic and many other Christian traditions officially recognize that the covenant of God with Abraham is still in effect and that Jews remain God's chosen people. The notion that Christianity has somehow replaced Judaism in God's favor, or that the Jewish people were responsible for the death of Jesus, is considered repugnant and condemnable.

The critical exploration of the Gospels is of crucial importance in this regard. It has become clear that "the diligent study of Judaism is of utmost importance for the correct understanding of the person of Jesus, as well as of the early Church" (*The Bible and Christology*, 1.2.5). Jesus must not be viewed as a sort of latter-day Christian who celebrated Christmas and Easter. He must be recognized as a Jew who was circumcised, bar mitzvahed, and who celebrated Chanukah and Passover. "The Gospels depict him as one deeply rooted in his own land and in the tradition of his people" (*The Bible and Christology*, 1.1.5.1). Modern research has demonstrated that Jesus proclaimed a very Jewish message of salvation. His announcement of the approach of God's reign was based upon Jewish expectations and conceptions. Far from being an inveterate foe of Judaism, Jesus was a deeply pious and religious Jew.

The Gospels' negative stereotyping of the Pharisees is seen as resulting from disputes with the synagogue at the time the Gospels were composed and not necessarily reflective of circumstances at the time of Jesus' ministry. In fact, Jesus appears to have been in considerable agreement with the Pharisaic school of Hillel. Similarly, Jesus' death was not primarily for religious reasons. It appears to have been orchestrated by the Romans in consort with their temple subordinates on largely political grounds. Jesus was seen as a threat to the established political order. His crucifixion as "King of the Jews" demonstrates this. The Gospels' attempts to blame Jews for his execution are a by-product of their own polemical situations later in the first century.

Furthermore, it has become obvious that depicting Judaism as a cold-hearted and legalistic religion is a gross injustice. The Jewish experience of God was above all else one of love and faithfulness. God had gifted his people with his way, his Torah, so that they could more perfectly live in his image. Thus the Torah is observed not to earn God's favor, but out of gratitude for having already undeservedly received it. I believe that any caricature of Jews or of Judaism leads inevitably to perversions of the Christian message. Modern critical awareness is necessary for correcting any lingering distortions in this regard.

The Central Importance of the Reign of God

The distancing of Jesus and his Church from their Jewish roots accompanied a similar sundering of Jesus from his proclamation of the reign of God. We have already seen in the New Testament period how an emphasis on Jesus the Son of God replaced his announcement of God's reign. The messenger had become the message.

As time passed, further redefining of the "reign of God" occurred. Perhaps taking their cue from the Gospel of Matthew's phrase "the kingdom of heaven," later Christians came to understand Jesus' message purely in terms of an afterlife. Heaven was a place which Jesus' death made accessible to his followers, who must, as far as possible, distance themselves from the sinful and degraded world. This focus on a sort of "pie-in-the-sky in the by-and-by when we die" tended to remove Christians from concern for human society. Rather than preserving the Jewish notion of the goodness of God's creation, many Christians came to regard the world as an evil, completely wretched place. Believers must not enjoy the sinful, physical pleasures of this world (especially sex), and must concentrate all their attention on the spiritual world above. This attitude more than smacked of the ancient heresy of dualism which declared that humanity and the world were beyond redemption and that to be saved one had to become pure spirit. It fostered a lessening of concern for social injustice and poverty because, after all, that was only part of life in this "vale of tears."

A critical reading of the Gospels clearly demonstrates how

alien such thoughts were to the ministry of Jesus. Rather than separating himself from the world as the Essenes had done, Jesus plunged right into the world, socializing with the dregs of society. He was criticized for the disreputable crowd he associated with, as well as for his frequent indulgence in fellowship meals. This was hardly the mark of one seeking to avoid the pleasure of a hearty meal. Jesus was also quite outspoken regarding injustice. He mocked the hypocrisy of the temple leaders and chastised them for failing to be faithful stewards of God's people. He proclaimed that the reign of God was commencing; a reign characterized by equality, mutual love, and pervading justice. His message and actions were so unsettling to the political status quo that he was crucified as a revolutionary criminal.

It seems to me that this means modern Christians must imitate Jesus' living-out of the values of the reign of God. We have a responsibility to promote God's reign by furthering the cause of peace and by combating poverty, disease, and social injustice. If the reign of God has been delayed in coming, perhaps it is because we have failed to really take that reign seriously and seek to implement its characteristics. It is a Jewish tradition that God made humanity his partners in bringing his creation to the completion that he intends for it. I suggest that our role as Christians is to assist in this creative process.

It may also be that our generally exclusive concern for asserting Jesus' status as Son of God has produced some unhealthy side-effects. We were so involved with the getting to heaven, where he is, that we failed to live the way he did here on earth. Jesus proclaimed a reign that was erupting into human history right here in this world. It seems to me that his followers can do no less. Perhaps the time has come for what might be called a more basileo-centric, or reign-centered, Christology. By this I mean a way of conceiving of Jesus which emphasizes his commitment to God and the inbreaking of God's reign. We have a good example to follow in this regard. Critically considered, the synoptic Gospels make clear that Jesus hardly ever talked about himself; he lived, breathed, and taught the reign of God.

Implications for Today's Church

This reign-oriented perspective, of course, poses many challenges to modern believers, both individually and as Church. Do I seek to foster the values of God in my own life? Do my relationships enable and empower people to freely exercise their gifts on behalf of all? Do I trust in the coming of God's reign as Jesus did? Does my life reflect the selfless and generous life of God as manifested in Jesus? Am I concerned with furthering God's reign in the world? Do I repeat the mistakes of some of Jesus' opponents who interpret the Scriptures in a literal and self-serving fashion, seeking to preserve power for myself?

As a Church, the critical awareness of the Gospel causes many questions which prod our communal conscience. Is the Church really reflective of the life lived by Christ? Do we accept people as they are, or do we seek to convert them to our preferences before we have anything to do with them? Do we believe that God loves all people, or do we unconsciously or overtly believe that others are not quite as good as we and therefore are "unsaved"? Are our Communion services as life-giving and as open to all as Jesus' fellowship meals were, or do we deny access to God's presence to some? Do we uphold institutional regulations, alienating and inflicting pain upon people in the process? Are our church communities marked by genuine love and heartfelt solidarity, or are they little different from clubs or organizations founded upon charters and constitutions? Does a radical equality unite all of those who believe in Christ, or are the people of God divided by the sins of clericalism and sexism? Do we as Church actively combat oppression, injustice, and poverty both within our ranks and in the world at large? Do we trust our Father enough to be willing to sacrifice our self-interests in the cause of God's reign?

All of these unsettling questions emerge from the critical exploration of the Gospels. This seems to me to be a very healthy thing. I suspect that when people read the Bible and come away feeling satisfied and complacent, they have read the Scriptures in an inappropriate and self-serving manner. When one reads the Bible and comes away challenged and uneasy, I believe that the voices of the sacred writers have really been heard. Perhaps by more accurately hearing the synoptic evangelists' inspired messages, we who are

Church today will be increasingly motivated to undertake Jesus' mission as heralds of the inbreaking reign of God.

QUESTIONS FOR REFLECTION AND DISCUSSION

1. Why is a critical understanding of the Bible important?

2. Why is a heartfelt belief in the God portrayed by Jesus so unsettling? Why do some seem more comfortable with a judgmental, vindictive God?

3. Why is it important to preserve the humanity of Jesus of Nazareth? What are the consequences of not doing this?

4. Why is a respect and admiration for Judaism a necessary part of being a Christian? How might one begin to grow in one's understanding of the Jewish tradition?

5. What would be the benefits of a renewed emphasis on Jesus' heralding of the reign of God? What challenges does such an orientation present?

BIBLIOGRAPHY

This is a listing of all the works consulted in researching this book and of works recommended for popular reading. For the sake of convenience all the items are combined alphabetically, whether they are popularizations, scholarly works, or journal articles. Items recommended for popular reading, or which avoid overly-technical language, are preceded by an asterisk and followed by a short description of the work in parentheses.

*Abbott, Walter M., S.J., ed. *The Documents of Vatican II*. New York: Guild Press, 1966.
(Important documents for all those interested in the changes in Roman Catholicism sparked by this Council.)

Achtemeier, Paul J. *Mark* (Proclamation Commentaries). Philadelphia: Fortress Press, 1975.

————. *The Quest for Unity in the New Testament Church*. Philadelphia: Fortress, 1987.

*Achtemeier, Paul J., gen. ed. *Harper's Bible Dictionary*. San Francisco: Harper & Row, 1985.
(An excellent and the most up-to-date collection of articles on biblical subjects. Prepared by members of the Society of Biblical Literature.)

Barth, Marcus. *Jesus the Jew*. Atlanta: John Knox Press, 1978.

Best, Ernest. *Disciples and Discipleship: Studies in the Gospel According to Mark*. Edinburgh: T & T Clark, 1986.

Best, Ernest. "The Role of the Disciples in Mark," *New Testament Studies*, 23 (1977), pp. 377–401.

*Boadt, Lawrence, et al., eds. *Biblical Studies: Meeting Ground of Jews and Christians*. New York: Paulist, 1980.
(A collection of articles which focus on the role of the Bible in the Jewish-Christian dialogue.)

*Boyd, Neil. *The Hidden Years: A Novel About Jesus*. Mystic: Twenty-Third, 1986.
(An excellent fictional account of the adult years of Jesus immediately prior to beginning his public ministry. The author is well-acquainted with modern scriptural insights into first-century Palestinian Judaism.)

*Brown, Raymond E. *An Adult Christ at Christmas*. Collegeville: Liturgical Press, 1984.
(Explores the infancy narratives in readable and pastoral terms.)

*————. *Biblical Exegesis and Church Doctrine*. New York: Paulist, 1985. (Separate articles which consider the relationship of Church teaching and biblical studies.)

*————. *Biblical Reflections on Crises Facing the Church*. New York: Paulist, 1975. (Applies modern Scripture scholarship to contemporary Church issues.)

————. *The Birth of the Messiah*. Garden City: Image Books, 1977.

*————. *The Churches the Apostles Left Behind*. New York: Paulist, 1984. (Examines seven church communities in the last third of the first century to discover how they coped with the deaths of the founding apostles.)

*————. *The Community of the Beloved Disciple*. New York: Paulist, 1979. (A reconstruction of the history of the church community in which were written the Gospel and Letters of John.)

*————. *The Critical Meaning of the Bible*. New York: Paulist, 1981. (Explores the necessity and consequences of understanding the Scriptures in a critical manner.)

*————. *A Crucified Christ in Holy Week*. Collegeville: Liturgical Press, 1986. (A discussion of the passion narratives. Useful for homilies and personal reflection.)

————. *The Gospel According to John* (Anchor Bible vols. 29 & 29a). Garden City: Doubleday, 1966 and 1970.

————. *Jesus: God and Man*. New York: Macmillan, 1967.

————. *New Testament Essays*. Garden City: Image Books, 1968.

*————. *Recent Discoveries and the Biblical World*. Wilmington: Michael Glazier, 1983. (Presents the impact of archaeological and linguistic discoveries on our understanding of the Bible.)

————. *The Virginal Conception and Bodily Resurrection of Jesus*. New York: Paulist, 1973.

*Brown, Raymond E., Karl P. Donfried, and John Reumann, eds. *Peter in the New Testament*. Minneapolis: Augsburg; New York: Paulist, 1973. (A team of scholars from a variety of Christian traditions considers each New Testament passage concerning Peter. Substantial unanimity is reached, indicating the positive ecumenical consequences of a common critical approach to Scripture.)

*Brown, Raymond E., Karl P. Donfried, Joseph A. Fitzmyer, and John Reumann, eds. *Mary in the New Testament*. Philadelphia: Fortress; New York: Paulist, 1978.
(A study like the preceding entry which considers all the New Testament Marian passages. Again, profound commonalities are apparent.)

*Brown, Raymond E., Joseph A. Fitzmyer, and Roland E. Murphy, eds. *The Jerome Biblical Commentary*. Englewood Cliffs: Prentice-Hall, 1968.
(A valuable, though now becoming dated, commentary on each biblical book by Catholic Scripture scholars. A new edition is promised shortly.)

*Brown, Raymond E. and John P. Meier. *Antioch and Rome*. New York: Paulist, 1983.
(An investigation of two early centers of Christianity which shows how their respective theologies developed.)

Brown, Schuyler. *The Origins of Christianity*. Oxford: Oxford University Press, 1984.

*Buttrick, George A., dictionary editor. *The Interpreter's Dictionary of the Bible* (4 vols). Nashville: Abingdon, 1962. (Keith Crim, gen. ed. Supplemental Vol., 1976.)
(A multi-volume encyclopedia of biblical topics.)

*Callan, Terrence. *Forgetting the Root*. New York: Paulist, 1986.
(Explores the reasons for the separation of Christianity from Judaism.)

Cassidy, Richard J. *Jesus, Politics, & Society*. Maryknoll: Orbis, 1978.

Cope, O. Lamar. *Matthew: A Scribe Trained for the Kingdom of Heaven* (The Catholic Biblical Quarterly Monograph Series, 5). Washington, D.C.: Catholic Biblical Association of America, 1976.

*Croner, Helga, ed. *Stepping Stones to Further Jewish-Christian Relations*. New York: Paulist, 1977.
(A collection of documents from various Christian traditions concerning Jewish-Christian relations. The recent Christian reappreciation of Judaism is apparent.)

Culbertson, Philip. "Changing Christian Images of the Pharisees," *Anglican Theological Review* (1982), Vol. LXIV, No. 4, pp. 539–561.

Cullman, Oscar. *The Christology of the New Testament*. Philadelphia: Westminster, rev. ed., 1963.

*Cunningham, Philip A. *The Apostle Paul: Male Chauvinist or Proponent of Equality?* Milwaukee: Hi-Time, 1986.

(A workbook which shows the consequences for women of Paul's belief that the messianic age had dawned.)

*————. *Jewish Apostle to the Gentiles: Paul As He Saw Himself.* Mystic: Twenty-Third, 1986.
(Presents Paul as an observant Jew, who believed that the time had come, because of the beginning of the messianic age, to save pagan Gentiles by admitting them into the community of Christ.)

Danker, Frederick W. *Luke* (Proclamation Commentaries). Philadelphia: Fortress, 1976.

Davies, Alan T. "Love and Law in Judaism and Christianity," *Anglican Theological Review* (1982), Vol. LXIV, No. 4, pp. 454–466.

*Edwards, O.C., Jr. *Luke's Story of Jesus.* Philadelphia: Fortress, 1981.
(Considers the meaning of the Luke's narrative for his readers. Valuable as a homily-aid.)

*Edwards, Richard A. *Matthew's Story of Jesus.* Philadelphia: Fortress, 1985.
(Similar to the preceding entry.)

*Falk, Harvey. *Jesus the Pharisee.* New York: Paulist, 1985.
(Written by a rabbi, this work proposes that (1) Jesus intended to begin a religion for Gentiles, and (2) Jesus was a Pharisee of the school of Hillel.)

*Farrell, Melvin L., S.S. *Getting To Know the Bible.* Milwaukee: Hi-Time, 1984.
(An excellent introduction to the Bible which gives a fine overview of the various books according to the modern, critical approach.)

*Fisher, Eugene J. *et al.*, eds. *Twenty Years of Jewish-Catholic Relations.* New York: Paulist, 1986.
(Contains interesting articles on the story of the Jewish-Catholic dialogue in the twenty years since Vatican II. Useful for appreciating Jewish viewpoints on Jesus and Christianity. The concluding article by Irving Greenberg is most thought-provoking.)

*———— *et al. Within Context: Guidelines for the Catechetical Presentation of Jews and Judaism in the New Testament* (4th draft). Washington, D.C.: Secretariat for Catholic-Jewish Relations, 1986.
(An absolute must for all who preach and teach. Presents important information on the proper understanding of Judaism in the New Testament.)

*Fitzmyer, Joseph A. *A Christological Catechism: New Testament Answers.* New York: Paulist, 1981.

(Provides well-considered and readable answers to common questions about Jesus.)

———. *The Gospel According to Luke* (Anchor Bible vols. 28 & 28a). Garden City: Doubleday, 1981 and 1985.

*———. *Scripture and Christology: A Statement of the Biblical Commission with a Commentary.* New York: Paulist, 1986.
(The Pontifical Biblical Commission's statement of the Bible and Jesus with comments from a leading American Catholic exegete.)

*Flannery, Edward H. *The Anguish of the Jews.* New York: Paulist, 1985.
(The scandalous history of Jewish-Christian relations from the first century to the present.)

*Freyne, Sean. *The World of the New Testament* (NT Message 2). Wilmington: Michael Glazier, 1980.
(A thorough introduction to first-century society and culture.)

*Funk, Robert W. *New Gospel Parallels* (Volumes One and Two). Philadelphia: Fortress, 1985.
(Presents in parallel columns the corresponding verses from all the Gospels, the Old Testament, and apocryphal literature.)

Haenchen, Ernst. *The Acts of the Apostles: A Commentary.* Philadelphia: Westminster, 1971.

*Harrington, Daniel J., S.J. *God's People in Christ.* Philadelphia: Fortress, 1980.
(Considers the relationships among the various Jewish and Gentile groups in early Christianity.)

Hayes, John H. and Carl R. Holladay. *Biblical Exegesis.* Atlanta: John Knox, 1982.

Hengel, Martin. *Acts and the History of Earliest Christianity.* Philadelphia: Fortress, 1979.

———. *The Atonement.* Philadelphia: Fortress, 1981.

———. *Between Jesus and Paul.* Philadelphia: Fortress, 1983.

*———. *Crucifixion.* Philadelphia: Fortress, 1977.
(Presents classical references to the practice of crucifixion.)

———. *Studies in Mark.* Philadelphia: Fortress, 1985.

Jeremias, Joachim. *Jesus' Promise to the Nations.* Philadelphia: Fortress, 1982.

————. *The Parables of Jesus.* New York: Scribner's, 2nd rev. ed., 1972.

Jervell, Jacob. *Luke and the People of God.* Minneapolis: Augsburg, 1972.

Jewett, Robert. *A Chronology of Paul's Life.* Philadelphia: Fortress, 1979.

Keck, Leander E. and J. Louis Martyn, eds. *Studies in Luke/Acts.* Philadelphia: Fortress, 1980.

Kingsbury, Jack Dean. *The Christology of Mark's Gospel.* Philadelphia: Fortress, 1983.

————. *Matthew* (Proclamation Commentaries). Philadelphia: Fortress, 1977.

Knox, John. *The Humanity and Divinity of Christ.* Cambridge: Cambridge University Press, 1967.

Kysar, Robert. *John: The Maverick Gospel.* Atlanta: John Knox, 1976.

Lane, Dermot A. *The Reality of Jesus.* New York: Paulist, 1975.

*LaVerdiere, Eugene, S.S. *Luke* (New Testament Message 5). Wilmington: Michael Glazier, 1983.
(A readable commentary on the Gospel of Luke.)

*Leary, James F. *A Light to the Nations.* New Jersey: Arena Lettres, 1983.
(An introduction to the books of the New Testament.)

Mackey, James P. *Jesus: The Man and the Myth.* New York: Paulist, 1979.

Mann, C.S. *Mark* (Anchor Bible, 27). Garden City: Doubleday, 1986.

Martyn, J. Louis. *History and Theology of the Fourth Gospel.* Nashville: Abingdon (rev. ed.), 1979.

*Matera, Frank. *Passion Narratives and Gospel Theologies.* New York: Paulist, 1986.
(Uses the passion accounts to demonstrate the theological perspectives of each evangelist.)

————. *What Are They Saying About Mark?* New York: Paulist, 1987.
(A fine survey of scholarly discussion are various Marcan questions, such as Mark's christology and the role of the disciples.)

*McKenzie, John L., S.J. *Dictionary of the Bible.* Milwaukee: Bruce Publishing Co., 1965.
(A classic compilation of essays on biblical topics.)

Meeks, Wayne A. *The First Urban Christians.* New Haven: Yale University Press, 1983.

Meyer, Ben F. *The Aims of Jesus.* London: SCM Press, 1979.

————. *The Early Christians: Their World Mission and Self-Discovery.* Wilmington: Michael Glazier, 1986.

*Miller, John W. *Step by Step Through the Parables.* New York: Paulist, 1981.
(A well-done introduction to Jesus' parables.)

Munck, Johannes. *Acts of the Apostles* (Anchor Bible, 31). Garden City: Doubleday, 1967.

*Murphy, Cullen. " 'Who Do Men Say That I Am?' " *The Atlantic,* Vol. 258, No. 6 (Dec. 1986), pp. 37ff.
(A comprehensive overview of modern scriptural and theological explorations of Jesus.)

*Neusner, Jacob. *Judaism in the Beginning of Christianity.* Philadelphia: Fortress, 1984.
(An excellent presentation of 1st-century Judaism, the various Jewish groups, and the consequences of the destruction of the temple.)

————. *The Pharisees—Rabbinic Perspectives.* Hoboken: KTAV, 1973.

————. "Two Pictures of the Pharisees: Philosophical Circle or Eating Club," *Anglican Theological Review* (1982), Vol. LXIV, No. 4, pp. 525–538.

*Perkins, Pheme. *Hearing the Parables of Jesus.* New York: Paulist, 1981.
(A popular introduction to the parables which compares Jesus' stories with extra-biblical accounts and which nicely relates the parables to today's world.)

*————. *Reading the New Testament: An Introduction.* New York: Paulist, 1988 (Revised Ed.).
(An excellent presentation of the New Testament.)

————. *Resurrection: New Testament Witness and Contemporary Reflection.* Garden City: Doubleday, 1984.

*Perrin, Norman and Dennis Duling. *The New Testament: An Introduction.* New York: Harcourt Brace Jovanovich (2nd. ed.), 1982.
(A more technical introduction to the New Testament.)

*Richards, H.J. *The First Christmas: What Really Happened?* Mystic: Twenty-Third, 1986.

(Explores the infancy narratives with an eye to reconstructing historical events.)

*Richards, H.J. *The First Easter: What Really Happened?* Mystic: Twenty-Third, 1986.
(Same as the above concerning the resurrection accounts.)

*Riley, William. *The Tale of Two Testaments*. Mystic: Twenty-Third, 1985.
(A pleasant introduction to the Bible.)

Robinson, James M. and Helmut Koester. *Trajectories through Early Christianity*. Philadelphia: Fortress, 1971.

Russell, D.S. *Between the Testaments*. Philadelphia: Fortress, 1965.

———. *From Early Judaism to Early Church*. Philadelphia: Fortress, 1986.

*Saldarini, Anthony. *Jesus and Passover*. New York: Paulist, 1984.
(Examines the Last Supper in the light of Jewish Passover and fellowship-meal rituals.)

Sanders, E.P. *Jesus and Judaism*. Philadelphia: Fortress, 1985.

———. *Paul and Palestinian Judaism*. Philadelphia: Fortress, 1977.

Sandmel, Samuel. *Judaism and Christian Beginnings*. New York: Oxford University Press, 1978.

Schillebeeckx, Edward. *Christ: The Experience of Jesus as Lord*. New York: Crossroad, 1981.

———. *Jesus: An Experiment in Christology*. New York: Crossroad, 1981.

Schineller, J. Peter, S.J. "Christ and Church: A Spectrum of Views," *Theological Studies* (1976) 37, pp. 545–566.

Schnackenburg, Rudolf. *The Church in the New Testament*. New York: Seabury, 1965.

Schüssler Fiorenza, Elisabeth. *In Memory of Her*. New York: Crossroad, 1983.

*Senior, Donald, C.P. *Jesus: A Gospel Portrait*. Dayton: Pflaum Press, 1975.
(A fine introduction to modern scholarly insights into the Gospels.)

*Sloyan, Gerald S. *Jesus in Focus: A Life in Its Setting*. Mystic: Twenty-Third, 1983.
(Presents a very readable overview of the culture and heritage in which Jesus was raised and preached.)

Stanton, Graham, ed. *The Interpretation of Matthew*. Philadelphia: Fortress, 1983.

*Stendahl, Krister. *Holy Week Preaching*. Philadelphia: Fortress (2nd ed.), 1985.
(Excellent homily suggestions based upon the passion narratives.)

*Swidler, Leonard. *Biblical Affirmations of Women*. Philadelphia: Westminster, 1979.
(Explores women in the Bible in a very positive manner.)

Theissen, Gerd. *The Miracle Stories of Early Christian Tradition*. Philadelphia: Fortress, 1983.

*———. *The Shadow of the Galilean*. Philadelphia: Fortress, 1987.
(A fictional account of a wealthy trader enmeshed in the politics of Roman-controlled Judea during the lifetime of Jesus. The author is a well-known European scripture scholar.)

———. *Sociology of Early Palestinian Christianity*. Philadelphia: Fortress, 1978.

*Throckmorton, Burton H., Jr. *Gospel Parallels*. Nashville: Nelson, 1979.
(Presents the synoptic Gospels in parallel columns.)

Townsend, John T. "Does the Study of Late Jewish Midrashim Have Any Place in the Study of the New Testament?" Unpublished paper read at the New England Regional Society of Biblical Literature meeting, March 22, 1985.

*Vermes, Geza. *The Dead Sea Scrolls: Qumran in Perspective*. Philadelphia: Fortress, 1977.
(A history and description of the Dead Sea Scrolls.)

———. *Jesus the Jew*. Philadelphia: Fortress, 1983.

Weeden, Theodore J. Sr. *Mark: Traditions in Conflict*. Philadelphia: Fortress, 1971.

Whiston, William, trans. *Josephus* (Complete works). Grand Rapids: Kregel Publ., 1981.

Wilken, Robert L. *The Christians as the Romans Saw Them*. New Haven: Yale University Press, 1984.

*Young, Robert. *Young's Analytical Concordance to the Bible*. Grand Rapids: Eerdmans, 1970.
(Lists all of the biblical occurrences of particular words.)

INDEX OF SCRIPTURAL PASSAGES

This index can be used to locate the page number(s) on which a particular scriptural passage is discussed.

OLD TESTAMENT

NEW TESTAMENT

TOPICAL INDEX